Holding Onto Love
Searching for Hope When a Child Dies

CHUCK COLLINS

Edited by Kimberly Alison Barry

iUniverse, Inc.
New York   Bloomington

Holding Onto Love
Searching for Hope When a Child Dies

Copyright © 2009 Chuck Collins

iUniverse books may be ordered through booksellers or by contacting:

iUniverse
1663 Liberty Drive
Bloomington, IN 47403
www.iuniverse.com
1-800-Authors (1-800-288-4677)

ISBN: 978-1-4401-2126-5 (pbk)
ISBN: 978-1-4401-2127-2 (ebk)

Printed in the United States of America

iUniverse rev. date: 3/10/2009

To our beloved Tiffanie - we'll always be a family of five!

Author royalties over production costs will be
donated to The Compassionate Friends.

Contents

Preface

My goal is to reach out to every heartbroken parent who has faced the death of your beloved child. Despite your agonizing pain, I hope that somewhere within these pages you can find comfort. As bereaved mothers and fathers, we face the constant challenge of searching for hope despite our anguish.

Over the years, my family has realized that our daughter Tiffanie still enriches our lives, despite her physical absence. Our world will always be a better place because she was in it. Holding onto her love makes each new day possible.

Acknowledgments

Special thanks to my wife, Kathy, for her insightful suggestions, constant support, and many hours dedicated to this effort. I am grateful to my sons, David and Christopher, for their honest perspectives on the impact of sibling grief. I am forever indebted to my talented niece Kimberly Alison Barry for devoting many hours to technical and content editing.

I want to acknowledge the generosity of my brother-in-law Daniel Barry in providing a beautiful New York setting where many of these chapters were written.

Lastly, I appreciate the invaluable personal insights of our wonderful friend Nancy Frank, a grieving mom who loves and misses her beloved son, Danny, every day.

Introduction - How Can This Book Possibly Help Me?

THIS BOOK HAS BEEN WRITTEN FOR parents who have suffered the unimaginable: the deaths of their precious children. We are totally blindsided when this inexplicable tragedy occurs. We suddenly face the harsh realization that our children have been robbed of the chance to follow their dreams. As mothers and fathers, we too are denied the opportunity to share in their future and witness as their lives unfold.

When we became parents, we had many hopes and dreams for our children's future. Whether newborns or adults: they are still *our* children and we love them deeply. Their passings shatter the very foundation of our universe, leaving behind an unmistakably clear message: in this life we control absolutely nothing.

As you grapple with the pain of your loss, I admire you for somehow finding the energy to open this book. I understand your aching pain as only another grieving parent can and still vividly remember the depths of that agony. It is a valley of sorrow that no human being could ever forget.

When my healthy, nineteen-year-old daughter, Tiffanie Amber, suddenly died, I was overcome with anguish and a sense of hopelessness. I was in a constant state of physical exhaustion, as though someone had disconnected my body from its energy source. My emotions seemed to fluctuate by the hour.

Because I recall the enormity of that torment, my heart aches just knowing you now have a reason to read these words. My goal is to provide some insight into the various aspects of grief I have experienced since my daughter's death. I have tried to write this book in a conversational style: as one parent talking informally to another. I have included my email[1] and website[2] and encourage your feedback about this book or any other topic related to the loss of a child.

Parents who have survived the horror of their child's death are uniquely qualified to offer comfort and hope to newly bereaved moms and dads. Facing the inconceivable prospect of life without their children, these emotionally-fragile men and women need strong emotional support.

Over the years as my wife, Kathy, and I attended various grief support seminars, we experienced an undeniable bond with the other families in attendance. Being surrounded by other bereaved parents provides a reassuring environment that allows us to feel safe and unconditionally accepted. This emotional safety net usually ensures no insensitive questions will be asked or awkward explanations expected.

Grief support groups tend to focus on assisting family members in learning how to survive, develop coping skills, and heal emotionally. They pay little attention to how our children died. They already understand something many of us cannot accept in the beginning: we are powerless to undo what has happened.

As your energy level gradually returns, I encourage you to read books by other authors who openly share their unique perspectives on dealing with parental grief. Many offer a deeply personal glimpse into how they learned to cope with their pain.

My wife, Kathy, emphatically praises *Hope for Bereaved: Understanding, Coping and Growing through Grief,* with its compilation of helpful articles.[3] This book was a source of tremendous comfort to her after our daughter died. I have also listed additional grief-related books for your consideration.[4]

After Tiffanie's death, I was desperate to find anyone who could give me "the answers" to ease my pain. It took considerable time to realize that parents who have suffered through this tragedy have no instant remedies for our agony. I discovered that we must travel this grief highway for the rest of our lives and it has no express lanes. Yet although the road remains the same, the scenery definitely improves over time.

The realization that there will never be any answers is an important step towards healing. Some parents cling desperately to their religious beliefs that their God has a plan for all of us. Yet even the most devout believer may struggle to accept that plan in the wake of their child's death.

What other bereaved parents *can* offer is their genuine understanding, compassion, and willingness to share their own experiences in coping with anguish. By interacting with them or reading books or articles about the grieving process, you gain a better understanding of how to deal with your pain. You can incorporate the approaches most compatible with your personality. It is you who ultimately must design your own customized survival strategy.

I will soon be retiring from the practice of law. Like any good lawyer, I am obligated to begin this book by disclaiming liability for anything I have written. Isn't that just like an attorney? I am not trained or licensed as a social worker, psychologist, psychiatrist, therapist, or grief counselor. This book also contains no legal advice whatsoever. Any law-related questions should be directed to a competent attorney practicing in the appropriate field of study within your community. The ideas and opinions expressed herein constitute my own personal opinions and are in no way endorsed by any organization of which I am currently a member or have ever held membership.

Before practicing law, I was a police officer for over twenty-five years and my bachelors and masters degrees are criminal justice related. Although I later obtained a Juris Doctor degree and practiced law in Virginia for over thirteen years, this in no way qualifies me to write this book.

No, I am definitely not a mental health professional. I am simply a loving, heartbroken father who watched my precious daughter live to the cusp of adulthood. Thirteen days before her twentieth birthday, this priceless treasure was ripped from our lives by an infection of bacterial meningitis. It didn't take a professional license for me to fully comprehend the devastating impact this horrific loss had on my family. I write this book as an anguished dad and only in that capacity.

Be forewarned, the aspects of grief that I describe are based on lessons learned through my own journey since Tiffanie's death. In some areas, my opinions may differ from those of noted authorities. However, as far as I can determine, the only real "experts" are the parents and siblings who have faced firsthand the nightmare of child loss.

As you enter this new, unwelcome phase of your life, you will undoubtedly hear the expression, "everyone grieves differently." This is one of the few accurate generalizations possible when describing grief associated with the death of a child. I accept this premise, but with the confidence that I do understand many aspects of your grief. This book will focus on the unique anguish parents experience when their children die. In my view, grieving the death of your own child is far different from other types of loss.

It is important to understand that the pain of losing a child is both emotional and physical. At times, your heart can seem to beat with alarming intensity as the ache of your tragedy permeates your entire body. If you experience unusual physical symptoms, don't assume they will wane in time. You should seek immediate medical assistance, depending on the severity of your condition. Don't take foolish chances with your health. If immediate emergency treatment is not required, notify your physician promptly and schedule a thorough physical examination to be safe.

I remember my own devastation when Tiffanie died. The rawness of my emotions and constant ache throughout my body were unrelenting. I experienced constant pressure in my chest, as though a giant vise had been placed across my body. In those early dreadful days, my wife and I openly entertained thoughts of suicide. We had lost the will to live without our daughter and regaining that desire seemed incomprehensible.

This book is not intended to be a biography. For illustration purposes only, I make periodic references to specific incidents occurring since we lost our daughter. When I mention Kathy, I refer to my wonderful wife of over thirty-four years. If you are interested in my personal account of Tiffanie's death, I have included a limited glimpse of our ordeal.[5]

My primary goal in writing this book is to help you survive this terrible void in your life. After we accomplish that together, my second purpose is to instill in you a sense of hope for the future. Traveling this particular path is a long, painstaking process that takes patience, caution, and courage. I will do my best to prepare you for your own personal grief journey. I hope that you can learn from my mistakes and be better prepared for the obstacles you will no doubt face along the way.

Over the years, the most common question Kathy and I have been asked by newly bereaved parents is, "Does it ever get any better?" The answer is an unqualified "yes!" Time does dull the sharpness of the constant ache that viciously stabs our hearts so brutally immediately after our loss.

Over time, the endless love we have for our child can overshadow the intensity of our heartache. We learn to maintain a delicate balance between our conflicting feelings of love and loss. We gradually discover how to manage our grief and better control how and when it manifests itself in our lives.

It has now been over twelve years since my family's tragic loss. Gradually, I have learned how to smile, to laugh, and yes, even to look forward to living again. I love my daughter deeply and have at times struggled to discover meaningful ways to keep her in my life. It bothers me that some relatives and friends have obviously forgotten her. And it has made us truly appreciate those who continue to find new ways to keep Tiffanie's memory alive.

Whenever I refer to our love for Tiffanie, I use the present tense. A parent's love doesn't fade simply because her child is physically gone. This enduring love becomes the bridge that keeps us connected to our children.

I will do my best to lead you through this pain and the many challenges you will encounter along the way. Despite this horrible tragedy, your life is still worth living. Although we will always miss the physical presence of our children, we can find a number of special ways to keep them in our lives.

It will not be an easy path, but eventually you can learn to enjoy your life again. Each day simply constitutes one small step in a long walk. Be patient with yourself and take each of those strides one at a time. Ultimately, the crucial key to our survival is this: As we awaken to face each new day, we do so always, always holding onto love.

Chapter 1 - Dealing with those First Moments of Loss

WHEN A CHILD DIES, THE OUTPOURING of love and support from family and friends is usually overwhelming. The constant noise from the telephone and doorbell eliminates any early opportunity for grief-stricken parents to absorb the full impact of their loss. While some families take comfort in the onslaught of these early personal calls and visits, others desperately yearn for solitude.

Parents will be given a variety of responsibilities during the funeral process, which serve as temporary distractions. In those early days of loss, they have barely begun to comprehend just how pervasively their lives have been altered forever. They will eventually be confronted with the foreboding prospect of life without their child.

If parents are left to handle this onslaught of activity themselves, it can leave them feeling overwhelmed and ill-equipped to handle the responsibility. A caring friend or relative who is willing to step up and take charge of the situation can be invaluable during this time.

Kathy and I are blessed to have close friend Claudia Soho in our lives. Claudia is a self-made success who worked her way through nursing school later in life. When we returned home from the hospital after Tiffanie's death, Claudia arrived soon after to provide her own brand of comfort. She hugged everyone and cried right along with us. Meanwhile, our life-long friend Margie Weiss offered to notify our relatives, neighbors, and acquaintances of Tiffanie's death, sparing us this dreadful responsibility.

As word of Tiffanie's death spread throughout the neighborhood, the telephone began ringing incessantly. A number of unscheduled visitors appeared at our front door to offer their condolences. My initial instinct was to flee through the back door, as I was emotionally unprepared to meet or talk with anyone.

Claudia's steady presence in our home helped keep us calm. She established an informal command center at our kitchen table to receive incoming calls. She meticulously recorded the messages and contact information left by each person. She also answered the door, escorting visitors in and out of our home. Her demeanor impressed upon each guest that their visit should be brief.

We never asked Claudia to take on these tasks. In fact, we were oblivious to virtually everything she was doing. We had just returned from the hospital and delivered the horrible news to Tiffanie's younger brothers, David and Chris, ages eleven and nine, respectively. We were emotionally shattered as a family and in a state of disbelief. Claudia's instinctive efforts placed a protective shield around all of us.

I hope that you have your own equivalent of Claudia in your life — that special friend or relative who realizes they have to think and function for you. He understands that you simply are unable to handle it.

Author Julia Wilcox Rathkey, whose husband, David, perished in the World Trade Center on September 11, 2001, wisely recommends the importance of establishing a network of family support in those early days:

> The initial, most important thing that friends and family can do to help is to set up a network. Put one trusted person in charge and delegate. Perhaps that individual could be the first one to get in touch with the family or the first one to come stay with the family, but someone should take over to assist in running the household, especially when children are involved.
>
> Once a person has stepped forward to be in charge of a support network, other helpers can follow. The support person can do only so much, so others can offer to take control of various tasks…[6]

Someone who assumes this role has the presence of mind to vacuum your home before visitors arrive and properly wrap any food items delivered by friends and family. They ensure that your home is clean when the last guest has departed. As an emotionally devastated parent, you should not face massive clean-up efforts when every ounce of your energy has been depleted.

During those first weeks of intense sadness, this person may organize a rotating schedule of donated dinners. These are often prepared by family, friends, and neighbors as a gesture of outreach and kindness. This person anticipates your family's requirements and ensures they are addressed. This may include things as simple as reminding you not to forget to pay pending bills, or transporting your children to and from ballet, ball practice, or other activities.

If you are very fortunate, this loyal caregiver will not just disappear once the funeral service has ended. Months and even years later, they remain a welcome companion and source of emotional support. They are always willing to make themselves available whenever you need a lift. Over the last twelve years, we have treasured Claudia's friendship. Having a loyal friend or relative with the courage to step forward during a crisis can be a blessing to a shattered family. The road through grief becomes far more difficult when inconsolable loved ones are forced to walk it alone.

Chapter 2 - Developing Your Comfort Zone

WHEN OUR CHILD DIES, THE UNIVERSE seems irreparably shattered as countless hopes and dreams are suddenly destroyed. Our fundamental beliefs about the natural order of life have been drastically shaken and our religious convictions may have been seriously tested.

After the funeral, we suddenly find ourselves waking each day to face an unending nightmare. In the beginning, it is not uncommon to awaken one morning with a sudden sense of cautious optimism. For a brief moment, we may contemplate the fragile hope that our child really didn't die. We take a deep breath of wary relief and wonder if it was all just a terrible nightmare.

When this happens, we lie in bed almost afraid to move. As reality sets in, we reluctantly recognize that our child really is gone - it was definitely not a dream. Those painful memories come rushing back and our spirits plummet yet again. Sadness overwhelms us and that painful sensation of a vise tightly gripping our chest suddenly resumes.

Bereaved parents may notice their energy level seems depleted. They may find themselves sobbing uncontrollably for extended periods of time. Even when composed, they may constantly feel only a moment away from breaking down again. During this early phase of grief, they often find themselves wandering from one room to another in search of the next place to lie down.

Experiencing this inexplicable catastrophe in our lives makes us no longer feel safe. We may unconsciously cling to a secluded area of our home to take refuge from the world. At first, our comfort zone is small - our bed can become a protective cocoon that offers privacy and solitude. There we are not compelled to communicate with anyone, go anywhere, or do anything. We lie there quietly wondering if we will ever find a respite from the terrible sadness that pervades our entire being.

Some parents spend time in their child's room instead of sleeping in their own beds. Lying among the child's possessions can temporarily ease the intensity of their suffering and instill a feeling of closeness to their child.

Regardless of where parents try to sleep, recapturing their energy level can seem an impossible goal. They may constantly feel too drained to do anything. They conceal themselves in their comfort zone in the faint hope that the world will simply leave them alone. While this sad description of the early days of grief does not apply to everyone, it is very common behavior for many newly bereaved parents.

Eventually, we expand our comfort zones and venture into the other rooms of our home. We interact with our spouse, significant other, and any surviving children, if we have them. We recognize that they are suffering too. We put on the bravest face possible, foolishly hoping to shield them from our pain. Usually, they are doing the same for us.

Most husbands and wives are confident that they understand each other by the time they become parents. Yet when their child has died, they are often surprised at the significant differences in how they grieve. One spouse may express grief outwardly, even displaying periodic fits of anger. She may be reluctant to get out of bed and lack the energy to even dress herself. Yet the other parent may bury the pain deep inside, presenting a calm outward appearance that masks the depths of his suffering.

These dramatic disparities in individual grief expressions can lead to verbal hostilities and even heated confrontations. The more vocal parent may misinterpret the spouse's passive behavior as an indication that he is not grieving "enough." This can be a difficult phase as parents are forced to distinguish how they grieve individually. They must learn to differentiate when a spouse needs a hug from those occasions when she would rather spend time alone.

In the beginning we may try to restrict our activities to whatever we cannot otherwise avoid doing. We dread making even the simplest of decisions while in such emotional pain. Eventually, we may turn on a television or radio as a temporary diversion from our punishing thoughts. We may even risk answering the telephone. Yet our sorrow is so fresh that each of these simple actions requires a very conscious, deliberate choice.

We also may prefer not to leave our homes for any reason. We venture out only for necessities, our job (when we return to work), groceries, or a visit to the cemetery. We are usually determined to accomplish our mission quickly and return home, unnoticed to sequester ourselves under the world's radar. Some parents are initially reluctant to drive, believing they are too distracted to safely control a motor vehicle. Their limited comfort zones will eventually expand as they begin to discover how to better manage their grief.

Both of our young sons, David and Chris, participated on soccer and Little League baseball teams during the months immediately following Tiffanie's death. We had always loved attending their games and cheering them to victory. Yet Kathy and I were so distraught over Tiffanie's death, we actually began to dread going to these games. We did our best to conceal that sentiment from our boys.

Without question, Kathy and I were the quietest fans in the stands. Yet David and Chris seemed gratified we were there. Most people did not realize how difficult it was for us to go anywhere, much less to attend our own children's ball games. We had to be there to encourage them, yet we felt emotionally detached. I don't know how much actual comfort our presence actually provided to either of them.

We were fortunate to have a few very loyal friends who made a concerted effort to attend those games and cheer enthusiastically for our boys. They obviously recognized that we were drowning in our sorrow. They sensed that David and Chris needed the kind of emotional encouragement that Kathy and I were too devastated to provide. They cheered their hearts out for two little heroic guys trying desperately to make their parents smile again. It was important for our sons to feel that support and our friends ensured that they did.

In time, as our comfort zone broadened, our enthusiastic passion for attending their games returned. With each passing day and week parents gradually expand their comfort zones as an increasing number of activities become less of a struggle. The first time they drive an automobile can be a significant breakthrough.

When bereaved parents attend a social gathering, they may do so with great reluctance. They harbor a natural fear about how they will be publicly treated. On arrival, they often try to blend virtually unnoticed into the crowd. Many experience great trepidation that they will have to engage in the "small talk" so customary at such events.

They are usually able to exchange greetings with friends and associates with a minimum of problems. However, when introduced to new people, these parents are suddenly placed in an emotional danger zone. Once the customary greetings have been exchanged, the conversation may eventually evolve to that dreaded question: "So, do you have any children?"

Hearing those words for the first time can stab like a dagger thrust through the heart. That question alone can be enough to consume inconsolable parents with panic. Yet unless they run away, the question begs an answer. It can take years before these aching mothers and fathers can respond to this question without being reduced to tears.

Once an answer is given, the questioner may suddenly find himself trapped in an uncomfortable situation. It was never anticipated that such a seemingly harmless question would evoke such painful emotions. The unforeseen response may result in an abrupt termination of the conversation as the questioner departs in search of less challenging dialogue.

When this occurs with enough regularity, we can develop low self-esteem around others and become severely distressed at the prospect of attending public gatherings. We fear becoming the large elephant in the room that everyone else is afraid to acknowledge. It can be tempting to avoid all public events completely.

Over time and with practice, you can eventually develop a ready response to better handle the "Do you have any children?" question. Some suggested responses include:

Do you have any children?

1) "Yes! Have you attended this event before? I don't remember seeing you." This response creates an instant diversion forcing a change of subject. In those early days, you may fear breaking down if you actually try to provide an answer.

2) "Yes! I have three children: My son David is twenty-four, Christopher is twenty-two, and a few years ago we lost our nineteen-year-old daughter, Tiffanie, to meningitis."

3) "Yes! I have two sons in college and my daughter is in heaven/the afterlife!"

Part of developing and eventually expanding your own comfort zone must include learning to anticipate potentially painful situations. If you have lost a baby or very young child, it can be difficult to attend a friend or relative's upcoming baby shower or his child's baptism. Depending on your child's age when she died, other potentially painful situations can include birthday parties, the first day of school, graduations, baby showers, and weddings. Just an unexpected glimpse of a school bus loading small children headed for nursery school can bring an emotionally struggling mother or father to tears.

Three years ago, I attended my young cousin John's wedding. Although I had gone to two other matrimonial ceremonies since Tiffanie's death, the couples involved were middle-aged. As I stood in church, the music began to play. We turned and watched as the pretty bridesmaids began their solemn procession down the aisle.

Suddenly, I caught a glimpse of Amy, the beautiful young bride. She was smiling and her eyes were beaming with love and dreams for the future. Walking next to her in measured steps was her father, smiling proudly. He marched in unison to present his precious daughter to John so they could begin their new life together.

It was then that the stark realization hit home that I would never share this moment with Tiffanie. I remember how much she loved the remake of the movie *"Father of the Bride"* with Steve Martin.[7] Tiffanie once commented that we had a similar relationship to the father-daughter bond depicted in that film. Tiffanie and I both anticipated that her wedding day would be a very special, happy time in our lives. Neither of us could have envisioned that it would never happen because she would die so young.

Standing in that church more than a decade after Tiffanie's death, I found myself gasping for air. It was just another painful reminder of how her loss had altered our hopes and dreams. Even many years after our child's death, we can be totally blindsided by our emotions. I should have anticipated this potentially painful situation. Yet with so much time having passed since her death, I let my guard down.

This proved to be a tough emotional reminder of my need to always anticipate the possibility of painful situations. I encourage you to consciously try to predict potentially difficult moments in your life. Developing a routine strategy for anticipating and dealing with them is an important healing step for parents as their comfort zones gradually expand.

Chapter 3 - The Initial Impact of Losing Your Child

I NEVER REALIZED JUST HOW OFTEN children die until Tiffanie passed away. Over the years, I recall other tragedies when families suffered the loss of a son or daughter. This was long before I became a bereaved parent myself. I remember that I never really understood the *proper way* to adequately express my concern.

I understood that it made no sense for children to die before their parents. When it happened, everyone in our local community became apprehensive. It seemed a harsh warning that a child can die in *any* family. Yet as tragic as these deaths were, they did not happen to *my* family. It was not *my* child. The onset of my own sadness over those families' losses waned in time.

After each funeral, I went on with my life like most people. I did not understand how to reach out to these families. Like so many of the people that I criticize now, I assumed the parents would eventually move on from their loss. None of us became grief experts until this horrific tragedy burst through our own front doors.

Your child's death is traumatic and emotionally paralyzing. Parents often experience varying stages of shock, anger, and even denial. This is particularly true when the death occurs suddenly without warning, e.g. a tragic accident, an undiagnosed medical condition, suicide, murder, etc.

When in such pain, it is important to recognize that you are vulnerable to impulse. You should avoid making any major, life-changing decisions immediately after your child has died. A sudden choice to retire, change jobs or careers, sell your home, or relocate to another city may be only a panicked reaction to your pain. You must carefully avoid rushing into a decision that you may deeply regret later.

Grieving After a Long Illness

Many parents whose son or daughter becomes seriously ill cling frantically to the hope their child will survive. As treatment continues and the medical prognosis gradually worsens, the parents' fears intensify. Still, they often cling desperately to the hope of a miraculous recovery. When their child's condition grows more serious, these heartbroken mothers and fathers may eventually come to understand, though not accept, that the condition is terminal.

Dealing with the impending death of their son or daughter places these families in a gut-wrenching situation. They face the enormous challenge of appearing upbeat and hopeful in the presence of their child. Even when the child is aware his condition will be fatal, parents and siblings try their best to smile and be positive. Yet emotionally, they may feel as though they too are dying.

The family struggles valiantly to hold it together for their child. These moms, dads, brothers, and sisters demonstrate incredible courage, dignity, and devotion in caring for their dying loved one. They epitomize the greatest example of unconditional love and are an inspiration to all of us.

Despite the advanced warning, the grief these parents face when their child dies is pervasive and unrelenting. To others, they may seem more organized, especially if some of the funeral arrangements were made in advance. Yet they are still grappling with the realization their child is really gone. Like all of us, their hopes and dreams have just been shattered.

Grieving as an Adoptive Parent, Stepparent, or Parent of an Only Child

I recall one situation in which ridiculous questions were raised about whether adoptive parents suffer as intensely as natural parents when their child dies. Generally, natural parents and adoptive parents do not love their children any differently. Adoptive parents are usually so devoted to their children; it is difficult to imagine why anyone would question their love.

Most adoptive parents have already dealt with a roller coaster of emotions by the time they become parents. They may have experienced intense sadness after initially learning they were unable to conceive a child naturally. Dealing with that news is devastating and life altering to a couple longing to start a family.

When they decided to pursue adoption, substantial time, energy, and resources were invested for the honor of becoming parents. They struggled through the complicated, expensive, and emotionally-draining adoption process. In willingly enduring the stress involved in dealing with these procedures, they made a far more determined commitment to raise a child than some natural parents ever did.

After the adoption was approved, their child became the answer to their prayers. When their beloved son or daughter is suddenly gone, how could they be anything but devastated? They suffer the same agonizing grief as any other parent. Sadly, since the adoption process is difficult, expensive, and at times gut-wrenching, adoptive parents are more likely to have lost their only child.

Parents who lose their only child suffer immensely. Sharon and Ben Smith describe the death of their only child Mark:

> We were devastated by the loss. As parents of an only child, we had lost our family and our future. I mourned for our child and the grandchildren that would never be. Ben and I had no reason for planning ahead. We had no real meaning in our lives – no purpose – no goals.
>
> Each new day brought more loneliness and unbearable silence. Ben longed for the son who was always at his side trying out a new wrestling hold, romping on the floor. I ached to hold my child again. [8]

It is a bit more difficult to generalize about stepparent relationships, which may depend on the age of the child when her father or mother remarried. Some stepparents accept their stepchildren unconditionally and develop the same, or an even closer relationship, than a natural or adoptive parent might. In other cases, relations may have been strained due to a variety of factors beyond the scope of this book.

Personally, I have never met a stepparent who was any less devastated by a child's death than a natural or adoptive parent. I have met several who are awesome parental role models and suffer just as intensely as any other parent. Their devotion has convinced me there is no such thing as "step-love" for a child

Appetite Issues and the Danger of Self-Medication

It is impossible to overstate the challenges faced by grieving parents who often lack the energy to even get out of bed in the morning. When they do finally manage to emerge, they feel virtually drained of their strength and desire to do anything. They may find themselves moving aimlessly around their home in search of a new place to lie down until they feel better.

Grief can have a dramatic effect on the appetite. While some parents completely lose the desire to eat, others resort to binge eating. I remember losing twelve pounds during the seven-day period from the onset of Tiffanie's hospitalization to her funeral. Kathy became dangerously thin as her loss of appetite continued for months. Sometimes, this may be only a temporary reaction to the initial shock. However, if this pattern continues without effective treatment, it can pose a serious health risk.

I remember arriving at home each day after my morning court appearance. I would often find Kathy, still clad in her pajamas, sitting in a dark corner of the house. She had eaten nothing, the television and radio were off, and the newspaper was still lying at the front door. While I tried desperately to convince Kathy to eat something in those early days, she had absolutely no appetite and ate very little.

Each day, Kathy grew more despondent. As her weight loss continued, I began to fear losing my wife in addition to my daughter. When I tactfully suggested that professional treatment at an in-patient facility might help her, she quickly dismissed the idea. Eventually, with the assistance of a professional counselor and strong emotional support from two close friends, Kathy gradually became more responsive.

In the early days of grief, parents are in such a state of agony, a gradual tendency to consume alcohol or become overly reliant on prescription medications can ensue. Parents sometimes receive a variety of legitimate prescriptions for medications to treat sleep disorders, anxiety, or pain immediately after their tragedies. Some of these have the potential for abuse, especially if they are taken in excess or mixed with alcohol.

My alcohol consumption increased dramatically during those early years. While I was careful not to drink and drive, once I was safely inside my home, some form of alcohol was usually in my glass. In the years that followed, I have often relied on beer, liquor, or wine to numb my emotional pain over losing Tiffanie. Take my advice, it doesn't work.

This reliance only magnified my feelings of loss and depression. At first my nerves were soothed by the initial effects of the alcohol. Yet intense feelings of sadness, anger, and despair soon followed. Drinking provided no emotional comfort whatsoever. It only magnified the pain I hoped to relieve and intensified my feelings of isolation.

In the long run, using substance abuse to ease your pain is a strategy for failure that can cause further turmoil in your family. If you are a social drinker, pay careful attention to your consumption habits as you deal with your grief. If you note changes in your drinking pattern, it can be an indication that you are falling into the same trap. Pay attention to these warning signs and learn from my mistakes.

Returning to Work

The year before Tiffanie's death, I retired after twenty-five years as a police officer. As I had already graduated from law school and passed the bar exam, I established a solo legal practice in Virginia. After a slow start, my cases began regularly appearing on the morning traffic and criminal court dockets. When Tiffanie died, I resisted the temptation to postpone my pending cases. Over the next three months, I only rescheduled two hearings.

I decided to take an entire month off from work for the sole purpose of grieving. To do so, I had to resolve my pending cases and discontinue accepting any new clients. To provide my clients with the most zealous legal representation possible, I had to find a way to shield myself from grief. I was convinced that if I avoided conscious thoughts of Tiffanie during the day, I could successfully focus on my work responsibilities. By blocking my emotions, I was initially successful in adhering to my grief-avoidance plan during the business day.

Kathy was totally distraught after Tiffanie's death and in no condition to return to her job. Two-and-a-half-months later, she resumed working on a part-time basis. One month later, she began working full-time.

As a career government employee, Kathy was fortunate to have a bank of accumulated sick leave to use during her absence. Those parents who are forced for financial reasons to immediately return to work after the funeral are amazing. They have no more energy than any other grief-stricken parent, yet somehow they find the strength to bravely make it through each work day without falling apart.

After returning to work, many parents struggle for a sense of normalcy. Initially, they may remain close to their assigned work areas, trying to go virtually unnoticed. They often keep to themselves, hoping to blend into their work environment. To the casual observer, they appear to be functioning normally in the workplace.

In reality, many of these parents are simply going through the motions. They make their way through each business day one second at a time and their raw emotions are often held in check with an almost robotic level of restraint. Using the same grief avoidance strategy that I relied upon, they attempt to block the tragedy from their mind for eight hours. At the end of the business day, they may find themselves sobbing again. The protective wall around their grief too often disintegrates during the trip home.

The initial period after a grieving parent returns to work is an inopportune time for an employer to change or add to her work responsibilities. What keeps these parents steady on the job in the early days is the security of dealing with the same familiar tasks. A lighter work load is certainly preferable and some concerned employers make that happen.[9] Adding additional or more complex duties can become a major stressor to an anguished employee just after her child's death.

One reason is that the magnitude of a parent's grief may hamper the ability to concentrate on anything for more than a few minutes. Even when at home, he may set out to complete a chore only to end up wandering in another room, having forgotten his original purpose.

The same problem can exist at work. A newly bereaved parent may experience great difficulty trying to continually focus on a project. This deficiency in her concentration level should eventually improve. However, during the initial weeks and months after a child's death, it can be a formidable obstacle to overcome. The struggle to maintain an adequate attention span can pose a constant challenge in all areas of a grief-stricken parent's life.

Regardless of when bereaved parents return to work, they may feel very isolated. Some co-workers who were friendly before their child's death may begin to either avoid the parent completely or limit conversations strictly to business. A few may dare to ask, "How are you doing?" Most don't have the courage to risk the possibility that you might actually tell them. Too often, these parents find themselves working in the midst of people who manage to get very busy whenever they are in the vicinity. This constructive isolation at the workplace only adds to their stress and depression.

When word spread that Kathy was returning to work two-and-a-half months after Tiffanie's death, one of her employees sought guidance from the agency's human resources division. This concerned young lady had the foresight to request information about how to interact with a bereaved coworker. Sadly, the personnel specialists had no research on the topic available. When my wife returned to work, the woman honestly confided her fear of saying something inappropriate.

This was a wonderful gesture by a concerned worker who had the prescience to request assistance. She didn't just assume that she would know what to say or how to act. It is surprising that a federal government personnel office would be totally unprepared to provide this type of guidance to its employees. Kathy later supplied her agency with handouts specifically designed to assist employers and co-workers in dealing with employees in mourning. Packets of these brochures are readily available at a modest cost from The Compassionate Friends, Inc. (TCF).[10]

As we deal with our sorrow, we can become less tolerant of the minor personal problems of others. Grieving parents who work in supervisory positions must be especially cautious. Employees routinely bring a variety of personal issues to the attention of their bosses to justify a request for approved leave, a change of schedule, or a number of other reasons. Yet what these workers perceive to be a serious dilemma may seem trivial to a supervisor who is struggling with the depths of her own emotional torment.

We have faced the worst situation imaginable for a parent. As one friend described it, we suddenly "develop a very low threshold for b.s." We can be tempted to inform the employee exactly how insignificant his problem really is, when compared to the emptiness we face every day.

However, in a supervisory role, we must remember that our employees are in a very different emotional place. These issues are very important to them, and as managers, we must fight the urge to tell them otherwise. Our goal should be to resolve these matters in the same professional manner we did prior to experiencing our tragedy.

Painful Reminders of Happier Days

When their child participated in organized recreational or athletic activities during his life, anguished parents often find themselves longing for happier times. They fondly remember driving their child to various practices for dance or drill teams, band, gymnastics, or various youth activities. If they later have occasion to see one of these groups practice or perform, it can bring a lump to their throats.

If surviving siblings attend the same school, it can be difficult for their parents to avoid direct contact with these activities. In fact, younger siblings may later join the same groups or teams, triggering an onslaught of bittersweet memories. As these mothers and fathers recall how much their child enjoyed participating, it can give them some level of comfort. Yet they are emotionally torn because they miss watching this child.

In high school, Tiffanie was a member of the "Precisionettes" drill team, which performed at halftime during W.T. Woodson varsity football and basketball games in Fairfax, Virginia. She cherished her years as a member of this talented, award-winning group. Her younger brothers, David and Chris, later attended the same school. While David enjoyed success as an indoor and outdoor track hurdler and ran cross country for four years, Chris excelled on the varsity football, basketball, and lacrosse teams.

During halftime at Chris' football and basketball games, Kathy and I would watch intently as the latest group of Precisionettes performed routines similar to those Tiffanie danced as a member. We found ourselves choking back tears the first few times they performed. Eventually, we were able to put aside our sadness and focus instead on our many happy memories of Tiffanie's participation on the squad. This taught us that we can sometimes use joyful memories of our children to temper the ache of our loss.

When our children moved away from home or left to attend college, they may have called home regularly prior to their death. With the ready availability of cell phones, email, text, and instant messaging, the ease of communications between college students and their families has improved dramatically over the last decade. In 1996, when Tiffanie was living on campus at Clemson University, she routinely called home every Sunday evening at 6:00 p.m. We looked forward to her weekly updates and made certain to be home for her call.

After Tiffanie died, Kathy and I could not imagine remaining at home on Sunday evenings when the telephone would no longer ring. We discovered a family bowling group operating on Sundays from 5:00 to 7:15 p.m. We joined the small, six-team league and began bowling every week. We knew that it would be too agonizing to stay home, so we did what we had to do to get through a very emotional dilemma.

David and Chris seemed to enjoy the new activity as it diverted their minds from their sadness. David in particular was constantly analyzing his ball delivery in search of the "right" way to bowl. It made us smile to watch our eleven-year-old son constantly unveil some new technique designed to perfect his performance.

Although we kept mostly to ourselves, bowling did provide an opportunity for the four of us to be together as a family. We continued to bowl in this league for two years before we finally faced remaining at home on Sunday nights. The first time we did, the telephone did not ring at 6:00 p.m. As Kathy and I glanced despondently at the clock, the silence was deafening.

Several years later, I was contacted by John and Jane Trimble, two parents in our family league. They were trying to locate our local Compassionate Friends support group after their beautiful daughter, Leisa, lost her life in an automobile accident. The information Jane was able to track down listed our home telephone as the contact number.

When Jane realized that I was the same "Chuck Collins" from the bowling league, she expressed surprise. I explained that we had lost Tiffanie and bowling was an escape from the loneliness of staying at home. I was stunned when Jane confided, "In the league we didn't know that you had lost your daughter. We just thought you weren't very friendly people!"

Jane's honest observation made us realize just how cold and distant we must have seemed to the other families. They had no idea that we were struggling with our daughter's death as we tried to survive the pain of another Sunday evening. It made Kathy and I realize that our outward appearance to others was drastically different from our own perception of it.

Handling Your Child's Possessions

When parents are able to begin sifting through their child's possessions, they may discover a diary or journal containing her innermost thoughts, recorded at various stages of life. This discovery poses a difficult emotional dilemma for parents. Reading the diary offers them an opportunity to gain new insight into their child and they may feel a desperate need to know everything possible about their son or daughter. Yet their child made these entries expecting that her personal privacy was assured.

A similar concern arises when the child leaves behind a personal computer. Depending on the child's age, his computer is likely to contain school-related assignments, a variety of correspondence, and other routine files. Yet it may also contain some very personal information. If access is not protected by a password, parents will face the same quandary of whether or not to read the files.

Tiffanie's computer sat virtually untouched for several years. Eventually, I was able to transfer her files from the computer's hard drive onto a portable disc without actually reading them. This information has been preserved and the decision of whether or not to read them has been postponed for another day.

After Tiffanie's files were copied, they were deleted from the hard drive. We then donated her computer to a friend with a desperate need for one. Unfortunately, since we waited so long to dispose of the computer, it was virtually obsolete within six months. The longer we hold onto our children's computers or other types of equipment, the less likely they will be of any practical value to others.

A child's automobile may present an emotional challenge for inconsolable parents. Deciding how and when to dispose of it can be agonizing. In some cases, other family members have a legitimate need for the vehicle. However, many families are left with no practical use for their child's auto.

Bereaved families may initially be reluctant to sell their child's car. However, it is definitely not wise to allow a motor vehicle to remain parked in the same position for an extended period of time. While I am no mechanic, common sense dictates that moving parts need to move periodically.

The summer before Tiffanie's junior year of high school, she frugally saved her income from her lifeguard job in hope of purchasing a car. She had her heart set on buying a new Saturn. By summer's end, Tiffanie had saved about $1800. When she realized the cost of a new Saturn at that time was about $12,000, her immense disappointment was obvious.

Kathy and I recognized that Tiffanie had learned an important lesson about the value of money. She had always maintained good grades in school, participated in wholesome after-school activities, and awoke very early to attend Young Life spiritual group meetings before her classes. Despite being confronted with the usual temptations all teenagers face, Tiffanie managed to avoid getting into trouble.

After weighing these factors, Kathy and I agreed that Tiffanie deserved the car. When we broke the news to her, she was ecstatic. We used her summer savings as the down payment and Tiffanie was allowed to special order a brand new automobile. Most of our friends and neighbors no doubt thought that we had totally lost our minds. Who allows their seventeen-year-old son or daughter to order a brand new automobile from a car dealership? Thank goodness we did!

Tiffanie enjoyed her distinctive, aquamarine Saturn during her junior and senior years of high school. Due to Clemson University's parking restrictions, the car remained at home during her freshman year. However, she did have it with her as a sophomore. Because she drove home from college on the Friday before her death, Tiffanie's Saturn remained parked in front of our residence.

We preserved the vehicle's shiny finish with a special protective cover Tiffanie had purchased. Yet each time I arrived home from work, the sight of that draped vehicle parked in front of our house was like a stab wound through the heart. For me, it was reminiscent of viewing her casket all over again. It brought back memories of too many police cruisers covered in black and parked in front of the stationhouse when a police officer died in the line of duty. Tiffanie's draped Saturn was a constant reminder to everyone in the neighborhood that she was gone forever.

Initially, there was no way I could bring myself to part with her car, so it remained in the same position for just over a year. Shortly after the first anniversary of Tiffanie's death, I placed an advertisement for the Saturn in our local newspaper. I eventually sold the vehicle at a very modest price to a father who purchased it for his teenage daughter.

When this gentleman arrived with a young girl, her eyes gleamed when she spotted the shiny Saturn. Her reaction brought tears to my eyes, as I vividly recalled Tiffanie's excitement the first time she spotted her new car at the dealership. We decided to place the money from this sale into a special savings account to be equally divided when David and Chris were mature enough to purchase their first automobiles. They would be reminded that it was a gift from Tiffanie to her brothers.

If your child lived at home or kept a room there even after moving out, more painful decisions arise after her death. You must first decide whether to keep the door to your child's room open or closed. If you normally kept it closed before the tragedy, the approach is obvious. The decision is more difficult if the door customarily remained open.

I recommend discussing this with everyone who lives in your home. Each person may be emotionally impacted by your choice, so requesting their input is important. When parents make this decision, the rationale should be explained to ensure everyone understands. If you decide to close the door to your child's room, reassure your family members that they are welcome to privately spend time there. It may give them some personal solace.

Another painful decision many of us face is what to do with the contents of our child's room. If your child died before birth or was stillborn, the room may have been painted a special color, especially if the gender was known. The room may contain a crib, changing table, and a variety of baby furniture, cuddly bears, etc. Facing an empty baby's room, so carefully planned with hope and dreams for the future, is agonizing for grief-stricken moms and dads.

Some parents may opt to close the door and preserve the furniture in its exact condition hoping, that eventually, they will bear or adopt another child. Others may feel the need to repaint the room or dispose of the furniture. I would strongly encourage them to close the door and defer making any decision, at least for the first few months.

Their initial inclination may be to clear out the room and start over. However, this can be a very expensive option. Try to remember that in most cases, it wasn't the room or its contents that caused this tragedy. The room was specially furnished as an act of love. Obviously, you have to make the choice that works best for your family. I encourage you to take your time because there is no deadline for making this sensitive determination.

Parents with older children face the same problem, as the decision whether or not to retain the furniture is distressing. In 2003, after twenty-three years in the same house, we decided to move to a newer home. I want to stress that it took us seven years after Tiffanie's death to leave the home where she was raised for most of her life. I strongly discourage newly bereaved parents from making the potentially life-altering decision to relocate in the early weeks and months after their child's death.

For seven years, Tiffanie's room remained in the exact condition as it was on the day she died. The moving process forced us to decide what to do with her furniture. We emptied the contents of her white desk, hutch, and bureau drawers into separate storage boxes and had her furniture delivered to our new home.

After we reassembled these items into a new room, it just wasn't the same. We realized that this had never been Tiffanie's bedroom and her possessions seemed out of place. A few months later, we decided to donate her matching bed, bureau drawers, and desk to a shelter for battered women. We knew Tiffanie would have been pleased by that gesture.

Some parents decide to dispose of their child's belongings in the first few months after their loss. Others wait, which is the approach that I encourage. Although it has now been twelve years since Tiffanie's death, her personal belongings remain stored in plastic boxes in our home. We have her prom dresses, warm-up outfits, and numerous other articles of clothing.

Since we remain emotionally unable to part with her personal possessions, we do what is best for us. Hopefully, as we continue to make progress in our healing, we will eventually be ready to properly dispose of them. Since there is no deadline for this decision, focus on determining when the time feels right for you and your family. I wish you the best of luck in making this very challenging decision.

Sadly, our friends Sue and Paul Lowden lost their handsome, eighteen-year-old son Will in 2004. At Will's funeral service, each of his shirts were neatly rolled and tied with decorative ribbons. They were placed in a hallway adjacent to where his memorial service was held. At the conclusion of the ceremony, Will's friends and relatives were invited to take an item of his clothing. Hundreds of people attended this service and the teenagers present seemed genuinely touched to leave the church with some special garment that belonged to Will.

When deciding how to dispose of your child's personal possessions, the best advice is to do what works for you. Try to learn as much as you can about how other people have handled their children's personal possessions. Then, create a customized approach that best satisfies the needs of your family. If you take your time and give this issue serious consideration, you are less likely to experience nagging regrets later.

If you are initially unable to dispose of your child's belongings, you might consider placing a date on the calendar to revisit the issue. At the very least, this will force you to periodically assess whether you are emotionally able to deal with this decision. If you're still not prepared at the specified time, you simply schedule another review date and hope that you will be ready then. The Collins family is definitely proof that there is no deadline. As I write this, I still have no idea when we will finally face this emotional task.

Keeping Your Child's Memory Alive at Home

After we donated Tiffanie's furniture and stored her personal belongings, we no longer had a room designated for her in our home. It was very important to us that she have a visible presence in our new house. We wanted any visitor to immediately know about our daughter.

After considerable research, we purchased a large display case, placing it just inside the entrance to our front door. We exhibited some of Tiffanie's personal belongings in this case, including several photographs, special memorabilia, and even her high school drill and dance team jackets.[11] A variety of beautiful angel figurines are also intermingled with these items.

Whenever guests visit our home, they almost always take a moment to peruse the contents of this case. Some will view the sentimental keepsakes without comment. Others openly ask questions about Tiffanie or express their condolences over her loss. Although the reactions are mixed, our goal of ensuring that Tiffanie is not forgotten has definitely been achieved.

We were also fortunate to have a unique painting done by David Cochran, a talented Alexandria, Virginia artist. I refer to his creation as "Our Dream Vacation" because it depicts all of us together surrounded by everything that we enjoy in life.[12] Whenever guests visit our family room, they are immediately drawn to this wonderful work of art. Tiffanie is prominently in the middle with her two brothers. This is another way we ensure that Tiffanie's memory is kept alive in our home.

Selecting a Marker

Many parents order a marker for their child's grave when they are making funeral arrangements. Kathy and I struggled with this gut-wrenching decision but were too distraught to make this purchase immediately after Tiffanie's death.

While there is usually no deadline for ordering a grave marker, some cemeteries do impose time limits on how long a temporary name plate can remain on a grave. Although Tiffanie's cemetery had this rule, our contact person understood that we were struggling with the decision and never pressured us.

The wording on a cemetery marker is extremely important to the family. I drafted a number of proposed inscriptions for Tiffanie's memorial plaque, but my first attempts were far too lengthy. Kathy reviewed each effort and tactfully offered her own counter-proposals. We knew that it was critical for both of us to agree on the final engraved message. This exasperating process continued for nearly five years. At times we grew desperate trying to capture the proper wording to pay tribute to our daughter's life. Yet nothing we initially generated seemed to achieve this purpose.

On one occasion, I ran into a friend whose daughter was very close to Tiffanie. She asked the usual questions, inquiring how our family was doing. Suddenly her compassionate demeanor seemed to change to one of complete distain. In a very accusatory tone she asked, "When are you going to put a marker on that child's grave?"

I tried to explain that Kathy and I were having great difficulty finding the right words. Yet her facial expressions made it obvious that my answer displeased her. She was outraged that we could bury our only daughter and yet be unable to promptly place a permanent memorial on her grave. She had no clue how much anguish Kathy and I suffered in trying to create just the right inscription. How could she? Her children are alive and enjoying their lives.

My naive hope was that anyone who stumbled across Tiffanie's grave would instantly know her. I believed the cemetery marker should be a tribute to her life and provide insight into Tiffanie's true personality. As the years passed and we continued to grapple with this process, I eventually realized this simply was not possible. Tiffanie was so much more than could ever be captured on a small stone memorial.

When this realization finally sunk in, I opted instead to create a message that would have pleased her. In the end, we settled on a memorial bearing her photograph and Kappa Kappa Gamma sorority emblem. The entire marker is encircled by her favorite roses and reads:

IN LIVING HER LIFE, SHE DEEPLY TOUCHED OUR HEARTS, OUR SPECIAL ANGEL TO CHERISH AND LOVE FOREVER. LIKE THE MOST PERFECT ROSE...GONE TOO SOON.[13]

Five days before the fifth anniversary of Tiffanie's death, this permanent tribute was finally placed on her grave.

Gazing at the marker on your child's grave for the first time is a very difficult experience because it symbolizes the permanency of death. The message has been engraved forever, so the pain of the finality can be overwhelming. No matter how long ago our child died, few of us are prepared for that first glimpse when a memorial is engraved at his grave.

Certified death educator Helen Fitzgerald tries to prepare teenagers for this experience in her book written for grieving teens:

I do want to warn you, though, that once a headstone is in place, visiting the grave can be a shock. Seeing the name of your loved one with a birth and death date etched in granite is powerful. It will again drive home the reality of the death.[14]

Issues Related to a Child's "Estate"

Children under the age of twenty-one generally own few, if any, major assets. Even when they are old enough to drive, their automobiles are often registered under the parents' names. Thus, there is usually no formal will in existence when a child or young adult dies. "One who has died without a valid will" is said to have died "intestate."[15]

The laws governing the handling of a child's intestate estate vary. Wills and trusts are statutory creations defined by the laws enacted in each jurisdiction. The distribution of assets can become an issue, particularly when the child has existing bank accounts or owned valuable property. It may also become important if a wrongful death civil litigation is later initiated on behalf of the child's estate.

A good first step is to visit your local court to obtain information on the procedures for handling "small estates." A consultation with a local trust and estates attorney is also a smart move. Most of the time, devastated parents are forced to struggle through this inquiry themselves. A close friend or relative willing to research the requirements and procedures governing the handling of small intestate estates in that jurisdiction is invaluable. She can also locate a competent attorney and relieve the grief-stricken family of that stressful responsibility.

Chapter 4 - Anger and Parental Guilt – Is it My Fault?

I DON'T KNOW HOW WE, AS parents, can avoid dealing with periods of intense anger and deep resentment after our child is suddenly ripped from our lives. Some of us may direct that anger at our God for not preventing this tragedy. If there is an identifiable person who directly or indirectly caused our child's death, we may be furious at them. A few examples include the drunk driver who caused the fatal accident, the dealer who supplied our child with drugs, the doctor who misdiagnosed our child's medical or psychological condition, to name a few. Some of us may be upset because we disagree with how our child's death was investigated or handled by the police.

We may also be angry at our child if he willingly placed himself in harm's way, or did something reckless that resulted in such a needless tragedy. It can be difficult for us to simultaneously reconcile our feelings of intense anger, pain, and love. If our child committed suicide, we may be torn between being incensed at her and feelings of deep remorse that we were unable to reach her emotionally.

We also may be infuriated because we simply don't understand "why." We are left to deal with the uncertainty of not knowing "the reason" our child suffered this fate. Why did death have to visit our family, our precious child? Why must our family bear this tragedy, when others seem to go through life trouble-free? We are enraged at the injustice of a child dying before his or her parents.

While anger can be a difficult burden for us to carry, self-imposed guilt is especially agonizing. Too often, inconsolable parents blame themselves for their child's death. Doing so can be paralyzing, as they constantly replay every detail leading up to the tragedy. Even when someone else is clearly identified as being responsible for their child's death, parents often continue to blame themselves.

If the death resulted from a car accident, we may blame ourselves for failing to purchase a "safer" vehicle. We may constantly second-guess ourselves as to why we didn't give them a ride instead of allowing them to drive or ride with someone else. If we had only done that, we reason, our child would still be alive.

If our child became ill due to disease, we may question the quality of medical care she received. We can ache with deep regret believing we should have purchased a better quality of health insurance that might have offered more highly-skilled physicians. We also may question why we failed to recognize our child's symptoms earlier so the illness could have been detected and more promptly treated. If parents made the agonizing decision to turn off their child's life support equipment, nagging regrets can haunt them for the rest of their lives.

If the death was drug-related, parents may question the quality of alcohol or drug counseling their child attended. Too often, these distraught mothers and fathers will torture themselves with a belief that their child could have been saved. They wonder if tragedy could have been avoided "if only" their child had been treated for substance abuse addiction sooner or in a more effective rehabilitation program.

If the child's death was attributed to suicide, some families may privately blame themselves for failing to recognize potential signs of their child's depression. If the child did undergo mental health counseling, the parents may wonder whether they should have insisted on alternative courses of treatment. Either way, the self-induced guilt that can result is suffocating. The death of their child may drive these parents, even more than other suffering families, to find ways to unjustifiably blame themselves.

Writer Albert Y. Hsu, who lost his father to suicide, describes the painful guilt that may accompany such a death:

> In our darker moments we answer the 'why did this happen' question by pointing the finger at ourselves. We think of ways we might have contributed to the death, signs we didn't see, steps we didn't take to prevent the suicide. This is called survivor's guilt, and it is tremendously common. Virtually all survivors of suicide wrestle with it to some degree.[16]

The underlying factors that may motivate someone to end his life are extremely complex and beyond the scope of this book. Even experts who have conducted extensive research into suicidology may disagree about the root causes.

If our child died while taking a trip, we may blame ourselves for failing to convince them not to go. Even if our child was randomly murdered, we torture ourselves because we didn't prevent them from being vulnerable to such violence. Too many guilt-ridden parents just can't resist blaming themselves. They will resort to the weakest-causation link possible to convince themselves that they are at fault.

For five years, I suffered with tremendous guilt, believing that I was directly responsible for Tiffanie's death from meningitis. If Tiffanie had only known that there were several other cases in the area, she could have taken a highly-effective vaccine to protect herself. A small percentage of the population carries meningitis bacteria, but they usually have the immunities in their system to prevent infection.

When meningitis entered Tiffanie's system, she had just finished a grueling week of final exams ending her sophomore year at Clemson University. Typically, many college students survive their test schedules by consuming junk food, often in a sleep-deprived state. During her exhausting week of examinations, Tiffanie was probably no exception, although she normally adhered to a very healthy diet. Whatever the reason, Tiffanie's immunities failed to protect her from infection.

After her death, I convinced myself that I may have been the "meningitis carrier" who infected Tiffanie. I was the person with her the most during the twenty-four hours before she became noticeably ill. My emotional torment continued for over two years until I learned that Tiffanie's exposure was far more likely attributed to a specific contact.

Even this new information was not enough to dissuade me from feeling responsible. I began blaming myself for failing to rush Tiffanie to a hospital as soon as I arrived to pick her up after her exams.[17] At dinner that evening, I discovered Tiffanie was dealing with a sore throat. She had visited the campus clinic the previous day and received a decongestant. Other than her sore throat, the typical symptoms of meningitis did not manifest themselves until about thirty-four hours later. For years, I went to Tiffanie's grave sobbing uncontrollably, convinced I had failed to get her medical attention soon enough.

There is yet another reason why many parents punish themselves emotionally for their child's death. They may share the unspoken fear that their God allowed the tragedy to punish them. A child's death goes against the natural order of life. When it occurs, it is so shocking that parents are often desperate for some logical reason.

When they are denied that explanation, it can spark a pervasive feeling that their child's death occurred to punish them. They may begin to believe their child was taken in retribution for past sins. They suffer inside as these horrible thoughts race through their minds. They rarely verbalize these painful suspicions to anyone. It is simply too agonizing to share these private fears.

The various guilt schemes we concoct to justify blaming ourselves may be only a smokescreen. The underlying reason why we may feel responsible is our failure as parents to protect our child from harm. This is particularly true of fathers, who are often raised to believe that family protection is the man's most important obligation.

If you suffer from this punishing guilt, part of the grieving process involves ultimately recognizing that you are most likely not responsible. The best explanation I can offer is that it was simply your child's time. As difficult as that is to reconcile, there is usually nothing you could reasonably have done to change it. All of us would have done anything in our power to save our child's life. We already suffer terribly over the reality that our child is gone. I encourage you to avoid adding unfounded guilt to your agony. You are already struggling with enough pain.

Chapter 5 - Miscarriages and Stillbirths

WHEN A WOMAN LEARNS THAT SHE is an expectant mother, there is usually a tremendous sense of excitement and hope for the future. If this is the first pregnancy, the expectant parents are especially ecstatic. Having a child represents a major transition in our lives. Expectant mothers and fathers will often purchase the latest books available to educate themselves about how to become "good" parents. Even if the couple already has other children, each pregnancy is a unique, exhilarating experience.

When I was accepted into law school, Kathy and I recognized that working full-time as a police captain while also attending night classes would drastically limit my free time. Since we would be staying close to home, we decided this would be an ideal time to try for a second child. Soon after entering my first semester, Kathy became pregnant. We were ecstatic as we anticipated how our second child would enrich our lives. We openly shared this joyous news with six-year-old Tiffanie, as well as our family and friends.

Upon discovering she was pregnant, Kathy took prenatal vitamins religiously and complied with her doctor's recommendations. She is not a smoker and avoided even a sip of wine, despite our urge to celebrate. It was an exciting time for our family, filled with preparations for our new son or daughter's arrival. Our emotional bond with our unborn child had already formed.

In an instant, our dreams came to a devastating halt when Kathy's pregnancy ended in a miscarriage at twelve weeks. We were shocked and totally unprepared. Since Kathy did not have any complications in her earlier pregnancy, we had no reason to anticipate this pregnancy would be any different.

Kathy's doctor could offer no logical explanation as to why this happened. He indicated that it occurs sometimes "when the child isn't developing properly." I remember pervasive feelings of sadness, anger, and disappointment in the subsequent weeks. Kathy searched for books about miscarriage, but was only able to locate a few. Yet she was amazed by how many women approached her privately and shared the fact that they too had suffered a miscarriage.

Apparently, miscarriages were one of society's best kept secrets. They occurred with far greater frequency than we had ever realized. Yet it was almost taboo for anyone to openly discuss them. Most of our friends and relatives expressed their regrets without further comment. Since so few people actually understood miscarriages, they didn't know how to react.

Some friends offered a variety of possible causes of miscarriages they had "heard about" in the past. Included among these were: being overworked, getting insufficient sleep or too much exercise, being exposed to paint fumes, and using alcohol or cigarettes. While none of these applied to Kathy, I resented the subtle insinuation that she could have somehow been at fault for her failed pregnancy.

I didn't realize at the time that many women blame themselves when a miscarriage occurs. James Van Praagh, a widely acclaimed medium and author, discusses this tendency:

> When a death occurs before birth, as in miscarriage, a mother-to-be feels not only cheated of her dream, but also feels at fault, as if she were directly responsible for the death. After all, the baby died inside her body, and she blames herself for not being a safe receptacle for her unborn child. Her grieving can involve excessive self-criticism and utter remorse. In the most severe of prenatal deaths, a few women may even feel like murderers. At the very least, a woman feels unimaginable inner conflict and turmoil and tremendous grief. Of course, a father feels disturbed, too. He may blame himself for not taking better care of mother and baby in some way.[18]

Kathy and I were never told about the existence of any support groups for families dealing with this type of loss. We were simply expected to work through our pain. A miscarriage is so traumatic, some women fear trying again. But since our doctor encouraged us to do exactly that, we did.

Six months later, Kathy was with child again. This time, we were more guarded in our optimism and only shared the news with a few people. As before, Kathy was meticulous in following her doctor's instructions. When she miscarried at ten weeks, our deep sense of sadness and loss was magnified. We feared that we might never have another child.

We were soon referred to a high-profile specialist for a consultation. The doctor attributed Kathy's difficulty to a condition called endometriosis. He recommended major surgery requiring months of recuperation and no guarantees the problem would not recur.

When Kathy's regular physician learned of this proposal, he suggested trying to become pregnant one more time. By now, both of us were afraid to get our hopes up and the fear of dealing with another loss was pervasive. Finally, we did try again and Kathy became pregnant. Although she experienced some problems during her pregnancy, a healthy David Barry Collins was born in 1984. Two-and-a-half years later, Christopher Charles Collins followed.

Kathy and I realize how fortunate we are that these subsequent pregnancies were successful. The fact that we were eventually able to have two more children did make it easier to heal and emotionally rebound from our earlier losses. Yet we still experience feelings of emptiness for the two children lost through miscarriages.

Those parents who are unable to have a child following a miscarriage may experience greater difficulty healing emotionally. This miscarriage ended their hopes of ever giving birth. The emotional bond the mother forms with the life she carries inside leads to intense pain when the pregnancy ends in a miscarriage.

Based in part on their personal experiences, Marie Allen, Ph.D. and Shelly Marks, M.S., describe a mother's bond in their book about miscarriage and its effects:

> ... So by the time a woman knows she is pregnant, she may already be deeply emotionally linked with her baby. She maintains constant awareness of her baby when making decisions throughout each day about what she will eat, what she might take for a headache, and how she will put on her seat belt. In everything she does, she holds her baby in her heart and in her mind. To her, the being she carries inside of her is already her very *real and whole* baby, and powerful maternal love is long under way...[19]

I realize that the population of the United States is heavily divided over the issue of when life actually begins. I am certainly not anxious to enter the pro-life versus pro-choice debate. However, Kathy and I personally believe we lost two children due to miscarriage. We remember the hope we had for each and feel an emotional attachment with them in our hearts.

One of Kathy's greatest frustrations is that there are no graves to honor them. We visit Tiffanie's grave each day. Yet there is no special place to pay tribute to our two other children who never had the chance to be born. Because both pregnancies ended so early, we never knew their gender or had the opportunity to consider names.

Today, hospitals and health care facilities are more willing to provide high-quality photos of the fetus to the parents. These can become a cherished keepsake for the family if a miscarriage later occurs. Hospital policies may vary with regard to the availability of photographs after a stillbirth. Many parents may be unreceptive to having such pictures, while others might cherish them.

Most child bereavement support groups officially welcome parents who have lost their child through miscarriages or stillbirths. I definitely don't want to discourage anyone from attending these bereavement meetings. Most parents who regularly attend are very supportive and anxious to offer comfort to distraught parents.

My opinion is that while the losses are different, the feelings of pain, sadness, anger, and despair are all devastating. Regardless of the fetus' stage of development, the emotional love bond between parent and child has formed.

However it can be especially difficult for parents who have suffered through miscarriages or stillbirths to attend regular child-loss support groups. There may occasionally be someone in attendance who does not consider a miscarriage or stillbirth to be equivalent to other child losses. Additionally, when others discuss experiences they shared during their child's life, these men and women are limited to talking about the pregnancies. This can make them feel isolated and uncomfortable. Too often, they attend one or two support group meetings and never return.

Today, there are a number of support groups devoted specifically to dealing with losses from stillbirths and miscarriages. Attending these groups may be preferable because everyone who attends had a similar experience. I have included a partial list of these groups on my website for your consideration.[20]

Chapter 6 - Visiting the Gravesite

SOME MOTHERS OR FATHERS EXPERIENCE IMMENSE anxiety about visiting their child's grave after the funeral. Sometimes one parent is emotionally able to go to the cemetery regularly, while the other is too distraught. Visiting your child's grave, especially in the beginning, evokes raw emotions. For some, it is a safe place where they can privately communicate with their loved one. Others may experience a closer connection merely by spending time alone in the child's room.

Parents who are continually overcome with anguish at the cemetery, may be incapable of regularly checking if their child's grave is being properly maintained. This can be especially difficult for single, divorced, or widowed parents with no spouse or significant other to fulfill this obligation. A caring relative or close friend can ease the burden by temporarily watching over the gravesite on the family's behalf.

A trip to the grave is inherently a very personal experience with different meanings for each individual. Kathy and I are fortunate that we both take comfort in visiting Tiffanie's grave each day. I visit her gravesite because it is the final resting place for her body. Sadly, it provides the only opportunity I have left to protect and care for her. I don't feel any closer to her when I visit the cemetery, but I feel her presence around me all of the time.

We, as fathers, deeply miss the roles as our children's protectors. Many of us were raised to believe that safeguarding the family is our most solemn responsibility. When our child dies, we may experience persistent, nagging pangs of guilt. We are tortured by the belief we have failed in our duty to keep our children from harm's way.

Grief-stricken fathers are often desperate to find ways to take care of their children. Many are compelled to check on their child's grave daily and the same may be true of mothers.

At the cemetery, I make certain Tiffanie's marker has not been damaged, ensure her flowers remain upright, and remove any trash from the immediate area. I also try to ensure Tiffanie's marker is kept reasonably polished. These daily inspections are admittedly a small contribution, yet they provide the only meaningful opportunity I have left to care for my daughter.

For the first few weeks after Tiffanie died, I was obsessed with visiting the cemetery five or six times a day. On one visit, I discovered the mum flowers on her grave had been meticulously taken apart, petal by petal, and strewn across the grass. I was instantly outraged and vowed to track down the person responsible.

This cult-like ritual of disassembling Tiffanie's flowers was repeated on several occasions over the next few weeks. Each time, I cleaned up the mess and replaced the flowers while quietly seething. Determined to identify the person responsible for this desecration, I began conducting surveillance on the grounds. I was confident all those years of law enforcement would now serve me well.

I suspected this was being done by some deranged person with a personal grudge against either Tiffanie or our family. At first, I parked just down the street from her grave and carefully hid myself in my automobile. I tried to remain out of sight while peering through a small side window.

Although I maintained my surveillance for several weeks without success, my frustration grew as the dismantling of flowers on Tiffanie's grave continued unabated. Yet these incidents always occurred when I was not in the area.

In desperation, I climbed a tall tree directly across the street. While it took considerable effort, the fullness of the leaves and multiple branches provided the perfect camouflage. From this vantage point, I was well hidden and had a direct view of Tiffanie's gravesite. Each time I was on the cemetery grounds, visitors came, paid their respects, and left without incident. Some brought new flowers, but no one disturbed the existing arrangements.

One afternoon, after several hours of uneventful surveillance, I left the grounds to purchase a drink from a local convenience store. When I returned fifteen minutes later, the vandal had struck again. I became totally incensed at having missed my opportunity. It seemed as though the person responsible was close enough to be watching my every move.

Despite the hours devoted to my cemetery stakeout, it was Kathy who actually discovered the culprit's true identity. During a morning visit, she looked on in disbelief as a fluffy grey squirrel systematically disassembled the flowers on Tiffanie's grave. It was only then we discovered that squirrels are especially attracted to small mums.

The moral of my naive experience is not to allow your grief to become an obsession. My determination to protect Tiffanie's grave clouded my good judgment; in retrospect, the answer should have been obvious. In my anguish, I was too caught up in my compulsion to protect Tiffanie's grave at all costs. It is so difficult to think rationally when your heart has been ripped apart.

One of the sad realities about cemeteries is that the general public has unlimited access to them throughout the day. Over the years, I have spoken to a number of parents who were upset after discovering some special memento missing from their child's grave. Expensive plants are especially vulnerable. A person who removes items from a cemetery would probably argue that any property left there has been abandoned and thus has no owner.

I spent over twenty-five years in law enforcement and another dozen years as a criminal defense attorney. Based on my range of experience, one might suspect that I would not easily be surprised at the things some people do. Yet the first time someone removed a plant from my daughter's grave, I was outraged.

Each incident has involved an expensive plant, left as a gesture of love in Tiffanie's memory. It would seem logical that whoever was responsible was motivated by its value, eliminating teenage pranksters as likely suspects. When someone removes articles from a child's grave, the family feels totally violated. It becomes one more way fathers may feel they failed to protect their children.

On one occasion, I observed a female visitor removing flowers from several graves and placing them on another in an adjacent area. I provided this information to our favorite cemetery representative. He checked into the situation, confirmed what I had reported, and the woman was later identified. Sadly, a combination of mental illness and deep anguish played a role in her bizarre behavior. The problem was resolved and I have never seen her again.

Many cemeteries restrict the quantity of items that may be placed on a grave, as well as their duration. These policies exist to ensure each site is properly maintained and presents a neat appearance. Depending on how rigidly these rules are enforced, even fresh flowers may be removed if they are deemed too excessive or otherwise in violation of the rules. This can be extremely frustrating for families because aggressive enforcement may result in removal of items left by other visitors. It brings special comfort to a bereaved parent to know that friends or relatives still visit their child's final resting place. If expressions of remembrance from others are removed prematurely, parents are denied the reassurance that others still care.

If you experience these types of problems, I recommend meeting with your cemetery representatives and apprising them of the situation. If enough concern is voiced about strict enforcement, administrators may be willing to re-evaluate their positions.

You should also notify them whenever items seem to selectively disappear from your child's grave. Most members of the grounds crew constantly move throughout the site, ensuring the grass is neatly trimmed and the hedges properly sheared. We can't always be there to watch over our children's graves. If these workers are made aware of any problems, they are often very willing to act as our eyes and ears.

Chapter 7 - The Stigma of a Child's Death

PARENTS MAY EVENTUALLY DISCOVER THAT SOME friends, coworkers, and even relatives begin to treat them differently after their child's death. One afternoon, several months after Tiffanie died, Kathy and I were shopping in our neighborhood grocery store. We spotted a woman whom we recognized because one of her daughters was Tiffanie's friend. We had met this woman during various activities in our neighborhood. She had attended Tiffanie's wake and sent a sympathy card to our family.

As we continued pushing our shopping cart in her direction, the woman suddenly glanced up, apparently sensing our approach. When she looked directly at us, her grimaced expression revealed her obvious panic. She made an immediate u-turn with her grocery cart and scurried off in the opposite direction. At the time, Kathy and I were too puzzled to realize the significance of what had just happened. This incident was only a precursor to the type of rejection we have learned to anticipate from too many others over the years.

When our children die, friends and family members are usually very supportive immediately after the tragedy. When the funeral services have ended and everyone returns to their normal routine, heartbroken parents are often left to pick up the pieces of their lives. We take a deep breath and seek refuge in a form of emotional hibernation. The world as we knew it has changed drastically. Over time, we learn to take small, cautious steps to interact with those around us.

As we gradually resume meaningful contact with others, we may notice that some people seem reluctant to be around us. Perhaps merely seeing us is too painful of a reminder to them that anyone's child can die. Being in our presence forces them to face the reality that it can happen to any family. Since they prefer to avoid considering that possibility, we apparently make them very uncomfortable.

Grieving parents must learn to expect a variety of adverse reactions from people. If it happens repeatedly, we can begin to develop a low self-image. We sense that we've become a black cloud that hovers over everyone else's sunny day. This stigma is something we have to bear to varying degrees for the rest of our lives. Eventually, we learn to consider this rejection as just another sad consequence of our child's death.

There will always be some people who consciously choose to avoid us after our children die. While this may hurt our feelings, there really is nothing we can do to change their minds. We may have to accept the unpleasant reality that we are far better off without them in our lives. Sadly, we usually have to suffer some emotional indignity before we realize someone falls into this category.

In Chapter 8, I describe the isolation many parents experience after their child's death. Initially we may find the lack of interaction with others preferable. It takes us off the public stage where everyone seems to be constantly watching. During those fragile early days, we are so consumed with emotional pain, we constantly seem on the verge of tears. Most of us would prefer to be left alone.

There are a variety of aggravating factors that can magnify our feelings of isolation. The manner in which a child dies can add a suffocating stigma that seems to swirl around the family. Sometimes medical experts are initially unable to identify the specific cause of death and the finalization of an autopsy report can take several months to be completed. While the family nervously waits and wonders, this delay may fuel speculation among neighborhood gossips. An unexplained death may be falsely attributed to a variety of "suspected" causes.

If the child was very young, unfounded allegations may circulate that she was the victim of physical trauma or abuse. Spreading this type of baseless gossip is at best negligent, and possibly intentionally hurtful. Eventually, these cruel rumors are likely to be reported back to the parents by a friend or relative. False accusations emotionally torture a family already suffocating from the crushing pain of its loss.

Law enforcement officials have to remain objective as they wait for the cause of death to be determined. Yet what the police may have intended to be a cautious, professional approach can be misinterpreted by the family as cold indifference or even distrust. Depending on the circumstances, parents may fear being accused of something they find incomprehensible. This only increases their feelings of guilt, insecurity, and isolation.

A child's murder can also be a catalyst for wagging tongues and leave parents feeling trapped, shattered, and alone. There is no logical reason to explain why a child is murdered. It can be the result of a personal relationship that turns violent. It may also result from a random act of violence, when no logical connection exists between the perpetrator and victim.

When a suspected murderer is apprehended, his defense attorney may raise potential legal defenses. In doing so, there may be a conscious effort to publicly portray older victims as having a propensity for violent behavior. When this occurs, the lawyer possibly intends to raise self-defense as an issue in the case. The family finds its child's reputation being publicly attacked with little or no recourse to undo the harm.

When the shattered parents of a murdered child find the energy and courage to walk into a large gathering, they may pretend not to notice the pervasive whispering in various corners of the room. Too frequently, baseless speculation can lead to the collective assumption the child was involved in dangerous and/or illegal behavior that contributed to his death. There may be a tendency for some people to rudely gawk at the parents from a distance while avoiding actual contact.

Regardless of how faultless the child may have been, the mere fact that she was murdered seems to fan the flames of incessant rumors. If the parents have other small children, they may find it difficult to maintain consistent playmates as a direct consequence of the neighborhood rumor mill. The family can feel ostracized at a time when it desperately needs emotional support from others to begin the healing process.

Psychotherapist and author Kathleen O'Hara, MA, whose son Aaron Land was brutally murdered, describes the impact of violent deaths on a family:

> You may feel shame about what happened and this may keep you from telling your story. You hold it inside because you feel it is too awful to tell. You may be afraid to tell people what happened because of their possible reactions regarding the victim, or for fear of what they might think of you. Many in this situation experience the stigma that surrounds violence. It is vital to your recovery that you find the courage to face and work through this.
>
> Silence is deadly; it leaves you feeling hopeless, angry, and isolated. Talking about what happened is an important step in removing the stigma, by stopping the denial our culture perpetrates. Survivors often feel as if they are the ones with the problem, as though they are rejected by the very society they thought they were part of. You may feel as if you did something wrong, and unfortunately there may be people who sometimes unconsciously or unintentionally reinforce this notion...[21]

According to the Centers for Disease Control and Prevention, suicide was the eighth leading cause of death for males in the United States in 2004. When categorized by age, the suicide rate rose to third for persons 10 - 14, 15 -19, and 20 - 24 years and was the second leading cause of death for males ranging in age from 25-34 years.[22]

A child's death by suicide presents another type of social stigma for an emotionally struggling family. The fact that the child consciously took his own life can cause people to speculate. They wonder aloud what was so terrible in the child's life that he was driven to escape.

As these local gossips spew their poisonous venom debating the child's motives, the devastated parents emotionally torture themselves with feelings of intense guilt that so often accompany such a terrible loss. As they constantly reassess what might have been done differently, the last thing this family needs is for hurtful rumors to add to their already intolerable pain.

Many people automatically assume that fatal drug overdoses are suicides. Although most of these deaths may have been intentional, some drug overdoses are accidental. When illegal drugs are purchased on the street, there is never any guarantee as to the strength or quality of the substance. There is no strictly-regulated manufacturing process for these drugs or cautionary documented procedures for their safe use. Anyone who resorts to using illegal substances definitely places her life at risk each time she does so.

Some drug overdoses are caused by the use of legally-prescribed medicines. These deaths may result because the medications were taken in the wrong quantity or mistakenly combined with other, incompatible medicines. Many of these medicines should never be combined with alcohol, yet that restriction can be easily forgotten in a social-drinking environment.

Thus, not all fatal overdoses are the result of intentional acts of suicide. If there was no actual intention to die, in my view the death was accidental. Parents may never know the real answer as to whether death resulted because their child was reckless, naive, or intended to take her life. Regardless of the child's actual intention, the result is the same and the family's pain is agonizing. They need support from friends and relatives, rather than endless conjecture over the cause of their child's death.

Even death by disease can carry a stigma. Two days after Tiffanie died, Kathy and I were totally distraught as we struggled to handle her funeral arrangements. Later that evening, I answered a telephone call from a close relative who informed us that her family was refusing to attend Tiffanie's wake and funeral. She explained that they did not want to risk possibly "catching meningitis" from my daughter's body. This is not exactly the type of love, emotional support, and compassion you would expect from a loving family during a time of extreme crisis.

As I listened to her voice, I was initially confused and didn't grasp the significance of her message. When I realized the actual purpose of her call, my first reaction was shock. It was incomprehensible that she and her family could abandon my daughter and our family so casually at such as disastrous time. My attitude quickly transitioned from total disbelief to complete outrage. I remember screaming into the telephone that I "disowned" them all.

One of the few constant memories I have of Tiffanie's wake is of continually watching the entrance to the visitation room. To the very end of each viewing session, I clung desperately to the hope these family members would change their minds and attend Tiffanie's wake or at least the funeral. They never did, and I have avoided contact with them ever since. Right or wrong, I have no place in my life for any of them.

Chapter 8 - I Am Hurting and Want to Die Too!

LIFE IS THE MOST PRECIOUS OF all gifts. As grieving parents, we understand that as well as anyone. When our child died, we were suddenly confronted with the fine line between life and death. One day our son or daughter was alive within our grasp in this world. In an instant, they were gone.

Many religious representatives are supportive during the period immediately after a child's death. However, too often, they virtually disappear once the funeral services have ended. Many fail to recognize the critical need for regular follow-up with a family after the funeral. During this time, emotional isolation can begin as parents may become more depressed and feel hopeless. During this period of intense anguish, dying can begin to hold an unhealthy fascination for despairing parents, who may experience fleeting thoughts of suicide.

Most of us were raised to believe death should be feared. We were taught to always protect ourselves and take safety precautions in everything we did. Yet when a child dies, parents may suddenly lose the fear of dying. Since their precious loved one died, they may no longer fear their own death. Self-destruction can even seem to be a means to a desirable end: unification with their child.

Tortured by the thought they can no longer protect their child, these grief-stricken moms and dads may feel helpless. The agony of facing a future without their child can make suicide seem a welcome respite from the physical and emotional pain they initially believe will never diminish.

Just after our child's death, we are often tormented by many irrational impulses which may include thoughts of suicide. The fresher our grief, the more compelling these impulses may seem. Since the early days can be especially dangerous, friends and family should always be alert for possible signs of self-destructive thoughts in grieving parents. The skewed logic that can lead a parent to consider taking his own life may seem insane to the rest of the world. Yet it can seem to be a perfectly reasonable alternative to a parent whose entire being aches with despair.

I understand that feeling of hopelessness and desperation. My wife is one of those "computer people" in a profession requiring intellect and the ability to exercise consistent, logical reasoning. Yet when Tiffanie died, Kathy and I spoke openly, even calmly, about suicide. We were both in such immense agony, dying seemed an attractive alternative to living in a world without our daughter. Common sense and logical reasoning did not enter into the equation.

Even though our two young sons, David and Chris, were only eleven and nine respectively, we were not initially dissuaded from considering suicide. Our rational judgment had been clouded by the depths of our anguish. We never reached the stage of discussing a possible method. Nor did we talk about whom we could trust to raise our sons after we were gone. We never eliminated suicide as an option; we simply stopped talking about it.

In retrospect, I believe our discussions about suicide were merely fleeting impulses of panic, fueled by our intense pain and sense of hopelessness. Any brokenhearted parent can be vulnerable to thoughts of self destruction. Most are consumed by a level of emotional pain unmatched by anything they have ever experienced. Just after our child's death, we can't fathom any way this intense level of agony will ever subside. We feel adrift without our children, believing our mission in life has been lost.

It is potentially very dangerous to allow grief and pain to dominate our reasoning process. This is why it is so important for religious leaders to recognize the vulnerability of parents during the period after the funeral. They must be more proactive, ensuring regular follow-up outreach is made to spend time with a family in mourning.

Even when distraught mothers or fathers don't consciously consider suicide, a self-destructive subconscious can pose an equal danger. After their child has died, some parents may begin to seriously neglect their overall health. Examples of this behavior can include refusing to eat, excessive overeating, excessive consumption of alcohol, or a sudden reliance on antidepressant medications. If parents already had medical conditions requiring daily medications, they may simply forget to take them.

Some parents may begin to drive their automobiles in a far more dangerous manner. They are suddenly more willing to engage in high-risk behavior probably because their fear of dying is gone. While they may give no outward indication of suicidal tendencies, their actions can provide subtle clues of a subconscious yearning for self destruction. They may not even realize their underlying motivation for suddenly behaving so recklessly. If they were to be killed or seriously injured, they would never want anyone to believe it was an intentional act.

A careful observer might notice this person is suddenly living his life on the edge. A pattern of self-destructive behavior poses great potential peril. This is a difficult problem to address, especially when these individuals will not admit their real motivation, even to themselves. If confronted, they are likely to dismiss any concern as overblown or unjustified. Although they may avoid that dreaded "suicidal" label, the end result – the risk of death or serious injury - would be the same.

If any of these feelings apply to you, understanding they exist is a good first step. If you have been experiencing self-destructive thoughts, it is a serious warning sign of danger that cannot be taken lightly. I urge you to seek immediate professional help. It is critical to reach out to someone qualified to provide the emotional and psychological support you need. There is no shame in asking for help if you suddenly find yourself overwhelmed by the magnitude of your loss. While I may not always agree with some mental health professionals, I have seen first-hand the miracles they can perform.

Some communities offer mental health resources to assist those suffering with depression. Suicide prevention hotlines are particularly helpful for those who feel the need to immediately and confidentially discuss their feelings. There are a number of these hotlines across the country. A National Suicide Prevention Lifeline is available twenty-four hours a day at 1-800-273-8255.[23]

When coping with these emotions, it is important to spend time around people who care and can be supportive, such as your family or close friends. Isolation can exacerbate feelings of depression and increase your vulnerability. In the early days of grief, you should try to reduce time spent alone. I recognize this advice is difficult to follow when solitude often becomes an integral part of our early comfort zones.

The vast majority of parents survive the loss of their child. Somewhere in the midst of grief, they rediscover hope and realize that suicide is not the answer. They recognize the distinction between a panic-driven obsession to die and a temporary loss of passion for living. In the latter, the parent's zest for life has understandably waned as a result of his child's death. The solution lies in finding new ways to recapture that enthusiasm.

Hopefully, parents who grieve are surrounded by a nurturing support system that reaches out to keep them continually engaged. They need constant emotional support, social interaction, and tactful reassurance from their friends and loved ones. Leaving them to fend for themselves only intensifies their sense of isolation and despair.

As time passes, parents may begin to fear their friends and family have forgotten their loss. This concern is usually heightened by those people around them who seem uncomfortable at the mere mention of their child's name. Organizing special events or activities in a child's memory can bring comfort to the anguished parents. This is a good way to coax them out of their solitude. It can also help them discover new ways to ensure their child is always remembered.

Regardless of how briefly they lived, our children will always be special to us. It becomes very important to us that they are not forgotten. Parents can find renewed enthusiasm by engaging in activities to preserve their child's memory.[24] This new purpose often invigorates their passion for life.

If we merely succumbed to our initial self-destructive impulses, our child would quickly be forgotten. Thus, most of us accept the challenge to find new ways to remind the world around us that our children deserve to be remembered. Our mission in life, as we understood it, has been drastically altered, as we are emotionally refreshed each time we succeed in having our son or daughter's life acknowledged.

In the early days after Tiffanie's death, The Compassionate Friends, Inc. (TCF), an international support group, became our lifeline. In the twelve years since Tiffanie's death, Kathy and I have made the transition from devastated parents to determined, caring social activists. We are driven to reach out and comfort everyone who has faced the loss of their beloved child. We share their pain right along with them, just as I ache for you. Through the depths of their suffering, we search for ways to help them rediscover hope.

We have been honored to play personally-rewarding roles as TCF chapter leaders and have learned the importance of helping those who grieve.[25] At each meeting, our children are remembered and celebrated. In our local support group, many parents wear pins bearing their child's photograph so everyone present can become more familiar with their child. Our wonderful friend John Trimble, Leisa's dad, brings a special machine to every meeting to create remembrance pins for every family member in attendance.

Kathy and I will always remember the depths of our pain when Tiffanie died. Our mission in life has now changed as we channel our grief into a committed desire to reach out and help others survive this horrible experience. This book is intended to help you rediscover hope, despite the intensity of your anguish.

Chapter 9 - Siblings

WHEN A CHILD DIES, PARENTS CAN be so devastated that they are unable to recognize the emotional needs of any surviving siblings. Blinded by their own mind-numbing grief, they may be incapable of assessing the tragedy's full impact on other children left behind. Surviving brothers or sisters can quickly become the forgotten grievers.

Well-intentioned friends and relatives often instill in siblings an expectation that they must "be strong" for their parents. This unfortunate advice can be offered as early as the wake or funeral. In the first few weeks and months after the funeral, this guidance is often reinforced as siblings encounter other adults who ask, "How are your parents coping?"

It is wonderful that these people show concern for the parents. Yet asking this question completely ignores the fact these siblings have also incurred a tremendous emotional shock. They too are intensely suffering. There seems to be an inherent presumption that since they "only" lost a brother or sister, their grief can't be as traumatizing as their parents. Siblings' roles can become strangely reversed as they suddenly become their parents' protectors.

Recognized grief experts Dr. Heidi Horsley and Dr. Gloria Horsley[26] describe some of the difficulties faced by surviving siblings in their recent book, *Teen Grief Relief: Parenting with Understanding, Support and Guidance*:
- If a family member has died, not only are you suffering from losing them but you're also dealing with losing the way your parents and family life used to be. You have a double loss.
- Parents sometimes focus too much on your life and projects.
- You're often the forgotten mourner, overlooked, unacknowledged or ignored. People tend to say, 'It must be really hard for your parents,' or 'Be strong for your parents.' [27]

Sibling grief is devastating as they face the after-effects of an intolerable tragedy that has drastically changed their lives forever. Although they may have a multitude of nagging questions, they resist the normal impulse to ask their parents. Their reluctance may be partially due to the advice they received to "be strong," as well as their fear that questions will only evoke more sadness for their parents. Unless they have a friend or relative who has suffered a similar loss, they may feel uncomfortable confiding in anyone. Too often, their concerns are left unanswered and their suffering is only exacerbated by the uncertainty.

Surviving siblings struggle immensely, often very privately, with their sadness. Depending on the relationship that existed with their deceased brother or sister at the time of death, siblings can experience tremendous guilt. Joey O'Connor, author of several books devoted to parents and young adults, describes the magnitude of a sibling's grief:

> Another common emotion children feel after the death of a loved one is guilt. For varying reasons, children may think that it is their fault the person died. Particularly with accidents, children can feel that they in some way caused the accident or that they could have prevented the accident.
>
> Children also feel guilty when they are helpless in comforting their inconsolable parents. Since death has a tremendous impact on the landscape of family life, the guilty feelings children experience are often related to not knowing how to respond to the various needs of family members. Unknowingly, grieving parents can look to surviving children for a sense of comfort and support. Guilt is felt when a child cannot meet the needs and expectations of grieving family members, whether the perceived needs are real or not.[28]

Periodic disagreements are very common among siblings. Yet if the surviving siblings had recent arguments with the brother or sister who died, it can torment them emotionally for the rest of their lives. They may replay these disputes over in their minds, only to be emotionally consumed with regret.

If surviving brothers or sisters were involved in the same activity that led to their sibling's death, they may be overwhelmed with guilt merely because they survived. One example of this would be an automobile accident in which one sibling dies while another lives. Surviving siblings may become extremely depressed as they wonder if they will ever be able to enjoy life after their sibling's death.

In her book written for grieving teenagers, certified death educator and author Helen Fitzgerald documents this problem:

> Feeling that you should be dead instead of the person who died is a common feeling, and there is even a name for it: survivor guilt. Survivor guilt is a very powerful emotion. It occurs to some extent after all deaths...[29]

In light of the severity and complexity of sibling grief, it is important for parents to maintain a supportive environment. The anguish of these brothers and sisters must be recognized and acknowledged. Since we all grieve differently, resources must be directed toward reaching out to them as individuals. They too need an outlet to share their feelings, as well as to help them cope with a myriad of emotions. If possible, counseling resources should be made available to each sibling. Sadly, the high cost of health insurance, as well as policy coverage limitations, can make counseling an unattainable option.

Another potential obstacle is the tendency of older brothers or sisters to refuse participation in counseling. My experience interacting with mourning family members has taught me that the older the sibling, the greater the likelihood she will resist therapy. Those older than fifteen can be very difficult to convince to confide their innermost thoughts to a professional counselor.

This reluctance may be partially due to early advice to "be strong" for their parents. They may fear that undergoing counseling would only make their parents more upset. To avoid adding to their parents' emotional burden, it is common for siblings to hide their pain.

This new role as our protectors can cause siblings a multitude of problems later. Deprived of the opportunity to grieve in the aftermath of their loss, siblings focus on hiding their pain to protect us from further suffering. If they can't share their feelings with a counselor or someone who has experienced the same tragedy, their voices are often muted. With no outlet for their stream of painful emotions, they are forced to bury their grief deep inside where it can gnaw away at them over time.

When parents are consumed by their child's death, siblings may mistakenly conclude they are not loved as much as the brother or sister who died. This can cause resentment and create a void in their lives. Vulnerable siblings may remember this period of their lives as one of emotional abandonment by their parents. To them, it may seem their mothers and fathers are so obsessed with the loss, they have lost interest in their living children. Bereaved brothers and sisters may express frustration, believing this tragedy has ruined their lives. They lost a sibling they loved, as well as the close relationship they previously enjoyed with their parents.

Siblings need to experience consistent, outward expressions of parental love, as well as our acknowledgement that they are grieving too. I urge you to do everything in your power to demonstrate your love and genuine interest in their lives. This may involve attending a ball game or a dance recital, helping with homework, or simply going somewhere together as a family. We joined a family bowling league soon after Tiffanie's death to get us out of the house.

Even though it only involved a couple of hours a week, the time we spent together as a family was definitely a blessing.

It is essential to be totally open and honest with our children. They are in great pain and should be encouraged not to shield us from their emotions. We need to educate them that we understand their pain is horrific. They should not be made to feel like "second-class" grievers.

This opens the door to improved communication between parents and siblings as they cope with tragedy in their own ways. Hopefully, it will make them more willing to share their feelings with us without fear of escalating our pain.

Our children must understand that we appreciate their desire to protect us, but they can put our minds more at ease by at least trying a professional counselor. If they consult with a therapist to help them better understand their own unique grief, we will have less reason to worry. With this proactive approach, we may convert the pressure to "be strong" into a willingness to participate in counseling to make us feel better. However, don't be surprised if they refuse. Some teenagers and young adults cannot bring themselves to discuss counseling issues with their parents. If this is the case, there may be a better chance for success if the topic is tactfully suggested by a close relative or friend.

When a sibling is willing to undergo counseling, the next hurdle is matching him with "the right" analyst. While handling juvenile court cases, I discovered the complexity in locating professionals capable of relating to adolescents effectively. If there is no chemistry between a young person and his counselor, the opportunity for therapy to have a beneficial effect is drastically reduced.

Finding a therapist for a grieving brother or sister adds an entirely different dimension to the challenge. She must have the same training and experience as any other professional. Yet her background should include experience with the intricacies of sibling grief. If you locate a professional who communicates well with a certain age group of young adults, teenagers, or children, impart that information to other families in need.

In addition to word-of-mouth, there are a number of other therapy referral options. School counselors can be a very helpful resource. While organized support groups may have strict policies against making referrals to professionals, individual group members are often willing to share their experiences with a particular therapist. Hospital social workers often have a firm grasp of the mental health resources available in their communities.

After Tiffanie's death, both our boys became noticeably quiet around us. We knew that they were suffering deeply with their own overwhelming sadness. Even in our fragile emotional state, we understood that both boys needed professional counseling.

Prior to our tragedy, our eleven-year-old son had written about his family as part of a class assignment. In describing Tiffanie, David wrote:

> She makes a difference in the family. She gives me advice and tips about things when I need them. She is the oldest child in the family and she's also the nicest and the most reasonable. She fills my eyes with happiness when she smiles at me. She always makes things seem more fun and more enjoyable from the way she describes them. She is the greatest, coolest, and the best sister in the world.

After her death, David became very upset when he could find no photographs of he and Tiffanie together. There were many photos of all three children, yet I was only able to locate a few with only the two of them. When David viewed these photos, they seemed to bring him comfort.

Whenever Kathy or I left home, our nine-year-old, Chris, suddenly began demanding to know exactly when we would return. It was obvious that because of his sister's death, he was now worried one of his parents might also die. Chris would work himself into a frenzy if he didn't know our whereabouts or estimated time of return.

After Tiffanie's funeral, Chris began writing a note to his sister every day on an index card. Each day we drove him over to the cemetery to leave his special message on Tiffanie's grave. Although it broke our heart each time he did this, we tried not to show our reaction. At the end of the week, Chris decided that he no longer wanted to leave a message. We didn't dare ask him to explain his reasons. We simply accepted his decision, hoping it was a positive sign of progress in his healing.

Younger siblings are usually more amenable to participation in counseling. Dr. Beverly Anderson[30] met with David and Chris individually over the next few months and provided a safe outlet where they could openly discuss their feelings.

Helen Fitzgerald[31] has done some groundbreaking work exploring grief in children. Although Mrs. Fitzgerald is nationally recognized, we were fortunate that she conducted a youth support group in our community. Kathy enrolled David and Chris in Mrs. Fitzgerald's program concurrently with their private counseling sessions.

The group focused on any type of loss and Helen Fitzgerald did a masterful job of creating a safe environment for the children to share their emotions. These boys and girls readily accepted each other and were open to expressing their innermost thoughts. They worked on a number of grief-related projects that enabled them to interact closely and share their feelings.

We must recognize that no matter what approach we take, older siblings will often refuse to attend counseling. It is critical to avoid getting into arguments over whether they are grieving *properly,* as they too are emotionally vulnerable. As all of us grieve differently; we must respect their approach. Our wisest course of action may be offering our assurance that counseling is always an option if they change their minds.

Making major life decisions immediately after suffering a tragedy is never recommended. Yet sometimes siblings attempt to do so while in a heightened state of emotional sadness. If they are away at college, they may seriously consider dropping out of school. If a sibling suggests this approach, a more reasonable alternative might be to request an approved sabbatical for the remainder of the semester. Colleges have different rules and regulations regarding temporary approved absences from the school.

This inactive status may allow students to return home without bearing the pressure of schoolwork at a time when their grief is so terribly fresh. Spending time with their parents can reassure them that mom and dad are gradually making progress. The period away from school will give them a chance to grieve, as well as to evaluate their next step. Hopefully, they will return to college for the following semester. Universities usually have professional staff available on or near campus to assist students in exploring counseling options.

Older brothers or sisters who have accepted employment in other areas of the country may be tempted to quit their jobs after their sibling's death. They may feel a responsibility to return to their parent's community to *be there* for them. Again, this type of potentially career-damaging decision should be avoided, if at all possible. Some employers offer emergency family leave programs that might authorize a temporary absence from the work site. Siblings should be cautioned against abandoning a favorable job opportunity during times of such emotional crisis.

As parents, it can be difficult to detect signs that our children are shielding us from their emotions. We should not be offended if they avoid going to the cemetery with us. Whether to visit their brother or sister's grave is a very private, individual choice that we must respect. As our children were growing, we were the strong ones who protected them. To suddenly witness their parents weeping and overcome with sadness only adds to the intensity of their sorrow. Thus, it is not surprising that they may avoid those early trips to the grave site, at least when accompanied by their parents.

When siblings eventually resume their normal activities, they are likely to remain very concerned about their parents. If they reside outside of the immediate area, they may communicate with each other, as well as local relatives or friends, to monitor their parent's progress. It is their way of trying to *be strong* for us.

Most grief-stricken parents privately wonder how their children are *really* doing. Since siblings often don't talk about their brother or sister, parents may wrongly conclude their children don't seem to be mourning. Yet they grieve for their brothers or sisters in their own personal ways. They do this very privately, and often don't share this with their family. We need to give them space to grieve in any way they choose. It is not for us to determine the *right way* for them to heal. Simply because they don't talk about their pain does not mean they are not agonizing over their loss.

My youngest son, Chris, was the quarterback of his high school football team. During his senior season, he scored eighteen touchdowns. When I later received copies of the game films, I noticed something unusual. Each time Chris scored, he raised his right arm for a split-second and pointed toward the sky. I later learned that he had dedicated each touchdown to Tiffanie, whom he described as his *missing fan*.

Chris never mentioned this special tribute to us. If copies of the game films had not been provided, we would never have discovered his special, heartfelt remembrance. This is just another example of how siblings grieve in their own personal ways.

The loss of a brother or sister is a terribly traumatic event for a sibling, but the death of a twin adds unique problems. Sharing the same birthday may cause the surviving twin tremendous anguish. What was once a day the twins looked forward to celebrating together suddenly becomes a stark reminder that he is now alone. The surviving twin may even wish his birthday could be changed to another date when a celebration without guilt might be possible.

Identical twins enjoy the unique experience of having the same physical attributes. Yet when a twin dies, the survivor loses that special relationship. Each time he glances in the mirror, the image presents a stark reminder that his sibling is gone forever. Because the twins were identical in appearance, a surviving sibling becomes a constant reminder to everyone of his brother or sister.

As the twin grows older, even the parents may look at her differently. Most parents privately wonder how their child's appearance would have changed as they matured. Yet parents of identical twins can see exactly how their child would have appeared. This also may cause the surviving sibling additional anxiety.

If they have other children, grieving parents may begin to worry that another child could die. This unspoken fear is very real to them because they may become convinced their family has been cursed. They ask themselves why else would something so horrible and unusual happen to their child?

Most parents are blessed with the opportunity to enjoy watching their children grow up, attend school, begin their work careers, fall in love, possibly get married, and maybe even raise their own families. Deprived of sharing these experiences with their child, grieving parents feel different from those around them. They may suspect their family is more vulnerable to tragedy and live in constant fear that bad news is just a telephone call away.

With this in mind, they rarely miss the opportunity to give their surviving children two important messages: "I love you" and "Be careful." Whether the conversation takes place over the telephone or in person, that message is constantly reinforced. Grieving parents and surviving siblings usually share this heightened understanding. They can't take the chance that something else will happen to prevent them from expressing their love. Their shared tragedy has made each of them acutely aware that tomorrow is never guaranteed.

Chapter 10 - Sources of Comfort

I WISH THERE WAS A UNIVERSAL source of comfort to help each of us heal. In reality, we find our emotional relief in many different ways. This chapter identifies sources of comfort that I have encountered along the way. I hope you find something here to facilitate your own personal healing.

This chapter begins with an important caveat: beware of artificial sources of comfort. One such trap is the temptation to make significant financial purchases hoping it will lesson the magnitude of your family's grief. Because this tragic loss has devastated our family members, we can become desperate to find something to ease their pain. It tortures us to see our loved ones suffer and magnifies our feelings of powerlessness.

About a year after Tiffanie died, we received an invitation to attend a vacation timeshare seminar. To this day, I am mystified as to how they ever coaxed us into attending. Although we had always avoided high-pressure sales presentations in the past, this time we decided to go.

After listening to the details, we entered into a six-thousand-dollar timeshare arrangement, justifying the cost as an investment in our sanity. We naively believed spending such a large amount of money would force us to travel. We assumed that taking a vacation would lift our spirits and ease our pain.

While we did manage to take three moderate trips over the next few years, they didn't provide enough benefit to justify such a large expenditure. In fact, the company eventually went out of business, leaving few options for its members to recoup their original investments. We would never have been susceptible to such an unwise venture had we not been reeling from Tiffanie's death. Our travel strategy for grief proved to be only an artificial source of comfort.

My advice is to avoid throwing money at your grief. It may give you and your family members a temporary escape from your anguish, but it will not drive away your pain. Any relief it provides is fleeting at best.

Spending money to feel better can make you particularly vulnerable to financial scams. Even if the purchase is actually legitimate, you can find yourself living beyond your means in a desperate attempt to comfort your family. The impulse to "buy now, pay later," hoping that it brings you relief, can place you in serious economic jeopardy. This stress will only add to your anxiety in the long run.

Counseling: Yes or No?

Losing a child is undeniably a life-changing event that shakes the very foundation of our beings. If there is ever an appropriate time to consider undergoing professional grief counseling, after a child's death is certainly one of them. If you have sufficient financial resources and are amenable to trying the services of a grief counselor, it seems foolish not to at least explore this option.

If you experience persistent thoughts of suicide or any other type of violent or self-destructive behavior, professional mental health counseling is no longer an option - it is an urgent necessity. These symptoms pose a potentially ominous threat to you and your family and emergency mental health treatment must be sought.

Some employers have extensive employee assistance programs that offer grief counseling. Many insurance companies will provide at least partial coverage for the mental health services of a qualified therapist. A variety of government programs also offer counseling services within their communities.

Kathy had been granted an approved absence from her job during the first week Tiffanie was scheduled to be home from college. They had hoped to spend that time together shopping and enjoying each other's company. Having to use that time to plan Tiffanie's funeral seemed the ultimate betrayal.

In the early days after our daughter's death, Kathy and I were overwhelmed by the intensity of our pain. I was actively handling several cases pending on various court dockets, but I immediately stopped accepting any new clients. I tried to keep as busy as possible to avoid having to think about Tiffanie's death.

Kathy became increasingly quiet and lethargic, and seemed to be slowly slipping into a deep depression. I tried to ensure that she actually ate something every day while I maintained a watchful eye over our boys. Yet there is no doubt all of us were struggling in different ways to cope with the enormity of our emotions.

Shortly before the funeral, we received a telephone call from Dr. Beverly J. Anderson, the Clinical Director/Administrator of the Employee Assistance

Program (EAP) for Washington D.C.'s Metropolitan Police Department. During my law enforcement career, my family was entitled to coverage for the variety of professional counseling services EAP offered. Since I was now retired, I was technically no longer entitled to these services.

At Dr. Anderson's insistence, I scheduled an appointment for Kathy to meet with her individually. I was very concerned because Kathy's depression seemed to be worsening each day as she became more withdrawn.

I drove my wife to her first appointment, which Dr. Anderson estimated would take about an hour. As Kathy exited our car, she seemed extremely apprehensive. Two-and-a-half hours later, she emerged from the building. I will never forget the dazed, almost "shell-shocked" expression on her face.

I inquired how her session with Dr. Anderson had gone. In an almost inaudible tone of voice, all Kathy could manage to say was, "She's pretty." I already knew Dr. Anderson was very attractive. I was hoping instead for some meaningful insight into Kathy's prognosis, but that simply didn't happen.

As the former head of several police investigative units, I had been trained in interrogation techniques. Yet I couldn't coax my own wife to reveal anything about her counseling session. I knew better than to pry any further because Kathy remained guarded. She was still in a very fragile emotional state, so I decided to give her some space. Dr. Anderson also remained tight-lipped because of the confidentiality required in a doctor-patient relationship.

My inability to obtain any meaningful insight into Kathy's emotional state was frustrating. I felt powerless to help her because I didn't know which approach might be most effective. She remained protective about her sessions with Dr. Anderson and continued to seclude herself in our home. Eventually, I realized Kathy's willingness to continue meeting with Dr. Anderson was a positive sign. For the time being, I would have to be satisfied with that small measure of progress.

After her initial meetings with Kathy, Dr. Anderson insisted that the next few sessions include both of us. Being the tough former cop, I was confident in my ability to finesse Dr. Anderson. I had been involved in three separate shootings during my police career and handled many highly emotional situations over the years. To survive this tragedy, I would just have to "suck it up," as I had done so many other times as a police officer. Besides, I was confident Dr. Anderson needed to concentrate on treating Kathy.

I quickly discovered how incredibly difficult it was to open up and express my own feelings about Tiffanie's death. I found myself physically aching and in tears throughout these meetings. Finally, after three torturous sessions, I begged out of further counseling. I just could not handle the volcano of painful emotions they evoked. I concluded that counseling was definitely not the right approach for me.

Kathy remained in therapy with Dr. Anderson and over time, she made great progress. I credit Dr. Anderson's excellent work and the emotional support Kathy received from her friends Sue Lowden and Claudia Soho with saving her life. I regret not being able to provide more direct help to Kathy myself. We were in two very different emotional places in our grief, although it was difficult to comprehend that at the time.

Dr. Anderson also met individually with my sons, David and Chris, on several occasions. In addition, we enrolled them in a special group bereavement class with other young children who had lost a loved one. These sessions were carefully designed to assist children in expressing their grief.

In addition to individual and group counseling, David and Chris were blessed to have a guidance counselor and several elementary school teachers who took a special interest in their wellbeing. They created a special bulletin board displaying several photos of Tiffanie during her years at the same elementary school.

The guidance counselor placed the boys in charge of a fundraising effort to purchase new books for the library. Each donated book would bear a dedication page to Tiffanie inside the front cover. This was an ingenious idea and both boys seemed very excited about the project. It gave them comfort to do something special to honor their sister. It also drew them out of their protective shells as they planned each step of the fundraising campaign.

Through these efforts, David and Chris raised enough money to buy fifteen books for the library and plant a tree in front of the school with an attractive memorial plaque as a tribute to Tiffanie.[32] Additionally, the teachers periodically had lunch with both boys to monitor their progress. This combination of private and group therapy, as well as the guidance counselor and teachers' proactive team approach, provided a very solid support system to enable our young sons to begin to heal.

Whether to allow a grief counselor to work with you and/or your family is a very personal decision. If you decide to do so, the next important step is a difficult one. Identifying the *right* grief counselor can be a very stressful process. It is important to find a counselor who has at least some training and/or experience working with families who have lost a child. I believe the grief that characterizes the loss of a child must be distinguished from other types of losses these professionals may have studied.

It is also important that you find a professional with whom your family has the right chemistry. Personality is a very important component in the counselor-patient relationship.

A favorable recommendation from a friend can be helpful, but it is only one factor to consider. Hospital social workers, religious leaders, or other bereaved parents may also be helpful. We all have different psychological needs and comfort levels and should select a professional whose personality gels with our own. This is critical in developing the trust necessary to confide our innermost thoughts to a therapist.

Religion and Grief

In the early stages of a family's tragedy, parents may experience disbelief that their child's death is final. Even after the funeral, they may find themselves on their knees pleading with their God to allow their child to return home. While it may seem bizarre to others, it is not uncommon for anguished parents to pray, "Please take me and let my child come home."

Other parents may resort to bargaining with their deity in other ways. They may pray, "If you give me back my child, I promise I will never ..." They solemnly pledge to discontinue whatever they consider their worst habit or human fault, such as failing to attend religious services, consuming excessive amounts of alcohol, gambling, or some other conduct they believe their God condemns.

This negotiating may stem from a subconscious belief that their child died as retribution for one of the parents. In desperation, they promise to eliminate whatever they believe is behind that punishment. This is the desperate act of a parent grasping for a miracle, unable to accept the reality his or her child is gone.

Losing a child can test and even shatter the deepest religious beliefs of grief-stricken families. They ask questions such as: "How could a loving, compassionate God do this to a child?" Many parents become so angry at their God, they stop attending religious services completely. For some, this may only be a temporary decision. For others, it can become a lifelong refusal because they are unable to forgive their God for their child's death.

The day after Tiffanie's funeral was Mother's Day and Kathy and I somehow managed to return to the same church where her funeral service was held. On that morning, two babies were scheduled to be baptized during the regular Sunday mass.

At the start of the baptismal ceremony, two young mothers were invited to the front of the church to introduce their infants to the congregation. Suddenly, the priest presiding over the mass called Kathy up to the altar to join them. He explained to the congregation that our daughter had just passed away. Somehow, he reasoned that including Kathy with these mothers who were celebrating the baptism of their children was appropriate. Kathy stood there in obvious discomfort, doing her best to conceal the natural desire to run toward the nearest exit.

This priest's gesture was surprisingly insensitive, however well-intentioned it may have been. He obviously did not understand the magnitude of a parent's grief. On her first Mother's Day without Tiffanie, having just buried her daughter on the previous day, Kathy was expected to stand in front of the entire church congregation for a joyful celebration. Did he really believe involving her in this ceremony would bring her comfort when she was clearly still in shock? He was obviously clueless and we have never returned to Sunday mass at that church.

Not long ago, my oldest son, David, asked if I was still angry with God over Tiffanie's death. I responded, "As far as I am concerned, when I die, God has some explaining to do!" That may shock some of my religious friends. Yet that answer reflects how I continue to struggle with my own faith. I remember begging my God during Tiffanie's illness to please allow her to survive, but those prayers were left unanswered. When I pray now for some special reason, my prayers are directed only to Tiffanie. I consider her my direct contact in heaven.

A significant number of mournful families really do manage to hold firmly onto their strong religious beliefs. Their deep faith and trust in their God is a great source of comfort and strength. These families are an inspiration because of the depth of their faith. They are usually very open about sharing how they have turned to their God for help during this horrible ordeal. Reading religious guides, such as the Bible, the Torah or the Koran, also seems to bring them comfort during the darkest of times.

Putting trust in one's God through the tears and anguish of a child's death requires the strongest of religious convictions. Carl and Pearl Douglas are examples of two grieving parents whose faith has sustained them through the painful loss of their son Barry:

> Is there a God, and, if so, when our child is taken from us, has He abandoned us? He lives! Just like He has for centuries. He loves us! He gave us these gifts and perhaps we did not recognize them as gifts. But the memories are beautiful and everlasting in spite of the pain of their departure.[33]

This does not mean that embracing their religious beliefs is not a struggle for grief-stricken parents. Carla Killough McClafferty, who suffered the loss of her young son, describes her conflicting feelings in her book *Forgiving God*:

> While I began to pray when I needed strength and comfort, I continued to struggle with bitterness and anger toward God...[34]

Carla read the scripture for comfort and enlightenment.

> I learned that God is sovereign. In His divine authority, God doesn't always answer our prayers the way we want Him to.

Sometimes, God doesn't change our circumstances, He changes us in our circumstances.[35]

People who attend support group meetings are at different stages of grief. Some are newly bereaved and struggling with the reality of their loss. Others have many years of experience working through their grief and remain involved to reach out and help others.

A potentially divisive environment can develop any time the group discussion focuses on religion. Parents whose faith sustains them can unwittingly find themselves at odds with others at the meeting, especially those so consumed with anger that they question their religious beliefs or feel they have lost their faith.

It is the job of a good meeting facilitator to acknowledge that strong religious beliefs can be a source of great comfort and support for some families. Yet because we all grieve differently, others may have difficultly reconciling their faith after their child has died. At these meetings, the facilitator must stress that we need to respect and embrace those differences.

Many religious institutions are supportive throughout the funeral services. Yet too often, there is very little effort devoted to aftercare with the families. Religious leaders frequently have a difficult time reassuring parents that their God has a plan that we are incapable of understanding until we die. That rationalization usually provides little comfort to a sobbing mother or father. Perhaps this explains why too many families return home after the funeral with little or no follow-up contact with representatives of their religious institution.

It is critically important for religious leaders to reach out to these families. They should consider it part of their responsibility to refer a bereaved family to available grief services within the community. Far too many families are left to fend for themselves once the funeral services have ended.

In the past, Kathy and I have been invited to speak to groups of people involved in the Stephen Ministries.[36] This unique organization, located in St. Louis, Missouri, assists a number of Christian churches around the country. It provides training to dedicated church volunteers committed to *being there* for parishioners experiencing a crisis. After the training, the volunteers return to their churches, determined to provide one-on-one follow-up support to those who are suffering. They listen to distraught family members and act as their companions, even when friends or relatives have turned their backs or moved on with their lives. This can be an invaluable gift, as long as personalities are compatible

While this approach may not be flawless, it is a major, positive step by the ministry to provide a meaningful form of aftercare to people in crisis. I am hopeful that religious leaders of all faiths will follow the organization's example. It is vitally important for these institutions to be proactive in providing emotional support to families as part of their regular post-funeral outreach efforts.

Grief Support Groups

Kathy and I have a long affiliation with The Compassionate Friends, Inc. (TCF), an international support group founded in 1969 by Reverend Simon Stephens, then an assistant hospital chaplain in England. This non-denominational organization has been a source of tremendous comfort to both of us over the years. Yet like any support group, it does not appeal to everyone.

There are a multitude of grief support groups across the nation that reach out to persons suffering from all types of losses. I have included some of them on my website, although this list is certainly not exhaustive.[37]

You can usually locate a grief support organization in your community through a variety of methods. Community websites or newspapers may contain listings of local grief support groups, usually under the heading "bereavement." Websites for these groups, if they exist, may provide insight into how meetings are conducted. Local religious leaders or hospital social workers may also be good referral sources. Of course, traditional word-of-mouth suggestions can lead you to a group that others found rewarding.

Support groups meet on a regular (often monthly) basis. These groups impose few, if any, obligations on their members and there are usually no fees or attendance requirements. While the actual format of the meetings may vary, they often involve brief introductions, group sharing sessions, and recognition of any children whose birth or death months coincide with the meeting date.

The general focus of grief support groups vary. In the beginning, you may be more amenable to participating in a general bereavement group. These sessions assist people who have suffered any type of loss, whether a relative or friend. Later, you may be more inclined to limit your participation to groups specifically focused on the death of a child.

These groups generally offer comfort, hope, and emotional nourishment to those who attend. They help grieving families gain new perspectives and better understand their emotions. Yet sometimes a struggling parent is simply not in the emotional frame of mind to attend a support group meeting. If he is too emotionally drained, or just doesn't feel the need to interact with others on the day of a meeting, there is no obligation to attend.

Parents may go through an extended period when they don't participate in any meetings at all. That is fine, as long as they do something else to provide an outlet for their grief. After taking a break from attending meetings, they may later be more amenable to returning. One major advantage of these groups is that family members are welcome to attend any meeting. Their leaders are committed to offering compassion and support whenever they are needed.

Just after your child's death, the intensity of anguish may compel you to attend any support group that might offer an ounce of hope. In desperation, you may drive long distances in search of anyone who might help you feel better. Eventually, the accessibility of these meetings is likely to become more important to you.

I have talked to countless brokenhearted parents over the years. In the beginning, many are frustrated that these sessions are only held once each month. Whenever they express this sentiment, I am reassured the meetings are giving them comfort. I always encourage people to attend meetings with other grief-related organizations available in the area. I also urge them to visit grief-related internet chat rooms for comfort when actual meetings are unavailable.

Once you have selected one or more support groups, be careful to verify either through a contact number or website that the meeting schedule or location has not changed. It can be quite helpful to ask a friend or relative to research the services of each one and verify assembly times and places on your behalf when you are particularly distraught. This is a small gesture that people can make to assist your family during this terrible time.

Our sister-in-law Dorothy Barry took the initiative to research available support organizations in our area. She located the nearest TCF chapter and provided the meeting schedule and location. If investigating these options had been left to us, Kathy and I would not have found a support group during that first year.

The next major step is making the decision to attend that first meeting. This can be a very difficult emotional step for many people. While these groups have traditionally been composed predominantly of females, a growing number of men attend these meetings to show support for their wives and some participate without a spouse or significant other. It doesn't matter whether you go alone or attend with your spouse. Most of these groups will greet you with open arms, compassion, and understanding.

Like many men, I harbored serious reservations about support groups. I survived over twenty-five years in an environment where police officers were expected to bury their emotions. Sitting around with a group of *do-gooder* strangers offered no appeal to me whatsoever.

Yet Kathy was in such a fragile, emotional state, there was no way I could risk leaving her to attend a support group session alone. The first time we drove into the parking lot of a TCF meeting site, my reluctance suddenly grew stronger. We sat in the car discussing whether we really wanted to do this. While Kathy and I had reservations about whether this meeting could possibly help us, she was more willing to try it.

Surrendering to my fears, I shifted the vehicle's gear from "park" to "reverse." As I did this, someone knocked on the driver's side window. A neatly dressed young man stood just outside the car door. He very politely asked, "Are you here for the Compassionate Friends meeting?" When I grudgingly acknowledged that we were, he tactfully coaxed us into the building.

I soon discovered this young man was Stu Schippereit, who along with his wife Marianne, were the chapter co-leaders of the TCF Burke-Springfield, Virginia Chapter. Years later, when I became a chapter leader, I adopted Stu's *parking lot patrol* strategy. It became an effective tool for encouraging reluctant visitors to take that first difficult step. Over the years, I have definitely nabbed a few hesitant husbands who were also ready to put their cars in reverse.

When you walk into your first TCF support group meeting, there is usually someone assigned to welcome you. There may be refreshments available before the meeting, although many groups reserve them for afterwards. There may also be a library cart or table available containing an assortment of books or brochures related to the loss of a child. These books are usually available for you to borrow at no cost until the next meeting.

I remember the tension in the room when we entered that first meeting. The entire experience is so emotionally conflicting for newly bereaved parents. You are there to share your feelings with others and gain a better understanding of your grief. However, you fear that if you try to talk, you will break down and cry.

Most groups invite you to share your feelings and experiences if you have the strength and composure to do so. Yet they are very understanding and supportive if you are not emotionally ready. They try to reassure you that it is acceptable to simply listen to the discussion. This is all part of that "comfort zone" you are learning to develop.[38]

If you decide to attend a support group meeting, be patient with yourself and proceed slowly. Don't feel undue pressure to speak about your child or the grief you are experiencing if you are not ready. Everyone present attended their first meeting at some point and will understand your reluctance to speak. While each of our circumstances is different, the agony of that pain is a horrible life experience we all share.

Before the meeting begins, you may observe some members huddled in small groups conversing informally. You may even notice a few laughing and joking. This can prompt you to wonder whether you can possibly be in the right place. After all, you overcame your initial reluctance to attend this meeting because you felt as though your world has ended.

It can be very disheartening to hear other parents, whom you assume have lost children, gathered around the room laughing. You may ask yourself, "Are these the people who are supposed to help me?" It can force you to seriously question how they could possibly understand your pain if they are actually enjoying themselves at these gatherings.

This is a perfectly normal reaction. I remember Kathy looking around the meeting room with complete disdain. She whispered to me in disbelief, "These people are actually laughing in here!" We didn't stand up and leave, but we considered doing exactly that. Our emotions were raw and we were so sensitive that it would have taken very little to offend us. Fortunately, we resisted our initial instincts to scurry out of there.

In time, Kathy and I learned that it is a positive sign of progress when grieving parents are finally able to laugh. It should provide a glimmer of hope that one day, we too will learn to smile and enjoy ourselves again. If you hear people laugh at a meeting, consider it as proof of their healing progress, not as an indication they are no longer struggling to deal with their loss. They most definitely are.

It is also important to recognize that meeting discussions are likely to touch many of your emotions. You may actually feel worse the day after a session and wonder why you tortured yourself by attending the group at all. Yet these meetings can provide an important outlet for expressing and understanding your pain. Your anguish after a group discussion may be a sign that you are making progress in your healing.

At our first meeting, I was anxious to hear how other families had dealt with a variety of issues. For example, after Tiffanie's death, Kathy and I disagreed over how to deal with her room. I strongly believed the door to Tiffanie's bedroom should be kept open. It gave me comfort to be able to gaze into her room.

Yet Kathy insisted the door should remain closed. For her, the open door was sheer torture because she could see Tiffanie's belongings, while knowing she was never coming home. In light of Kathy's depressed emotional state, I agreed to leave the door closed. Still, I was driven to know the *right* way to handle this decision.

I learned this is just another one of those issues for which there is no correct answer. There are only options each family should consider when making its own decision. In our case, I agreed to keep the door closed, because Kathy was having enough problems.

I chose instead to periodically go into Tiffanie's room for personal reflection. I would lie across her bed or sit at her desk and drink in memories that were so much a part of Tiffanie. While it would often bring me to tears, it also gave me comfort. I felt particularly connected to Tiffanie whenever I was in her room. For me, these visits became a regular therapeutic experience.

I also raised another issue at one support group meeting. I tried to send a birthday card to my mother shortly after Tiffanie died. As I was about to sign it, my mind went blank. For years we had signed our greeting cards "Chuck, Kathy, Tiffanie, David & Chris." I panicked at the thought that we could never sign a card that way again. I was so distraught when this realization hit home that I gave up trying to send the card at all. I hoped the support group could help us better understand how to resolve this concern.

Over time, a variety of suggestions were offered, and each seemed to have worked for the families that tried them. Some parents continue to sign their child's name along with the rest of the family. Others place a halo over their child's name to signify their child's "angel" status. Some draw a heart or angel wings around their child's name. Ultimately, we opted to follow another suggestion which was the least painful approach for us -- we sign all of our cards "The Collins Family."

As these and other questions were discussed, I gained a better understanding of our options and experienced genuine concern from those around us. We also visited other groups, especially in those early days.

I encourage you to visit as many grief-related support groups as you can locate in your area. This will allow you to experience the chemistry of each one and make an informed decision about which ones satisfy your needs. When you have attended at least two sessions with each, select the sessions that best fit your comfort zone. There is no need to limit your participation to a single support group – you can involve yourself in as many as you have the time and energy to attend.

Our own quest for comfort led us to the TCF Arlington, Virginia Chapter led by John and Mary Bell. Many parents who attend these meetings eventually bond with another family who suffered a loss similar in either cause of death or the child's age. John and Mary lost their beautiful daughter, Susan, while she was attending college, just as we had lost Tiffanie at the end of her sophomore year. The wonderful Bells took us under their protective wings and were a great source of encouragement during the darkest time of our lives. We will always be grateful for their compassion and warmth.

We have met so many great friends over the years through our support group participation. Although all of us wish we never had occasion to meet, these close friendships will last a lifetime.

The strengths and weaknesses of a support group vary depending on a number of factors, particularly the composition of each group. Like any gathering, the personalities assembled can either encourage or discourage continued participation. Leaders openly acknowledge their chapters are made up of family members, not trained therapists. Their primary qualification to head the group is usually that they survived the death of their own child and dedicated themselves to assist others in finding hope in their lives.

Visiting Internet Grief Chat Rooms

The Internet offers a number of grief-related chat rooms. This is an especially valuable resource because not everyone has the luxury of grief support sessions in their community. The idea of turning to a chat room for comfort initially appealed to me because it offered a non-threatening environment. Since no one would know my identity, I could remain in the privacy of my home and still have the opportunity to express my feelings. I was able to ask questions that I was reluctant to pose to anyone in person. If I broke down emotionally, no one else would know.

One of the advantages of a chat room is that it affords anonymity. People who can't bring themselves to attend a regular support meeting can enter a chat room without having to face anyone. In those early days when these inconsolable parents may have no desire to leave their homes, the chat room can seem a more viable option. They can share their thoughts and pain without fear of embarrassment.

When I first experimented with this medium, I was only able to locate a few websites. Some offered "bulletin-board" style forums with no live interaction among the participants. In this format, visitors submit messages that are later screened by someone else. If the content is approved, it is subsequently posted on a message board. As each new person visits the website, she then has the option to respond to any bulletin board comments.

I found this approach undesirable because it offered no live interaction. The delay between posting messages and receiving responses was frustrating. If I was going to openly express my feelings or pose a question, I wanted an instant reply. I didn't have the patience to keep checking back to see if anyone had responded to my comment.

When I entered grief-related chat rooms, there were generally about four to seven people online at any one time depending on the time of day. The majority of those present identified themselves with some reference to the person they had lost. Most registered their nicknames on the site so they could use the same identifiers each time. I generally used "Tiffsdad" or "Tiffaniesdad" as my username.

I always found other chat room visitors to be very welcoming and genuinely concerned about my pain. Interacting with them provided a rare opportunity to honestly share my feelings. They offered the same type of emotional comfort and support that I had experienced at actual support group meetings.

By participating in an online support community, you can learn more about coping ideas from others who have suffered a similar loss. It is important to remember that no one in a chat room has *the* answer. There is no universal approach to grief that is effective for everyone. There are only options for each of us to consider.

Besides anonymity, the beauty of the chat room in those early days was its availability twenty-four hours a day. I didn't have to wait for a scheduled meeting. If I awoke at 2:00 a.m. unable to sleep, I could enter a chat room and compare notes with anyone who happened to be there.

Chat rooms today are likely to be more professionally managed, with assigned hours of operation and trained moderators to facilitate the discussions. These online leaders are usually experienced bereaved parents or sibling volunteers. Most are just as dedicated to reaching out to struggling families as those who facilitate actual support group meetings. Some actually serve in both capacities.

When I first started using chat rooms, most of them had no designated moderator. Anyone could log into the room and comment, free of content supervision. Fortunately, I never had any negative experiences. However, without a moderator supervising the chat room, the potential for abuse was very high.

The advantage of moderated chats is that all visitors are protected, as technical controls enable a moderator to "boot" or "mute" anyone who acts inappropriately, uses profanity, or becomes abusive. This is one of the major reasons why chat rooms need supervision. The last thing a sorrowful parent needs when seeking emotional reassurance is abusive treatment during an online session.

Seven years after Tiffanie's death, I volunteered as a chat moderator in the TCF online support community, which is directly accessible from the national website.[39] Initially, I was paired with a more senior moderator. After two months of training, I was assigned to moderate a one-hour session on Monday nights with another relative newcomer, Nicole Rinehart from Warner Robbins, Georgia. Nicole and her husband, Bob, lost their adorable nine-month-old son, Chase Preston Rinehart, to carnatine deficiency metabolic disorder.

In 2006, Pat Loder, the always progressive TCF Executive Director, recognized the need to enhance online services. She modernized the technical capabilities of the online support community and instituted more extensive moderator training. These innovations improved the ability of moderators to provide a safe, caring environment for each online visitor.

Most grief chat room guests are suffering and searching for the same level of comfort and support provided at meetings. Regular participants in these rooms go out of their way to provide exactly that. Good moderators try to ensure each visitor has the opportunity to share their comments. Those who are dealing with recent losses may initially prefer to monitor the conversations without actually making comments. Even in a chat room, it can be difficult to express themselves in the early months after their child's death.

My partner, Nicole, has experience as a TCF chapter leader in her community and is a very warm, caring moderator. The significant age differences of our children enabled us to appeal to a wide range of people. Over our four years together, we interacted with hundreds of grief-stricken family members. We hope to have touched their hearts as much as they did ours. In the fall of 2007, Nicole and I stepped down as moderators, believing it was important for new moderators with a "fresh perspective" to take over this important role.

Generally, grief-related chat rooms may have varying themes. Some sessions may be exclusively designated for siblings or men. Other categories may include general bereavement, pregnancy/infant loss, newly bereaved, parents with no surviving children, sibling grief, and murder/suicide survivors, among others.

While moderators may try to focus on a specific topic during sessions, the constant flux of visitors in and out requires more flexibility than a regular support group discussion. As more people join the discussion, the pace of the dialogue intensifies and several conversations on different topics may occur simultaneously.

Experienced moderators often encourage participants to seek out local support groups in addition to their online involvement. A chat room should only be a supplemental resource to attendance at an actual meeting. Unfortunately, for too many families in remote locations, the chat room may be their only form of grief support.

Although the presence of moderators reduces the potential for abuse, you still must use extreme caution when visiting an online chat room. When people frequent these rooms on a regular basis, personal relationships can sometimes develop. No matter how touching someone's story may seem, always proceed with caution.

You simply don't know whether someone in a chat room is genuine. You should always protect your identifiable information, including your real name, address, cell, home or office telephone numbers, as well as email or IM addresses. Disclosing any type of personal information in a chat room can enable strangers to gain access to it for criminal purposes.

You should view with great suspicion those chatters who seem to focus on their financial problems. Even a subtle request or hint for funds is a potential sign that a scam artist may have infiltrated. Too many loving people can be tempted to send monetary gifts or a loan to help someone whom they are convinced is suffering. Yet in doing so, they may become just another victim of an elaborate scam.

Other chatters may describe in vivid detail the most heartbreaking descriptions of how they lost their child. Yet in reality, their accounts may be completely fabricated. Perhaps they do this because they are desperately seeking the kind of attention that eludes them in their real lives. Online moderators usually try to identify these people, but they can be difficult to detect.

However, in my experience, the vast majority of visitors to online support communities have suffered life-altering losses and their pain is evident in the comments. Yet you must always keep in mind that someone's personal account could be fictitious. If you cautiously keep chatters at arm's length, hopefully you're less likely to run into problems.

There are no experts in these chat rooms and any advice you receive from another visitor simply constitutes one personal opinion. If you visit a chat room, let it be for the purpose of sharing your feelings, or asking any nagging questions you may have. Those who are legitimate grieving parents or siblings are very willing to offer their advice and share their experiences. You can adopt or disregard these suggestions, based on whether they are compatible with your situation.

The most realistic way to view a chat room is as a short-term opportunity to express your feelings or pose a question to others who have suffered the same loss. Hopefully, someone will offer a suggestion or comment that you find helpful. If you don't find the chat room to be a positive experience, you usually haven't lost anything by experimenting with this approach.

Consulting Psychic Mediums

Some bereaved parents are comforted by consulting with psychic mediums who claim the ability to relay messages from *the other side*. The decision whether to try the services of a medium can be emotionally conflicting. Parents can be so desperate to communicate with their children, they become vulnerable to con artist scams. Yet if the faintest hope of actually communicating with their child exists, it may overshadow the potential negatives and make consulting a medium an acceptable risk. Every parent wants reassurance that his or her child is safe.

This topic is discussed extensively later in this book.[40] However, if the concept of after-death communication greatly conflicts with your individual philosophical or religious beliefs, I encourage you to skip that chapter and any addendum or website references to this topic.

Use of Photographs and Video Cameras

As our children grow, we often take photographs or videos to document each phase of their development and record many of their activities, including birthday parties, dance recitals, recreational activities, and school graduations. We hope these keepsakes will be special to them when they reach adulthood.

If you are fortunate enough to have these photographs and/or videos of your child, they can be priceless treasures. Yet when a child dies, photographs and movies can cause a mixture of reactions. We all grieve differently, and not all bereaved parents are comforted by browsing through old family photo albums or viewing movies of their child. Some families at least initially find it necessary to take down their child's photographs because they cause them too much pain.

Others display their child's photos prominently, determined to ensure they are remembered. Friends and relatives may privately wonder if we are hurting ourselves emotionally by creating what they consider to be photographic "shrines" to our children inside our homes. Ultimately, each family must do whatever provides the greatest comfort or causes the least amount of emotional pain. Remember that regardless of how harshly others may judge your approach, the only opinion that matters is your own.

Personally, I believe it is an invaluable gift to be able to view Tiffanie's face in life, listen to her voice, and observe her unique mannerisms that I so cherish. I often watch these videos with tears running down my face, yet I treasure the chance to view them nonetheless. They give me one more opportunity to experience my daughter as she was in life.

Kathy is able to watch and seems to genuinely enjoy videos of Tiffanie when she was a child. She experiences greater trepidation when viewing movies of our daughter after she grew older. Tiffanie was in a videotaped bridal fashion show about one month prior to her death. This is particularly painful for Kathy to view for a number of reasons. It was the last film taken of Tiffanie and it reminds us exactly how she appeared immediately before she became ill.

It is also painful to watch this video because Tiffanie is wearing a bridal gown, signifying a special milestone in her life that we will never have the privilege of sharing with her. I usually watch these videos alone on Tiffanie's birthday or during other times when Kathy and I are not together. We all need our own space from time to time.

Many parents are in the same situation - one derives great comfort from videos or photos of their children, while the other is reluctant. The level of anguish that sometimes results can prevent both parents from sitting down together to share this experience. This is all part of that awkward phase of grief wherein each parent must learn to carefully navigate his partner's respective comfort zone.

Parents who are comforted by browsing through photos or watching videos don't have to deprive themselves of the opportunity if doing so is too painful for their spouse. They merely have to plan these activities during times when they will be alone to avoid causing their husband or wife further heartache.

Parents who lose children as a result of miscarriages or stillbirths may have no photographs. Although most medical health facilities provide photos of the fetus at various stages of development, sometimes miscarriages occur before these photos can be taken.

When stillbirths occur, the family rarely has the opportunity to take photos of the child. Whether the hospital routinely takes these photographs depends on the policy of each medical facility. While some parents may later cherish the opportunity to have these pictures, others may cringe at the mere idea such photos might exist.

Writing – Journaling

Although this book is not an autobiography, I have included my personal account of the events leading up to Tiffanie's death for your information.[41] In the early days of my grief, I became obsessed with documenting everything that happened because I was very concerned about memory loss. I made several unsuccessful attempts, but each time I was too overwhelmed by my pain to properly focus.

Eventually, I had to settle for creating an outline of the sequence of events. When I finished, I put the outline aside, hoping to return to it later when I was less emotional. Two years passed before I garnered the strength to try again. This time I was more determined than ever to record the events that led to Tiffanie's death. Yet I discovered it was still extremely painful. As I wrote each word, I found myself re-living this horrible experience and was overcome with the same anguish.

After several attempts, I was unable to work my way through the tears and grew extremely frustrated by this mental block. Finally, I tried writing in third-person from a disinterested observer's perspective. While I still found this to be a very emotional exercise, it was effective in partially shielding me from the full impact of the pain.

Although I had some emotional rough spots, this approach facilitated the completion of my first draft. I then put it aside and did not try again for several years. When I later reviewed the original draft, I was able to convert it to a first-person account. So many years later, I was amazed at how painful the process remained. When I finally finished writing my personal summary, I felt a tremendous sense of relief. An enormous weight had been lifted from my shoulders.

I realize now that the writing process was intensely therapeutic. It forced me to self-examine my thoughts and emotions and helped me gain a clearer understanding of what happened. This is important because when a child dies, the facts can sometimes be obscured by the sheer enormity of emotions that overwhelm the parents.

If you try writing in one form or another, remember that what you write is for you alone. It is a form of self-help therapy designed to allow you to express your thoughts and feelings. Don't put pressure on yourself to create a masterpiece destined for some literary best-sellers list. All that matters is that your written expression contains the message you want to convey. Be patient with yourself if you try this approach. It is likely to take multiple attempts and considerable time to write something you find personally satisfactory.

Over the years, I have met several bereaved parents who found comfort in writing letters to their children. Some took the approach that they were writing to their child who was away from home. This exercise can provide a valuable outlet for expression by a grieving parent. I tried this writing exercise at a recent grief workshop and found it to be very therapeutic.

Because of the strong emotions sparked by your child's birthday or date of loss, you might consider trying written expression to work through your feelings on these or other special occasions. Writing a letter to your child is a form of expression that can bring you comfort. I experimented with this approach during a recent grief workshop and found it an emotional experience. It gave me comfort to organize my thoughts into a special message intended only for Tiffanie.

This approach enables anguished parents to get more in touch with their inner feelings. It is an emotionally-rewarding exercise that provides a unique opportunity for a parent to formulate the exact message she hopes to convey to her son or daughter.

Other parents find solace in maintaining a chronological life journal or diary-style record that documents how they are feeling each day. This technique provides the same benefits as a letter, but also serves as a historical record of their personal grief journey and experiences. When reviewed months or even years later, this journal can provide a glimpse of the author's healing progress over time.

The opportunity to express your innermost thoughts in writing can provide a valuable outlet for your grief. In the weeks and months after our child's funeral, some parents discover that only a few close friends or relatives are actually willing to really listen to them. Taking a few moments to document their feelings can provide a valuable grief outlet for them. Writing can become our substitute companion during those lonely times when no one else can bear to hear the sadness of our thoughts.

However, journaling is not likely to comfort anyone who normally dreads written expression. This approach is best utilized by people who already enjoy personal writing and for whom it was already well within their comfort zone before the tragedy. Although it doesn't work for everyone, writing has the potential to provide great therapeutic value, if the process doesn't intimidate you.

Some grief support groups publish a newsletter that contains poems or articles written by family members. You might consider submitting a personal message to be published in your local newsletter dedicated to your child during the month of his birth or date of loss. Your expression may touch the heart of another parent and inspire them to do the same.

Music

Listening to music allows many grieving parents to experience a feeling of connection to their son or daughter. It is not uncommon for parents to be driving when a song begins playing on the radio with special meaning to their child. If tears start streaming down their face, a potentially dangerous situation can result.

If this happens to you, there are two options. The first is to stop driving and pull over to a safe location. There you can take a minute and listen to the song that touches your heart. When the song is over, you can compose yourself and resume your trip. Do not simply pull over on the side of the road, especially on a major highway. To do so could be extremely dangerous. Parking on the shoulder of a highway, even briefly, violates the law in many jurisdictions.

If you don't have the opportunity or inclination to interrupt your travel, a less popular alternative is to carefully turn off the radio. If you continue to listen and become upset, a significant danger exists to every motorist on the road. You can always listen to the song another time, but driving requires your full attention. You must resist the temptation to allow your emotions to cloud your good judgment.

Sometimes these songs begin playing at particularly meaningful times, such as when we walk into our child's room or as we park our car at the cemetery. We often can't dismiss the coincidence that a song began playing at an especially significant moment. Those melodies can bring us such sadness when our grief is still fresh.

In time, this same music can comfort us as we remember how much our children loved to hear it. We listen despite our tears because through these songs, we experience a close connection to our child. The music can soothe our pain and remind us of happier times.

There are a number of remarkable songs written specifically about grief or loss that touch our hearts. I have included a list of some songs Kathy and I have found especially comforting over the years for various reasons.[42] For example, Josh Groban's song, "To Where You Are" touched the hearts of countless families around the world.[43] His song embraces just how close we are to those we have lost and offers comfort and hope.

One afternoon, our local radio station played the song "Gone Too Soon" by Michael Jackson.[44] As I listened to the beautiful words, I was immediately touched. The lyrics prompted me to try once again to create an inscription for Tiffanie's memorial marker after more than four years of unsuccessful attempts. In a matter of hours, I came up with the words that now appear on her grave marker. It took one beautiful song to inspire a creative process that seemed unattainable for years.

Rediscovering Sexual Intimacy

I was uncertain whether a discussion about the effects of grief on our sex drives would be appropriate, but I decided to raise the issue. I was then unsure as to where it should be included in the book. Finally, I concluded that if making love isn't a significant source of comfort, what is?

In my experience the most common question parents ask at support group meetings in the early days after their loss is, "Does it ever get any better?" At some point, these same parents wonder privately about another important issue. Yet rarely are they bold enough to raise that question in a support group setting: "Will we ever want to make love again?"

The devastation of losing a child attacks our energy level, appetite, attention span, and memories, among other things. At times, our entire body aches as we struggle with conflicting feelings of anger and guilt. We are also vulnerable to prolonged bouts of anxiety and depression. Thus it is not surprising our desire for sexual intimacy is adversely impacted by this trauma.

As long as parents live in such a heightened state of anxiety, the ability to mentally relax remains elusive. Thoughts race through their minds at warped speed. Their child's death has physically and emotionally traumatized them.

There is no magic time when the desire for sexual intimacy returns. Gradually, one parent may regain interest in sexual contact with her partner, yet the other's drive may remain diminished or nonexistent. When this occurs, I recommend patience, planning, and honest communication on the part of both parents.

While the need for patience is obvious, careful planning is also important since couples co-exist on different grief timetables. Each partner must be given the opportunity to work through the initial shock of his loss. The more amorous spouse should be alert for opportunities to gradually inject romance back into the relationship. Consideration should be given to scheduling activities that enable the couple to spend time together alone.

They may begin by going places together that offer the chance for both parents to relax, such as to a movie or a play. This is a temporary, usually non-threatening escape from the pressure of the sadness that hangs over them. Weekend trips or brief vacations can also provide an excellent opportunity for both partners to rediscover how to relax.

Honest communication is crucial to ensuring both parents are on the same page. All aspects of the healing process involve each parent's gradual recognition of the differences in how they handle their grief. When one partner hopes to rekindle the sexual interest of his spouse, it is important for him to openly, but tactfully discuss it. When this desire is acknowledged, the couple can gradually work through the steps necessary to restore sexual intimacy into the marriage. I cannot overemphasize the importance of being subtle and using patience, not pressure, to achieve this end.

Hopefully, the couple can work through this phase. While I am certainly not a doctor, I believe approaching this problem together, not struggling with it individually, offers the greatest potential for resolution. Each partner must be open about his feelings and needs, while being careful to avoid imposing guilt or pressure on the other.

If the problem does not resolve itself over time, marital counseling is always an option. Yet a loving hug between a husband and wife offers great promise. It reinforces one partner's affection for the other, while sending that subtle signal of sexual attraction. My best advice is when in doubt, send flowers and try a hug first!

Chapter 11 – Grieving through Litigation or Investigations

In this chapter, I lightly touch upon some of the issues grieving families face when a child's death culminates in a criminal prosecution, civil lawsuit, or protracted investigation of the circumstances. If you don't personally have to deal with these issues, I encourage you to spare yourself the effort and move onto the next chapter; you already have enough frustration in your life.

Pending Criminal Prosecutions

The facts surrounding a child's death sometimes result in the filing of criminal charges. We lose far too many of our beloved children as a result of motor vehicle accidents. Whether they died while driving or riding as passengers, police officers will investigate to determine the cause. Based on their findings, criminal conduct may be attributed to one or more of the drivers involved. Potential charges include manslaughter, driving while intoxicated, reckless driving, racing, or driving on suspension, among others.

When the child's death resulted from physical trauma, charges of murder or manslaughter may eventually be brought against the suspected assailant. Once the criminal justice system becomes involved, the victim's family is forced to divert its energy away from absorbing its loss to ensure those responsible for this tragedy are held accountable.

Pending criminal charges pose an immense emotional burden for heartbroken parents. The family, already struggling to handle its agonizing sorrow, must face a pending trial likely to become a major distraction. This can produce further emotional trauma, especially if the defendant was their child's friend.

In preliminary meetings with investigators or prosecutors, parents bravely strive to put aside their raw emotions. I encourage these family members to ask every question they have, so everyone is aware of their concerns. The prosecutor will usually explain that every defendant in a criminal matter is presumed innocent. This presumption of innocence is defined as:

> The fundamental principle that a person may not be convicted of a crime unless the government proves guilt beyond a reasonable doubt, without any burden placed on the accused to prove innocence. [45]

The prosecutor faces a very tough burden to prove the defendant is guilty "beyond a reasonable doubt." According to *Black's Law Dictionary*, the "reasonable doubt" standard is defined as:

> The doubt that prevents one from being firmly convinced of a defendant's guilt, or the belief that there is a real possibility that a defendant is not guilty... [46]

The prosecutor in this process is entrusted with an important responsibility and is placed under considerable pressure. She must seek a just disposition that the victim's family will understand and hopefully accept.

As the family patiently listens, the prosecutor will usually provide an assessment of the case's strengths and weaknesses. They will likely be informed about the basic elements required to be proven, as well as how a court may interpret them based on similar judicial decisions over the years.

Criminal offenses carry a statutory penalty which usually includes a broad range of punishment. A convicted person may receive a sentence up to the maximum authorized in the statute. Many parents anticipate the maximum sentence will be imposed when a person is convicted of criminal responsibility for their child's death. Yet during these pretrial discussions, the family may discover the maximum sentence is unlikely, especially if the defendant has no prior convictions.

Over the years, federal and state sentencing guidelines have been enacted for a variety of reasons, including the imposition of fair and consistent penalties in each case. Under predetermined criteria, each offender is assigned various scores based on a wide range of factors, including the nature of the crime, his individual criminal history, and whether a weapon was involved. The figures are totaled and the final calculation is then compared to a chart of recommended punishments to determine the appropriate disposition for a particular defendant. While these guidelines are only advisory in nature, judges give them serious consideration in rendering their decisions.

Although parents try to understand how the trial will be conducted, they may become frustrated with the procedural and legal complexities of the criminal process. Good prosecutors are usually very willing to devote time to answering a family's questions. Many courts also have victims' rights advocates available to assist parents through each stage of the trial.

Prosecutors and defense attorneys normally "run" (calculate) the guidelines. A defendant's score provides a firm basis on which to negotiate, if a plea agreement is possible. In most cases where there is a strong likelihood the defendant may be convicted, both sides will at least make a good faith attempt to negotiate a recommended sentence. This usually means that in return for the defendant's agreement to plead guilty (often to a lesser offense), the prosecutor will recommend to the judge that a mutually-agreed-upon sentence should be imposed.

When the matter is discussed with family members, they may consider the sentence totally inadequate. Yet the prosecutor has to consider potential evidentiary flaws in the case that could be exploited by a skillful defense attorney during a trial. She must balance the option of offering a reduced charge or recommended sentence in exchange for a guilty plea against the overall risk of losing the case.

In the final analysis, prosecutors understand that conviction to a lesser charge or imposition of a more lenient sentence is distasteful to the victim's relatives. Yet they also realize the family would be far more devastated if the defendant was acquitted at trial.

Despite the existence of guidelines, the family often still has the opportunity to influence a defendant's eventual sentence. Jurisdictions may differ as to the type and source of relevant information a court will consider during the penalty phase. Most at least allow immediate family members to submit written victim impact statements. Some victims, relatives, and other relevant persons are afforded the opportunity to testify at the hearing.

It is important to keep one rule in mind when either preparing a victim impact statement or actual court testimony. Regardless of how much you despise the person responsible for your child's death, don't waste time presenting arguments attacking the defendant. The court is likely to receive an extensive pre-sentence report that should fully document the defendant's criminal and personal history. It will also gain a thorough understanding of the crime this person committed.

Instead of focusing on the defendant, it is important to introduce the judge and/or jury to *your* child. Your goal is to ensure the judge and/or jury leaves the courtroom feeling as though they actually knew your son or daughter. I recommend enlarging to poster-size a photograph of your loved one, and making it available to the prosecutor for introduction into evidence. You want the judge and jury to see your child as a person, not just another case on the docket. Introducing this large photo into evidence will also force the defendant to gaze upon your son or daughter's face one last time.

For the court to render a fair decision, the judge and/or jury should be educated about how your life has changed since your child's death. Be certain to mention any physical, mental, or emotional problems you have experienced since the tragedy. This should include any treatment, therapy, medicines, physical or emotional injuries sustained, support groups attended, loss of time from work, and anything else you have experienced. These victim impact statements are usually given strong consideration by the court. I have witnessed the toughest of judges reduced to tears by the sheer enormity of emotions evoked during testimony at a sentencing hearing.

An additional frustration for a family dealing with a criminal trial is the possibility that news organizations may publish or broadcast detailed descriptions of the evidence presented. The family is usually offered an option to leave the courtroom whenever sensitive forensic evidence is being introduced that may be particularly difficult for them to hear. Yet the media may cover this evidence in daily television, radio, or newspaper reports.

Thus, the family, friends, and associates may be exposed to the same painful information they sought to avoid hearing in the courtroom. Sadly, too often there is some annoying acquaintance that closely follows every detail of these news accounts. At some point, they may even have the nerve to ask a family member directly about some forensic issue they read or heard about during news coverage of the trial.

It is difficult to comprehend the level of sheer courage demonstrated by the families of Nicole Brown and Ronald Goldman, who were brutally murdered in 1994. On January 25, 1995, the criminal trial of O.J. Simpson began. During the proceedings, these heartbroken families had to publicly deal with the most gruesome evidence imaginable being heavily covered by the media each day. It would be difficult to find a case where more horrific details were communicated directly to the public.

Each of these families suffered a vicious, senseless loss. Yet they were forced to put on a brave face because the constant, smothering media coverage was inescapable. I cannot imagine their agony and frustration when the jury eventually acquitted Simpson on October 3, 1995. I can only hope that Simpson's unrelated 2008 Nevada convictions and incarceration provided some solace to these families

Even when the defendant has been sentenced, it may not be the end point for some of these families. Many jurisdictions have enacted statutes requiring that victims or their families be notified whenever an incarcerated felon is being considered for possible parole. Hearings are scheduled and victims or their family members often have the opportunity to testify about whether or not the defendant should be released.

While some relatives choose not to have any further involvement, others may consider it a sacred obligation to attend these hearings. It is an emotionally challenging decision either way. There is no right answer. Faced with this agonizing option, you should ultimately do what will give you the most peace in the long run.

Civil Litigation

The circumstances surrounding a child's death can also result in civil litigation. The inherent purpose of a civil lawsuit differs greatly from that of a criminal trial, where a finding of guilt and possible incarceration is being sought. In civil litigation, a specified sum of money is being demanded by the plaintiff. It is difficult for parents to quantify the value of their child's life. Yet monetary relief is usually one of the main goals of a civil lawsuit, although other forms of relief can also be included.

The formal civil litigation process usually begins with the filing of a wrongful death action. However, a great deal of extensive preparation must be completed before this step is even considered. Due to statute-of-limitations concerns, civil actions must be filed within a strictly prescribed time period set forth in the applicable laws.

If a lawsuit is initiated that does not comply with all statutory requirements, the opportunity for civil litigation can be lost forever. If the filing deadline is missed, a court will likely conclude that the opportunity to bring a lawsuit against the person, persons, or entities responsible for the child's death was forfeited. Thus, it is critical to determine as soon as possible when the statute of limitations expires.

It is also crucial to determine whether there are any additional "notice" requirements. Some jurisdictions may have special laws requiring additional forms of notice when the defendant is a government agency or falls within some other protected class of defendants. Failure to provide the required advance notice could exempt these entities from being sued. Thus, a timely determination of the type and form of required notice is also very important.

A prompt inquiry should be initiated to determine your family's legal rights. However, I understand that you and your family are likely too grief-stricken to even consider it. At a time when you lack the energy to get out of bed in the morning, the prospect of having to explain the circumstances of your child's death to an attorney seems equivalent to torture.

Often, families reeling from tragedy are initially reluctant to pursue a legal remedy at all. In addition to being preoccupied with their pain, they are uncertain whether anything legally actionable was done. Parents may rightfully question why they should get involved in a protracted civil litigation that won't bring their child back. Nothing else really matters to them in those early days of their grief.

Yet despite our suffering, we may feel an obligation to our child to find out the truth. We cannot fail to investigate the possibility that someone's actions caused their death. This is the only motivation that drove me to eventually file a lawsuit in Tiffanie's case. It was important that I knew everything in my power was done to thoroughly explore whether someone's actions or inaction caused her death.

When a person or entity may bear civil liability for your child's death, it is crucial that competent legal representation be obtained as soon as possible. Hiring an attorney can ensure the statute-of-limitations and notice requirements are satisfied. Procrastination can result in missing important opportunities to gather evidence. An attorney can use timely interviews and subsequent depositions to preserve each witness' recollection of the facts. If the family doesn't feel up to it, a trusted friend or relative can make the initial efforts to locate the right attorney.

In a criminal trial, family members usually have no voice in which prosecutor is assigned to handle the case. They can only hope the attorney assigned is a tenacious litigator who will be sensitive to their fragile state of mind. In contrast, the family can carefully select its own lawyer in civil cases. Obviously the legal skills, experience, reputation, and track record of a civil litigation attorney are important considerations. However, it is also important to find a legal counselor who is sensitive to the emotional rollercoaster parents will experience while dealing with the various stages of their child's case.

Once an attorney has been recommended, an interview can be scheduled for at least one of the parents to meet and provide an overview of the facts. The lawyer selected should strive to understand the family's motivation in filing a lawsuit. Discussing their goals and specific concerns will likely affect his or her overall approach.

For example, a family who lost its child due to some form of negligence may be seeking procedural changes within an organization to prevent future deaths. Occasionally, the family may even be demanding a public apology, a remedy that can be far more difficult to obtain than one might reasonably expect.

The filing and notice deadlines can be fully explained during the interview. Once a competent attorney is retained, he can conduct an initial investigation of the case to evaluate whether a legal justification exists for pursuing civil litigation. In the interim, the family should take solace in knowing their rights are being preserved and the matter thoroughly investigated by the lawyer. This reduces the family's anxiety level so they can focus on dealing with their grief.

Unlike criminal trials, the plaintiff in a civil proceeding only has to establish the proof in its case by a "preponderance of the evidence." *Black's Law Dictionary* defines the "preponderance of the evidence" standard as:

> The greater weight of the evidence, not necessarily established by the greater number of witnesses testifying to a fact but by evidence that has the most convincing force; superior evidentiary weight that, though not sufficient to free the mind wholly from all reasonable doubt, is still sufficient to incline a fair and impartial mind to one side of the issue rather than the other... [47]

Thus, civil cases require a less demanding standard of proof than that of a criminal trial.

Virginia litigator Stephen H. Ratliff,[48] whose civil practice includes handling wrongful death cases, observed:

> In my experience, relatives may become frustrated at either the lack of a criminal prosecution against the person responsible or an unsatisfactory outcome, if someone was charged. When this happens, families sometimes pursue a civil case (in most jurisdictions it is referred to as a wrongful death action). The O.J. Simpson case is a classic example of this situation.
>
> One advantage of civil litigation is that a lower burden of proof applies, as compared to a criminal prosecution. Another benefit is that the person (defendant) can be compelled to testify by way of deposition and/or at trial in a civil case, unlike a criminal prosecution. However, timing is very important because as long as criminal charges are pending or remain a possibility, a defendant in a civil suit can still invoke his/her Constitutional Fifth Amendment privilege against self-incrimination.

Civil litigation usually involves a multitude of motions and witness depositions. While family members are not usually required to appear at these motion hearings or formal depositions, many attend to ensure they are kept fully informed about the status of the case. Some parents insist on being included in every phase of the process, while others prefer to appear only when absolutely necessary.

When parents are dealing with a pending criminal or civil trial, they may be filled with rage at those they blame for their child's death. With emotions running so high, the prosecutor or civil litigation attorney can find himself on the wrong side of the family's anger. The parents are determined to ensure their child's case is handled properly. On occasion, they may voice loud opposition to the prosecutor's or civil attorney's approach to the case. This difference of opinion can result in confrontational, even accusatory, words.

Family members must recognize that by directing anger at their lawyers, they may be unfairly misdirecting their frustrations during this difficult process. The attorney should be concentrating his or her efforts on achieving the best results possible in the child's case and parents must be kept abreast of these efforts.

However, it is unfair to unnecessarily direct suppressed rage at attorneys who are competently striving to protect the family's interests. This may stifle future communication between the family and their legal counsel, prompting some lawyers to withdraw from further representation in the case.

Donna Miller Rostant, Esq. of Fairfax, Virginia is the attorney who represented Tiffanie's estate in a civil action. Although she did a masterful job in representing Tiffanie's interest, Donna later remarked that having a grieving attorney as a client was a challenge at times.

In retrospect, I realize that on at least one occasion I was guilty of transferring to Donna my own suppressed anger and frustration. Donna definitely did not deserve to bear the brunt of my anger and I regret the mistake. I sincerely urge you not to make the same error in judgment with your attorney. This book is intended to help you learn from my mistakes and this is definitely an important one to avoid.

Investigations

Local authorities may be initially unable to determine the cause of a child's death and a prolonged investigation can ensue. Sadly, there are many medical conditions that can occasion a young child's death. When a baby dies suddenly without any obvious explanation, authorities may initially consider family members as potential suspects.

As more information about shaken baby syndrome has become available, law enforcement investigators must be careful not to classify these cases prematurely. Thus, police are likely to conduct extensive, sometimes seemingly repetitive interviews to identify any potential issues or conflicts. In these cases, they may tend to rely heavily on the official autopsy reports before deciding how to proceed. These investigations can sometimes take months to conclude, to the deep frustration of the suffering family.

When investigations are undertaken to determine whether trauma was involved in a young child's death, innocent grieving parents may suffer greatly. They interact with law enforcement authorities who may seem indifferent, or even confrontational and accusatory. The parents experience tremendous emotional anguish at the mere inference they would ever harm a child they loved so much.

Their pain is magnified when these investigations are covered by the media. Unfounded public perception that the parents played some role in their child's death can make people less inclined to offer expressions of sympathy to the family. This can even affect the number of visitors who attend the child's wake or funeral service.

Sadly, when the final report is issued months later, the story too often does not make the news if the family is cleared of any wrongdoing. Yet rarely are the parents ever "exonerated" by the authorities. If no charges result from the investigation, police are more likely to conclude there was "insufficient evidence" to bring charges in the child's death. This *safe* disposition requires no apology and may leave a cloud of groundless suspicion over the family. When this occurs, there is no effective way for the family to undo the harm done to their emotions or reputation in the community.

When a teenager or young adult dies under unexplained circumstances, there may be a substantial delay before the exact cause of death is determined. This happens far more often than many people realize and can again fuel the fires of baseless speculation. As rumors spread that the child's death was connected to alcohol poisoning or drug use, among other causes, the final autopsy report may attribute the death to an undiagnosed heart condition or some other natural cause. Undiagnosed heart problems occur far more frequently than many people realize.

The same delay can occur when authorities suspect suicide as the cause of death. Too often, parents believe the death resulted from an accidental drug overdose while authorities conclude their child intentionally ended his or her life. Although the family may wish to challenge these findings, government officials are rarely willing to reconsider. They are usually inclined to issue a final report and move onto the next case.

Sadly, the use of illegal drugs is an enormous problem in our society. While some people consider a drug overdose to be synonymous with suicide, that is not always the case. One of the inherent risks of using drugs is that there are no safeguards in the manufacturing process. Drugs are illegally smuggled into the country and distributed to street dealers. These criminals must balance the risk of apprehension while in possession of these drugs against the desire to maximize profits by taking the time to dilute illegal substances.

If a supplier fears police are closing in, he may prematurely rush the drugs "uncut" to street dealers to avoid being arrested with contraband in his possession. Thus, there are occasions when overdose deaths occur because the drug was more potent than expected. Death can also result when an individual's drug tolerance is below that of a more regular drug user.

Occasionally, the evidence may fail to establish exactly what happened. If the child consumed alcohol or used drugs immediately prior to death, determining the facts becomes more difficult. Unexplained injuries to the victim's body, such as bruises or abrasions, may be falsely attributed to falls or other behavior normally associated with intoxication. Those who actually caused the child's death may use the victim's lack of sobriety as a smokescreen to shield themselves from detection.

These types of carefully-crafted explanations may enable criminal behavior to go undetected. Thus, drug or alcohol usage can provide a convenient distraction that draws attention away from the true cause of the fatal injury. This is so painful for anguished parents who will probably never know the truth. The feelings of helplessness that can result only add to their pain.

In summary, whether there is a criminal prosecution, a civil lawsuit, or an extensive investigation of the facts surrounding a child's death, the devastated parents are greatly affected. They have lost their child and still face the emotional pressure of the pending litigation or investigation. Rather than seeking refuge within their zone of comfort, they are forced to monitor the status of their child's case.

I believe this can effectively toll the grieving progress. This does not mean family members are not experiencing terrible pain, because they clearly are. Rather, they are simply unable to fully grieve their loss without distraction. Their mind is kept busy worrying about the court case or the investigation. It is not until their child's case is resolved that they can begin to fully deal with the anguish of their loss absent other outside diversions.

Once the legal or investigative process has concluded, parents must find a way to let it go, unless their attorney recommends otherwise. While they may not be satisfied with the disposition, they did their best to resolve the matter.

Regardless of the outcome, nothing can bring our child back to us. I remember receiving a call from a reporter soon after a civil action was filed in Tiffanie's case. The young writer asked me, "What will you do if you win this lawsuit?" I was amazed at the cold insensitivity of the question. I took a deep breath and politely told him, "There is no way that I can ever win. My daughter will still be dead, no matter what happens with this lawsuit!"

At the end of the trial or investigation, many parents discover that they overestimated their progress in dealing with their grief. They may experience renewed episodes of depression, isolation, and anger. Don't get caught blindsided. This sudden detachment after being so actively involved with the litigation or investigation can be quite abrupt.

It is important that you recognize the immense strain placed on your fragile emotions. When the process ends, you may wish to reach out to a trained counselor, a support group, or a close friend or family member for emotional support. This is not a good time to be alone.

Chapter 12 - Mourning the Child Who Wasn't "Perfect"

WHILE MOST OF US CONSTANTLY SING their praises, our children were not perfect during their lives. Kathy and I adore our daughter and like most parents, we love her unconditionally. Yet like all human beings, Tiffanie had her own weaknesses and faults. She lived a normal life facing the usual range of challenges like most people her age. Tiffanie made no secret of her love for her family and she cherished her friendships. While she was a bit shy as a youngster, she became more extroverted as she matured.

I recall having my share of verbal disagreements with Tiffanie during her middle and early high school years. These usually involved rather loud discussions about setting her boundaries. Like many fathers, I was concerned about where she was going, who was accompanying her, and most importantly, when she was coming home. As Tiffanie grew more accustomed to her *overbearing* dad's rules, our arguments waned. I suspect that she merely decided to humor the old cop and avoid more conflict.

Although Tiffanie had her faults, she was perfect for us. By the time she died at age nineteen, Tiffanie had achieved an impressive number of accomplishments. When Kathy and I talk about her, we focus on every wonderful memory we have. It is difficult to discuss anything other than what an awesome daughter she was.

When grieving parents describe their children it is natural for them to focus on the most positive aspects of their lives. Some parents refer to their children in almost angelic terms after their death. They are already dealing with enough pain. Why would they want to dwell on any negative attributes? It is obviously more soothing to cherish the happiest of memories as they struggle with the horror of their loss. However, this tendency can cause unintentional anguish for other parents when support group interaction occurs.

In group sessions, parents are usually given the opportunity to talk about their loved ones. They feel comfortable doing so because everyone present has suffered the same devastating loss. Yet deaths occur from an endless variety of causes, including suicide, drug overdoses, alcohol abuse, and criminal behavior, among others.

When some parents continually offer glowing accounts of their children's flawless lives during support group meetings, others may find themselves intimidated by the conversation. Their children may have experienced significant problems during their lives which kept their parents in a constant state of worry and turmoil. These issues may have been medical or psychological in origin. Their children may have struggled with significant personality disorders, substance abuse, or repeated confrontations with the law.

Each time the telephone rang, these mothers and fathers may have felt extreme trepidation. Some have dealt with years of school disciplinary problems, periodic trips to juvenile or even adult courts, recurring incidents of substance abuse, unsuccessful rehabilitation attempts, or even thefts of valuables within their own home. This assortment of traumatic experiences can cause severe emotional family scars over time.

Yet, when facing the anguish of their child's death, these parents struggle with deep regrets. They agonize because their children didn't enjoy better lives or suffered unique problems other families are spared. Their son or daughter may have faced difficult obstacles or lacked the opportunities other families are able to provide.

The difficulties troubled children faced in life don't diminish their parents' love, nor the depths of their anguish when they are gone. These moms and dads love their children just as deeply, while understanding and accepting that they were not perfect. Repeatedly listening as other parents describe their sons or daughters in saint-like terms can cause these grieving parents to feel isolated and reluctant to share details of their own children's lives.

They may feel insecure because of the understandable fear their child will be compared. They worry that revealing their own personal experiences will set them apart in a negative light. The last thing they need is to share their feelings with a group of people who may harshly judge their child's life. The resulting apprehension only adds another emotional obstacle for them to overcome. Parents who attend support groups need acceptance, not further isolation, to facilitate their healing process.

An effective support group facilitator will be alert for parents who attend meetings regularly but rarely say anything. As long as this continues, the opportunity to provide a meaningful outlet for them is limited. Sharing our thoughts and emotions is an important part of the healing process. These parents need an opportunity to discuss their feelings, which is why most were drawn there in the first place.

It is therefore crucial to locate a support group that generates honest discussions about all of our children and offers comfort instead of judgment. A good facilitator will periodically remind each group that our children were all unique and faced different challenges in their lives. This should encourage people to be more open in discussing their children realistically during these sessions.

Support groups can also provide additional opportunities for these parents by scheduling special topic sessions, such as deaths related to murder, suicide, substance abuse, or grieving the problem child. If your support group does not offer these types of special topic discussions, don't hesitate to suggest they do so. Most group leaders will welcome your honest feedback.

Parents who do feel inhibited during support group interaction should definitely consider consulting a professional therapist. It is very important that they find a meaningful outlet. Hopefully, a combination of private counseling and support group interaction can provide these parents with the emotional support and reassurance they desperately deserve.

Chapter 13 - Remembering our Children

BEREAVED PARENTS ARE OFTEN CONCERNED THEIR child will eventually be forgotten by family and friends. At some point after the funeral, parents suddenly realize the rest of the world has continued on without their son or daughter. Because our loved one's death impacted our lives so drastically, it is a shock to discover the community around us considers it just another tragedy. It was a very sad experience, but they have healed and moved on with their lives.

At family gatherings, parents can become irritated if their child is not brought up during the conversation. If they try to interject their son or daughter's name into the discussion, their family's reluctance to discuss the child can be quite obvious. This can produce more anguish and even a sense of betrayal.

Kathy was in tears driving home from our first family Thanksgiving about six months after Tiffanie's death. Not one family member had mentioned our daughter throughout the entire day. Tiffanie had participated in this annual tradition for the previous nineteen years. It was heartbreaking to believe she could be forgotten so easily by the same people with whom she shared so many other holidays.

I now realize that Tiffanie wasn't forgotten by her relatives. Facing our first Thanksgiving without Tiffanie, we were definitely emotionally distraught and our relatives had no clue how to offer us comfort. Rather than risk saying the "wrong thing" and causing us to become upset, they simply chose to avoid talking about our daughter. We were crushed when it happened during such a meaningful holiday with so many memories. Although I believe it was the wrong choice by our family, it was a well-intentioned one nonetheless.

In the beginning, you may be emotionally unable to communicate the fear your child will be forgotten. You may even be too consumed with sadness to discuss your son or daughter. In those early days, our grief is so fresh, we don't understand it ourselves.

In the first few months after Tiffanie's death, it was too painful for me to talk about her. The mere mention of her name would bring me to tears. Because I had several court cases on the docket after her funeral, I had an obligation to zealously represent my clients without falling apart. My strategy was to focus on my work responsibilities while blocking out my grief.

For the most part, this strategy enabled me to get through my immediate day-to-day responsibilities. Yet it did nothing to facilitate my need to grieve. After work, I would drive over to the cemetery where I routinely broke down at the gravesite.

One week after Tiffanie's death, I was seated in a courtroom waiting for a traffic case to be called. The prosecutor and I had discussed the legal issues and reached an impasse. A trial would be necessary to potentially achieve a more favorable outcome than the prosecutor was willing to offer. My client sat by my side, nervously waiting for his case to be called.

Then something very unusual happened. I noticed that the prosecutor was signaling for me to return to the conference room. I immediately exited, wondering if there was some new development in the case. After I seated myself, the prosecutor closed the door. He then informed me that he had just realized I was "the attorney whose daughter died last week." He genuinely wanted to offer his own words of heartfelt sympathy.

When he mentioned Tiffanie's death, my protective emotional wall instantly came crumbling down. As I sat in the conference room just a few feet from the courtroom, I began sobbing uncontrollably. This poor, well-intentioned prosecutor was frantic, having no clue how to handle my unanticipated response. Our case was scheduled to be called at any moment. Yet I was clearly in no condition to argue it. He tried to calm me down, but the floodgates had opened and I was in a devastated emotional state.

Driven by equal measures of desperation and compassion, he offered to resolve the case in the manner I had initially requested. He urged me to compose myself and return to the courtroom and promised to do "all of the talking." He reassured me, "I just want to get you out of here!" After a few moments, I managed to calm myself and return to the courtroom. I already knew my client would be satisfied with this result and only hoped I could stand in front of the judge without falling apart.

True to his word, the prosecutor did all of the talking when the case was called. I stood there like a robot and said nothing. At one point, the judge glanced over at me with an inquisitive expression, as if to invite my comments. Yet I continued to stand there stoic and silent. Hearing no opposition, the judge approved the agreed disposition. I am eternally grateful to this now-former prosecutor. There was no way he could have anticipated that a few words of kindness would bring me to my knees.

Yet this incident is a prime example of the danger inherent in erecting emotional walls to block out our grief. These protective barriers are very fragile and it takes little effort for someone to knock them down. When they collapse, the pain can totally overwhelm us.

I never experienced this problem in any other case. I suspect that a warning quickly spread to the entire cadre of prosecutors: "When you deal with Mr. Collins, *never* mention his daughter's death." I am glad this message circulated because it enabled me to keep my head above water during the grueling weeks and months of immense sadness that followed.

In my professional life, I continued using this pain-avoidance approach to block thoughts of Tiffanie. Many months later, I became more comfortable discussing her, but by then most people had grown accustomed to evading the subject. I could only blame myself for this result. The price of dodging our pain is that it teaches others to avoid any reference to our children.

Eventually, Kathy and I began wearing an angel pin in Tiffanie's honor. During each court appearance and client interview, this small remembrance was affixed to the right lapel of my suit coat. On my casual wear, the pin was placed near my right collar. This small gesture gave me reassurance that Tiffanie was always with me. One year after her death I had an angel tattooed on my right arm.

On most days, thoughts of Tiffanie abound. Still, there are rare occasions when life's daily challenges preoccupy my thoughts. When I attach the pin to my clothes each morning or remove it later that night, I always think of Tiffanie. No matter how demanding my days may become, adding that pin to my wardrobe as part of my daily routine gives me one more opportunity to think of my daughter.

What I did not initially anticipate was the response this pin would evoke. During my informal conversations with other attorneys at court, they would inevitably inquire about it. In the beginning, I was too emotional to offer much explanation and would simply say the pin held a special, personal meaning.

Gradually I became more receptive to discussing Tiffanie in my work environment. It gave me a unique opportunity to introduce my beautiful daughter to people who did not know her. Instead of reinforcing my earlier message to avoid the topic, the angel pin created an opening to talk about her once again.

Being able to talk about Tiffanie outside of the insulated support group environment was very comforting. The angel pin undid the damage I caused by blocking her from my thoughts in the early months of my grief. This small symbol became a therapeutic companion that helps me feel connected to Tiffanie and invites others to ask about its significance.

Now, twelve years later, I must admit that I lie in wait for the poor, unsuspecting attorney who innocently inquires about the small ornament on my lapel. Once she has taken the bait, photos of Tiffanie instantly appear as I aggressively bend her ears explaining all about my daughter. Some attorneys are caught so totally unprepared, they can be seen either gripping the wall for support or fumbling for their briefcase in desperate search of an escape route. When I finish, I always thank him or her for asking. I love doing it.

Over the years, I have met many wonderful northern Virginia lawyers. Once I overcame my inability to talk about Tiffanie, most people in my work environment were receptive to hearing about her.

I have been particularly blessed to meet and learn a great deal from Ron Smith, Esq., a very skilled Virginia litigator.[49] One morning, as we waited to resolve our respective cases in court, Ron noticed my angel pin and inquired about its meaning. Upon hearing my explanation, Ron shared his own personal experience. He revealed that in 1964, when he was in his early twenties, his nineteen-year-old sister Lorraine Maria Smith died after struggling for years with a kidney disease.

As I listened to Ron's tragic experience, the deep anguish of his sister's death over three decades earlier was evident on his face. Choking back his emotions, Ron vividly recalled the pain of her loss. In a quivering voice he said, "I remember what that did to my parents... I remember what that did to me..."

Ron paused and took a deep breath. Patting me gently on the back, he then returned to the courtroom in silence. I instantly understood that Ron had just revisited the depths of his grief so many years after his sister's death. The pain of her loss had come rushing back at a time when he least expected it. His anguish was just as strong as ever.

Ironically, just a few days earlier I had been told by some genius that after five years, parents and siblings are healed from the pain of their loss. Since I was only in my third year at the time, I naively hoped there was some validity to that prognosis. After witnessing Ron's anguish as he vividly recalled his family's tragedy, I immediately disregarded the *five year* rule.

Ron's emotional response taught me that there is simply no magic time when our pain completely ends. His reaction was a stark reminder that grieving is a lifelong process. As we heal, we get better at managing our pain, but we never get over it. We also never forget the depths of our anguish.

Over time I learned that it is our responsibility to ensure our children are not forgotten. When we are emotionally ready, it is important to encourage our friends, family, and co-workers to talk openly about our child. Unless we educate them, they simply have no clue how to reach out and help us. They often unintentionally hurt our feelings, sometimes without realizing they have done so.

It is imperative for them to understand that sharing memories of our son or daughter often brings us comfort – it refreshes us to know our child is still remembered and loved. Even when our tears flow during these conversations, it provides a therapeutic outlet for us. It lifts our spirits and makes our pain just a little more bearable.

In an effort to assist you in this regard, I have included a chapter written especially for your family and friends.[50] I have also added a checklist outlining suggested ways they can reach out to comfort your family.[51] I invite you to make a copy of that chapter and checklist and mail it to anyone whom you hope to educate about grief. Feel free to add any suggestions to my checklist or use it as a starting point in creating your own.

I make this gesture in the hope that it will promote better understanding and improved communication between bereaved parents and their family, friends, and coworkers. By improving their awareness, hopefully you will give the important people in your life insight into how to really *be there* for you. If they are genuinely concerned about you, I am optimistic they will.

The quest to ensure our children are remembered can become an obsession. Life after our loss involves constantly searching for new opportunities to remember our children. A few years ago, I was asked to contact a grief-stricken parent in another part of the country. When I did so, I met a heartbroken father struggling desperately to come to grips with the tragic loss of his daughter. One of his natural concerns was that his daughter would soon be forgotten.

During our ongoing discussions, I suggested focusing on ways to ensure his daughter could be remembered. To his credit, this loving parent set about creating an impressive number of special events, including five kilometer runs, memorial walks, and golf tournaments dedicated to his daughter's memory. He did an amazing job of organizing these activities.

I admire his determination in ensuring his child is remembered in her community. In reaching out to comfort a devastated parent, I tried to fan the small flame of healing through remembrance. This loving dad transformed it into a blazing forest fire.

There are many traditional ways our children are remembered, ranging from small bushes planted in their honor to far more elaborate displays. The Vietnam Veterans Memorial in Washington, D.C. pays tribute to the brave sacrifices of more than fifty-eight thousand people.[52] Many were young soldiers serving this country in the prime of their lives. This is just one of several memorials built to honor our dedicated military personnel throughout our nation's history. Whenever I have viewed the names engraved on that wall, my heart always goes out to the heartbroken families left behind.

A national memorial in Oklahoma includes a "Field of Empty Chairs" honoring one hundred sixty-eight people who perished when the Alfred P. Murrah Federal Building was bombed on April 19, 1995.[53] This exhibit includes nineteen small chairs symbolizing the children killed in the tragedy. Three chairs pay tribute to pregnant mothers and their unborn children.

On September 11, 2008, Kathy and I attended a touching tribute in memory of 184 people who perished seven years earlier at the Pentagon or on American Airlines Flight 77. At the Pentagon Memorial, each victim is honored with a unique bench over lighted flowing water.[54] The victims ranged in age from three to seventy-one. Five benches stand together honoring the children who died on the aircraft. This hallowed ground includes eighty-five maple trees, a gravel surface, and a wall documenting each victim's age. The national memorial provides comfort to families, friends, and a nation of Americans who will never forget the horrific events of September 11, 2001.

Sadly, gun violence has taken the lives of innocent students and teachers in schools across this country. Memorials honor the memory of those killed or wounded at Columbine High School in Littleton, Colorado on April 20, 1999[55] and Virginia Tech in Blacksburg, Virginia on April 16, 2007.[56]

Many parents honor their child's memory by becoming active in special ways, large and small, to make a positive difference in the lives of others. I have included a few examples of bereaved parents whose outstanding efforts continue to have a major national impact.

In 1981, six-year-old Adam Walsh was abducted and murdered in Florida. His devastated parents, John and Revé Walsh, were determined to achieve better legal safeguards to protect children and spare other families the same anguish. They created the Adam Walsh Child Resource Center, which later merged with the National Center for Missing & Exploited Children (1-800-TheLost or http://www.missingkids.com.) This organization assists families and provides resource support to law enforcement agencies worldwide.

John Walsh also became the host of "America's Most Wanted," a popular Fox television show that has led to the capture of hundreds of fugitives (http://www.amw.com). In 2006, the Adam Walsh Child Protection and Safety Act became law, mandating victims' rights protections, including a national sex offender registry and community sex offender tracking systems. John and Revé Walsh's dedicated efforts on behalf of children and crime victims everywhere have ensured Adam will always be remembered.

In 1980, Candy Lynne Lightner's thirteen-year-old daughter Cari was killed by a hit-and-run drunk driver in California. Despite her grief, Candy organized concerned mothers determined to prevent the needless deaths and injuries that can result from drunk driving. Candy's group evolved to become the nationally-recognized Mothers Against Drunk Driving (MADD).[57] Her contributions have likely saved countless lives over the years - a wonderful tribute to Cari.

In 1991, Stephanie and Stephen Loder, ages eight and five respectively, died tragically in a vehicular accident. Their devastated parents, Pat and Wayne Loder, became active in The Compassionate Friends, Inc. (TCF), an international support group for parents, siblings, and grandparents who have suffered the loss of a child.[58] They eventually became chapter leaders, reaching out to bereaved families in Michigan for over eight years.

After becoming national newsletter co-editors, Pat and Wayne created *We Don't Walk Alone*, an award-winning TCF magazine that provides grief support information to grieving families around the country. In 2001, Wayne became the national TCF Public Awareness Coordinator and Pat was named TCF's Executive Director. Their efforts have made emotional support available without cost to families through more than six hundred chapters nationwide. Pat and Wayne have ensured that Stephanie and Stephen are remembered as they touch the lives and hearts of countless people across the nation.

In 1977, Therese S. Schoeneck lost her twenty-one-year-old daughter, Mary, in a car accident. In dealing with her anguish, Therese recognized the critical void in available grief resources. In 1981, she compiled a wonderful assortment of grief-related articles from a variety of perspectives and made copies available for distribution. Since those early days, her inspiring publication, *Hope for Bereaved: Understanding, Coping And Growing Through Grief*, has been widely available to families in desperate need of something to give them comfort and hope.[59] In 2007, with the publication of her book's eleventh edition, Therese continues to honor the memory of her daughter, while reaching out to assist many families in need.

Not all parents can make a nationwide impact through their individual gestures to honor their children. Contributions on a local scale are equally meaningful and make a positive difference in the lives of others.

Kathy and I were blessed to meet Bill and Andi Baker through our local TCF chapter. They lost their beautiful nineteen-year-old daughter, Kelly Elizabeth Baker, in August, 2005. Six months after Kelly's death, Bill and Andi channeled their grief into establishing the Kelly Elizabeth Baker Memorial Scholarship. This monetary award is annually presented to a graduating student at the Notre Dame Academy in Middleburg, Virginia, where Kelly attended school.

Scholarship applicants are required to submit an essay explaining how their senior year of high school has enabled them to improve artistically, scholastically, emotionally, and spiritually. Each year when this award is presented, it is emotionally difficult for both parents. Yet Bill and Andi take great comfort in knowing that Kelly Elizabeth is remembered every time this special scholarship is presented in her name.[60]

Kathy and I grew up in Washington, D.C. with our good friend Rhea Nader (McVicker). In 1997, Rhea lost her twenty-two-year-old son, Nicholas Cristarella, as a result of a substance abuse addiction dating back to his early teens. In his memory, Rhea created Nick's Place, Inc. to counsel young males struggling with addiction.[61] In doing so, Rhea channeled her grief into reaching out to help others. Through her unselfish efforts, Nick's Place, Inc. touches the lives of young men suffering the type of addictions that tragically cost her son his life. This is a wonderful way to ensure that Nick will always be remembered, while striving to spare another family this same type of tragedy in the future.

I have included a brief summary of a few special parental tributes honoring their children.[62] Some are relatively simple to accomplish, while others require considerable effort. Just remember that any gesture you make to honor your child is likely to bring you comfort. If you have created a special remembrance to your son or daughter, I would love to hear about it. Please feel free to email me at tiffaniesdad@holdingontolove.com and share your story. I promise not to include it in any future editions of this book or on the website without your express permission.

Some families whose strong religious beliefs helped them during their sadness may arrange an annual religious service to honor their child. They can invite friends and family to attend and actively involve them in the program. It can be an uplifting, positive experience celebrating a special life that touched the hearts of many.

Some grief support groups or individual families organize butterfly or balloon release ceremonies in memory of children, often on Mother's Day. When organized by a family, this event is customarily scheduled on the anniversary of the child's birthday or date of loss. Family and friends will usually gather at the cemetery or some other place of special significance in the child's life. These events often include brief remarks, readings, and even musical accompaniment. At the conclusion of the ceremony, butterflies or balloons are released by everyone in attendance as a special tribute to each child.

The release of butterflies is very symbolic because, like our children, they are beautiful and have short life spans. Butterflies may be ordered in advance from a multitude of vendors that ship them across the country in small individual packets. However, this can be an expensive undertaking requiring careful storage precautions, including maintenance of an ideal temperature range. It is important to research these requirements before ordering butterflies.

If a butterfly release is planned, it is wise to order more butterflies than needed as a small number may die in transit. Immediately before butterfly packets are distributed to family members or friends, each one should be quickly inspected. The last thing emotionally fragile parents or siblings need is to be handed a dead butterfly at a time when they are hoping to honor their child.

The practice of releasing butterflies is not without controversy. A number of groups express vehement opposition to the exercise for a variety of environmental reasons too detailed to outline in this book. A great deal of information on both sides of the issue is available on the Internet. I encourage you to familiarize yourself with these concerns before considering a butterfly release.

A balloon tribute in your child's memory can also be very touching, albeit controversial. Opponents argue this practice has an adverse impact on the environment and some jurisdictions prohibit the practice. To address these concerns, a few commercial companies now sell biodegradable balloons which are advertised as environmentally safe. You should carefully research this issue before undertaking a balloon release ceremony to honor your child.

The Compassionate Friends, Inc., an international grief support group, dedicates an annual worldwide candle lighting event to honor and remember every child who has died.[63] Held on the second Sunday in December, families and friends around the world are invited to light a candle of remembrance at 7:00 p.m. their time. Our children are remembered globally, as small flames are illuminated across different time zones over a twenty-four hour period.

Many support groups across the country organize candle lighting ceremonies in conjunction with this event that are usually very well-attended. The beauty of this celebration of life is that it can just as easily be done privately. A family can remain at home and still join millions of other families in honoring their children. Either way, our children are loved and always remembered.

Special Anniversary Dates

The year after Tiffanie died, everything we did constituted our first time without her. Over the years, Kathy has begun to track events by whether they happened before or after our daughter's death. Obviously, activities that you previously shared with your child can trigger a volcano of emotions the first time you attempt to do them after he dies.

The anniversary of a child's death, often referred to as the "sunset" or "angel" date, is a time grieving parents dread throughout the year. Other days with special significance include your child's birthday, Mother's Day, Father's Day, Thanksgiving, Christmas, and Hanukkah, among others. These dates can be particularly painful and pose yet another obstacle for us to face. How we deal with each of these milestones throughout the year affects our healing progress. Any of them can trigger a sudden onset of anguish or depression, especially in the first few years.

Life after the loss of your child involves learning to anticipate upcoming events that may cause further anguish. If we can recognize the possibility of emotional discomfort in advance, we can be more prepared to successfully confront it. Once we realize a potentially painful anniversary or holiday is approaching, we can formulate our strategy to get through this occasion with the least amount of heartache. Otherwise, we can find ourselves blindsided by painful reactions to situations we never anticipated would arise.

Over the years, Kathy and I have tried various coping methods in dealing with these special occasions. I need to stress that holidays take on added emotional trauma if your child's death occurred around the same time. When this occurs, the particular holiday can seem to merge with the anniversary of your child's death to cause a constant state of anguish until both dates have passed. This prolonged period of heightened anxiety presents an additional burden for a mournful parent to overcome.

To prepare for each of these occasions, we must formulate our own approach to guide ourselves safely through them. In this chapter I have included a few of these key dates, along with my suggestions for your consideration.

Birthdays

Each time our child's birthday arrives, a once joyous occasion can become an excruciating ordeal. It seems the ultimate betrayal that this day, which brought us so much happiness before, is now marred by the reality our child is gone. Yet we cannot forget that our child's birthday is a special milestone in our lives. While it will definitely produce sweet memories of your child's birth, these are tempered by the sadness of her death.

I prefer to spend Tiffanie's birthday alone, watching family videos or browsing through old photo albums. In the past, Kathy has experienced some emotional difficulty when viewing Tiffanie's videos. For Kathy, watching these movies might constitute a step backwards in her healing progress. Although she initially remained home from work on Tiffanie's birthday, Kathy began working a regular day after a few years. She always visits the cemetery on her way home to place a special remembrance on our daughter's grave.

Some families schedule birthday parties to honor their child, especially in the first few years after their loss. They may invite family members and friends to visit their homes and celebrate their child's life. In the beginning, this can be a great opportunity to reach out to relatives and friends. Most genuinely want to help you, but they are uncertain exactly how to do so.

A birthday party offers a unique chance for family and friends to smile as they celebrate your child's life. The day accentuates positive memories and the myriad of emotions can provide a form of positive group therapy for attendees. However, you must realize when emotions run high, tears are likely to flow. Yet the overall celebratory tone can make this a healing experience for everyone involved.

If your child was very young, having a birthday tribute in his honor may be particularly difficult. Since your child's friends are also very young, inviting them is probably not the most appropriate approach, as they are incapable of understanding the significance of such an event. Yet this birthday celebration can still be a meaningful experience if you restrict your invitations to family and close friends.

If your child was older, inviting his or her friends can be very meaningful. It allows them to talk about experiences they shared with your child. It is such a gift when friends recall special memories of which you were unaware. Each revelation reveals something new your child said or did. These are cherished by bereaved parents as newly discovered treasures.

In this lighthearted atmosphere, friends become more relaxed and less emotionally guarded. As they realize the parents' spirits seem lifted by the discussion, it encourages them to share their memories. The warm feelings generated by openly recalling the "good times" can reduce everyone's anxiety about saying the *wrong thing*.

However, if you decide to hold a special gathering to honor your child's birthday, you should understand the potential emotional drawbacks. As much as you may be attached to your child's friends, it can be difficult for you to actually be around them. First, you will notice they are physically maturing.

Second, you are likely to hear them exchange stories about their day-to-day activities. Hearing these discussions can be very painful as you realize these young men and women are enjoying opportunities that your child has been denied. You may want nothing but the best in life for all of them. However, seeing them living their normal lives after your child is gone often triggers your own punishing *what if* thoughts.

After the first time this session has been held, it is important to expect a decline in attendance if future birthday events are planned. The fact is that as time goes on, people move on with their lives. They may feel less obligated to attend a second birthday celebration, assuming the family has "gotten over" its tragedy. Some may believe parents who hold these birthday celebrations are stuck in their grief. Others are simply unwilling to revisit those painful memories.

There are perfectly logical reasons why some people may be unable to attend future gatherings. Some may relocate, attend college, or become inaccessible for other valid reasons. Still, a birthday remembrance can be a very positive experience. If subsequent gatherings are held, they may be limited to a small group of your relatives or close friends. These occasions can still be very positive because they celebrate the joy of our child's birth instead of the sadness of our loss.

Date of Loss

As the first anniversary of their child's death approaches, parents usually dread its arrival and struggle to decide how to spend the day. Some people refer to this day as the *sunset date, angel date,* or by several other references that speak to the sadness of the occasion. In my opinion, the first two anniversaries of your child's loss are the most difficult. Yet the date of loss is always likely to bring on some level of anxiety.

The best advice I can offer to help you through this painful, annual reminder of your tragedy is to mentally prepare for it. If possible, plan an activity that honors your child's memory. Our intensifying anguish over the days and weeks leading up to our child's sunset date are often far more punishing than the actual day itself.

Every year, Kathy and I arrange to have Tiffanie's photo published in the "In Memoriam" section of our local newspaper on her sunset date. This is usually accompanied by a special message or poem written in her honor. When this remembrance appears in print, it often generates telephone calls or special "Thinking of You" cards from those who recognize Tiffanie's face. We have found that newspaper tributes ensure that people who may have forgotten will at least remember Tiffanie one more time. That alone makes it well worth the effort for our family.

One year, I received a package in the mail in response to our newspaper tribute. Inside was a thoughtful card from Ann Aurelia Kennedy, a childhood friend who had recently lost her brother, Daniel. I remember how Ann and Danny always enjoyed a close relationship. He was an immensely talented artist who painted, sculpted, and created a variety of works during his lifetime.

Attached to the card was one of Danny's actual pieces, entitled "Angel," which Ann offered "as a token of shared condolences." This was a wonderful tribute to Tiffanie, especially since I know how much Ann loves her brother and cherishes his artistic creations.

Kathy and I have spent the anniversaries of Tiffanie's death in a variety of ways, but always together. Some years we go to a local nursery to purchase a small tree to plant in her memory. Other years we visit local shops and browse in search of something with special significance that reminds us of our daughter. Frequently, we return home laden with angels, butterflies, and a variety of other special holiday ornaments. Since Tiffanie was blessed with beautiful strawberry-blonde hair, we are especially drawn to figurines bearing a similar distinctive hair color.

It is wonderful if parents can manage to be together on their child's date of death but I recognize not everyone has that luxury. If you are without a spouse or significant other, consider spending the day with a relative or trusted friend. I understand that some parents may prefer to be alone or find it awkward to ask someone to spend the day with them.

Yet for most of us, this is the saddest, most depressing day of the year. I usually spend Tiffanie's birthday alone, pouring through photo albums and watching videos. Yet that is the anniversary of one of the happiest days of my life. On the anniversary of her death I am more vulnerable to depressing thoughts. For this reason, I seriously urge you to avoid spending this day alone.

Try to take it easy on yourself and consider doing something that enables you to leave your home for the day, rather than staring at the walls. Do something that enables you to remember your child in a meaningful way. It could be as simple as placing flowers on your child's grave, attending a religious service, or visiting special places your child loved. However you elect to spend the day, even if circumstances require that you have to work, do something special to honor your child's memory.

Vacations

Taking that first vacation without our child can be a very depressing experience. We often hope getting away from home will clear our heads and make us feel better. Too often we discover that traveling only seems to make us miss our child even more. Each time we do something special while on vacation, we may feel unfulfilled because our child is unable to share the experience. Although we try to enjoy ourselves, our hearts remind us how wonderful this trip could have been if only our child was there.

Sometimes we select a location our son or daughter never visited to avoid the sadness our past memories may bring. Yet soon after arrival, we can find ourselves pondering how much he or she would have enjoyed this trip. With each new activity, our thoughts drift back to our child. Everything we try to do without our son or daughter can make us feel incomplete and unsatisfied.

If we return to a prior family vacation place, our emotions may become very raw, especially soon after the tragedy. We remember being there with our family when our lives were so very different. We find ourselves constantly tearing up as we recall specific things our child said or did at particular spots. In the future, these same memories can bring us great comfort as we sense a special closeness with each visit.

In the early days of my grief, I was especially drawn to locations where I had special memories of Tiffanie. The first few times I returned, it only intensified my pain. As I envisioned Tiffanie at particular spots and recalled what she said or did, my anguish was overwhelming. My first few visits seemed to only magnify the harsh reality of her absence.

Although many years have passed, I can still visualize Tiffanie at these same personal landmarks. When I return now, I focus on how much she enjoyed herself on vacation. In doing so, it makes me feel especially close to her. These visits are no longer the source of intense pain they were in the beginning. My vacation memories of Tiffanie now give me comfort rather than punish me with regret.

The widespread belief that going on vacation will make you feel better is a faulty concept at best. At first, we may find ourselves feeling guilty for being on vacation without our child. Because we miss her so desperately, we can feel miserable and tempted to return home early.

My best advice is to plan a family getaway when you are emotionally ready to understand and accept the drawbacks. Do so with the realistic expectation that vacationing is unlikely to lessen your emotional pain. Whether you are at home or away, you still carry that same hole in your heart.

A family excursion can still be a positive first step in your healing process. It can provide a welcome respite for your family to privately spend time together. It liberates you from the constant fear of running into neighbors or associates and from the negative reactions you dread while at home or work. Away from home, you generally face fewer delicate questions or uncomfortable situations.

Take the opportunity to physically and emotionally rest yourself. Hopefully, you can fade invisibly into this new environment, taking solace in the one real benefit a vacation normally provides: the emotional safety afforded by anonymity.

Mother's Day/Father's Day

I was at work one afternoon when a woman emerged from an adjacent office. I recognized her immediately because her daughter had been close friends with Tiffanie when they were children. Although I had not seen this lady in several years, she turned and recognized me immediately. She greeted me with this question, "Weren't you Tiffanie's dad?" Stung by the knife-twist effect of her words, I looked her in the eye and confidently responded, "I still am!" Apparently grasping the ignorance of her remark, she turned and hurried off without further comment.

We have lost a child, but we will never stop being his mother or father. That is an honor no one can ever strip away from us. In the early years after their child's death, parents often dread Mother's Day and Father's Day for months beforehand. These occasions can seem meaningless after our child is gone.

If you have surviving children, they may desperately search for ways to make the day special. Despite your sadness, you are their parent too! They may make an extra effort to honor their mother or father because they miss seeing you smile. Try to avoid resisting their attempts to honor you. By celebrating these special days, you may help them with their own healing. They need reassurance that you still cherish being a parent to *all* your children.

If you have no surviving children, the silence of the morning can magnify the emptiness you feel inside. The title of mother or father can seem less meaningful after your child's death. There is no escape for any of us from the overwhelming sadness we experience on Mother's Day or Father's Day, especially during that first year. This can be an agonizing time that seems to punish, rather than honor us. It will do exactly that if we dwell totally on the pain of our loss.

Being parents is one of the greatest honors we have ever been given. We have a special connection to our sons or daughters, regardless of whether they died before birth or lived well into adulthood. This incredible bond we share with our children is defined by love, not time. Mother's Day and Father's Day recognize our status as parents. Over time, we can allow ourselves to cherish that role, rather than becoming fixated on our loss.

I am still Tiffanie's father! I will always be her dad. That is what I focus on when another Father's Day approaches. Those words always bring me comfort in the face of sadness. I would rather have suffered the agony of her loss than never have had the privilege of being her dad. If I hide away in my room rather than celebrate that honor, I am not doing justice to my daughter's memory.

Veterans Day/Memorial Day

Veterans Day and Memorial Day take on added significance if your child was a soldier during her life, died while in military service, or had military career aspirations. Military families tend to be a close-knit community. These special days dedicated to our military personnel are a good time for grieving families to spend time together. The military organizes special events on days of remembrance to honor the brave sacrifices of our soldiers. Some of these families choose to participate in these solemn ceremonies while others prefer to keep to themselves.

American Gold Star Mothers, Inc. is available to mothers who have lost a son or daughter in military service, and their husbands and children may join as "associate" members.[64] This organization apprises its members of various memorial ceremonies held throughout the year to remember the sacrifices of our fallen soldiers.

Many parents who are dealing with the loss of a soldier are likely to display an American flag on their property throughout the year. Certainly on special days dedicated to military personnel, flying an American flag symbolizes a special tribute to their child. During these times, cemeteries are filled with small flags adorning the graves of those who proudly served and defended their country.

Tragedy Assistance Program for Survivors, Inc. (TAPS) is an organization dedicated to reaching out to families who have lost loved ones during their military service.[65] Among the variety of benefits it provides is a national hotline available twenty-four hours each day.

Bereaved military parents may prefer to use military-oriented support services rather than attend a community-based group. One of the reasons for this preference is the potential that political differences might draw unwelcome comments from others. Parents of children who died fighting a war should not bear the pain of having someone question its' political justification, thus inferring their child died in vain.

It is difficult to imagine anything more painful for a parent whose beloved child gave his life while answering this country's call to service. Regardless of political viewpoints, the sacrifices of these soldiers and their families must be greatly respected, deeply appreciated, and never minimized in the name of political activism.

Veterans' and Memorial Days are occasions when all of us can recognize and remember our brave soldiers by displaying an American flag in their honor. In doing so, we pay tribute to each soldier and the loving families left behind to grieve their loss.

Thanksgiving

If your family gathers together as a Thanksgiving tradition, it is heartbreaking when you do this for the very first time without your child. Too often, relatives carefully avoid any mention of your child's name. As they sense that you are just trying to get through the holidays, they try not to say or do anything that might upset you further.

Deprived of the chance to celebrate with your child, Thanksgiving can become yet another emotional obstacle that only intensifies your grief. I remember how empty all holidays seemed during those first few years without our daughter. They later became more tolerable as our family grew more willing to talk about Tiffanie.

It may be difficult to get beyond our anger during that first holiday. The sadness of missing our son or daughter becomes our constant companion. As depressing as it is to be without our child, Thanksgiving is an opportunity to give thanks that she was in our lives, albeit far too briefly.

Our lives have been greatly enriched by our children's love. Thanksgiving is the one day during the year dedicated to cherishing each of our blessings. If we focus on our gratitude for having that special love in our lives, Thanksgiving can still be meaningful, despite our pain.

It is also comforting when we find a way to include our child in this holiday. If your child was older, you can bring up her name in conversation by saying, "If _____ was here, she would be laughing about _____." The fact that you mention your child's name and reference a happy time in her life should send a strong signal that you openly welcome such a discussion.

Reserving a special moment to remember your child can become a permanent part of your family ritual each Thanksgiving. Your family can still remember your son or daughter by carefully lighting a special candle or offering a dinner toast in his or her honor. Although our children are no longer physically present to share this day with us, we can ensure they are not forgotten on Thanksgiving or any other special day by incorporating a few meaningful gestures of loving remembrance.

Christmas, Hanukkah, and Similar Holidays

Whether you celebrate Christmas, Hanukkah, Kwanza, or another similar December holiday, it is one of the most dreaded periods of the year after your child has died. Since I am most familiar with Christmas traditions, I will limit my references to that holiday. However, most of these observations will likely apply to other similar celebrations.

As the holiday season approaches, the air is thick with excitement. Yet you may find yourself struggling with bouts of intense loneliness and depression. Even if you have a spouse, significant other, and/or surviving children, facing that first Christmas without your child can be emotionally devastating. You may feel isolated and overcome with sadness at a time when much of the world is overjoyed.

You remember how much your child loved the unique customs and fanfare associated with Christmas. It seems incredibly unfair that you are denied the chance to celebrate with him like every other family. If you have other children, you search for ways to accomplish the impossible: providing a normal Christmas for your family. Yet masking your immense pain from surviving siblings is not easily accomplished.

Siblings are often hopeful their holidays can still be joyous. Young children are usually in awe over Santa Claus, elves, reindeer, colorful parades, religious services, and of course, gifts. These are the yuletide symbols so many children cherish and part of why they usually look forward to Christmas all year long.

Yet surviving brothers or sisters may feel robbed of the wondrous experience they treasured in years past. They desperately want their family to be as happy as everyone else around them. The death of their brother or sister seems to have altered everything they now do as a family and they may privately wonder if their family will ever be able to truly celebrate anything again.

Kathy and I were totally overwhelmed with dread as our first Christmas without Tiffanie approached. Our daughter adored these special holidays and our closets are filled with videos documenting her excitement over the years. Yet as that first Christmas without her drew closer, our heartache only intensified. There was no way we could become enthusiastic about celebrating without her. Our attic was filled with boxes of decorations that remained untouched. We found ourselves incapable of buying our traditional live holiday tree, a family ritual that our daughter particularly treasured.

For many years before Tiffanie died, Kathy and I mailed greeting cards bearing a photograph of our children. It was so much fun to review the different poses each year and select one that would be the official Collins' Christmas card. Yet on December 1st, we were struck with a cruel dose of reality. It was the time of year when we would normally prepare these special cards. We realized that we would never be able to place a photo of our children on a greeting card again.

When we considered sending a more traditional, non-photo holiday card, we ran into another problem: How would we possibly sign it? In the past, our greeting cards were always signed, "Chuck, Kathy, Tiffanie, David and

Chris." To sign it any other way would cause tremendous emotional pain. As all of these worries brought on too much anguish, we decided against sending cards at all.

Some professional counselors might label our decision as "grief avoidance." Yet as struggling parents, we did what caused us the least amount of pain that wasn't harmful in the long run. By opting not to send holiday cards, we faced one less emotional mountain. We were suffering under an avalanche of grief. The world would not come to an end merely because we didn't send cards.

Knowing we were facing the prospect of a horrendous Christmas, our friends Sue and Paul Lowden from Las Vegas, Nevada came to our rescue. They invited our family to visit during the week immediately following Christmas. Sue, Paul, and their young sons Paul and Will graciously shared their holidays with a family that couldn't have been very jovial companions.

This was the most unselfish, loving gesture anyone could possibly make to a family in mourning. Being in Las Vegas made it easier to pretend that it really wasn't Christmas at all. We found ourselves in one of the few places in this country where bright lights twinkle twenty-four hours every day of the year. Thanks to the Lowden family, we left our normal environment to escape the emotional hardship we would have faced at home.

I suspect the experts will beat me up on this one too. My best advice for surviving that first Christmas is to run to the nearest exit. Get out of town! Take your family somewhere else, anywhere other than home. I understand that not everyone has the financial resources or employment flexibility to make this a viable option. However, if you have the opportunity, I encourage you to escape the emptiness that first Christmas holiday brings. I would encourage newly bereaved parents to consider traveling anywhere, especially Vegas… Vegas… Vegas!

Most grieving parents don't have caring friends in Las Vegas to come to their aid. They have to face their first Christmas surrounded by so many painful reminders of past celebrations together. If they suffered a miscarriage, stillbirth, or if their child died as an infant, they may feel betrayed. Their dreams of spending that first Christmas with their baby have been destroyed. It seems so effortless for neighbors and friends to come together in joy. These distraught parents wonder why they couldn't have been given that same special blessing in their lives. I understand the depths of their frustration. They feel trapped in a world that rejoices while they struggle with the greatest loss imaginable.

They face each day devoid of the excitement that permeates their community. Being constantly reminded of the seasonal festivities everywhere they go, too many suffer in self-imposed isolation because they can't stand to leave the house. They also must decide whether to decorate their homes, and if so, how extensively. If they have small children, the desire to present some sense of normalcy may force them to decorate, at least to a moderate degree. My heart goes out to them. I recognize how painful it is to decorate your home with symbols of love and joy while your heart is breaking.

Thanks to the generosity of the Lowden family, we actually traveled to Las Vegas for two years before we faced our first Christmas at home without Tiffanie. David and Chris finally asked if we could resume our regular celebrations as they missed spending time with our relatives and their friends at home.

When we finally had to confront this emotional challenge, Kathy decorated the interior of our home with traditional ornaments. We bought a live tree, remembering Tiffanie's excitement each time we did so in the past. As we examined the ornaments, we discovered a few special ones our daughter made when she was in elementary school. When we decorated the tree, we reserved a space near the top to hang her decorations.

The boys and I used every outdoor light imaginable to decorate our yard. They seemed so excited by the return of those colorful lights symbolizing that our family was finally able to celebrate again. By the time we were finished, there were so many decorations in our front yard, we won the annual neighborhood association ham for the most decorative home. I suspect that John Bowles, one of our loyal and sympathetic neighbors, influenced the voting. However, Chris and David were very excited when we were notified of our selection.

For many years, an electric angel ornament has adorned the top of our holiday trees. She holds a candle-like light in her hand and when activated, her arms rotate gracefully back and forth. Before our first Christmas at home without Tiffanie, we unpacked the angel, placing it in its usual position on the tree. When we connected the electrical cord, we realized the bulb in the angel's hand was no longer illuminated.

When I later reviewed the video from our last Christmas with Tiffanie, the bulb in the angel's hand was clearly shining brightly. To honor her, we decided never to replace the light bulb. The angel still gracefully adorns the top of our tree each year, but the light in her hand no longer shines. This has special significance for our family. Although the light may be gone, the angel still remains very much a part of our lives.

Since Tiffanie's death, we have purchased a variety of special angels, many with Tiffanie-like strawberry-blonde hair. As these gradually accumulated, they were initially hung near the top of our tree to honor Tiffanie. One day, we received an ornament in the mail bearing a photo of Tiffanie when she was in the first grade. During that school year, each child handmade a special holiday ornament bearing her photo and presented this special gift to the teacher.

After hearing of Tiffanie's death, her former teacher was kind enough to mail the ornament back to us. Her thoughtful gesture touched our hearts and we continue to hang the ornament on our tree each year. We cherish it and take solace in knowing it was created with Tiffanie's love.

As the number of angel ornaments in our home multiplied over the years, a separate "angel tree" had to be created. Tiffanie's personal ornaments still hang at the top of our tree in the family room, but a special tree stands in our living room displaying all kinds of unique angels. It has become a special feature of our holiday that friends and family enjoy during visits.

In the last few years, Kathy began purchasing a small ornament, usually an angel or a butterfly, to give to visitors during the Christmas holidays. Our hope is that they will take the ornament home and hang it on their own trees as a tribute to Tiffanie. It is yet another small gesture to ensure our daughter is remembered.

New Year's Eve

As the world prepares to welcome a new year filled with hope for the future, in the first year of our loss we may find ourselves struggling to hold onto the past. We may have lost our optimism that good things are even possible. The last year brought us the death of our child. We may fear that another will only bring us more pain.

On our first New Year's Eve after Tiffanie's death, Kathy and I had dinner at a terrific restaurant in Las Vegas. Sue Lowden's parents arranged a separate New Year's dinner for the four boys, who spent the night together at their home. Kathy and I planned to return to our hotel room after dining. There, we could spend New Years Eve together, while strategically avoiding the midnight celebrations.

We had a great conversation with Sue and Paul during dinner, which extended longer than we had anticipated. When we finished our meal and thanked our gracious hosts, we made our way through a crowded hallway in the direction of our adjacent hotel. Although it was still two hours before midnight, the large corridor was jammed with enthusiastic people, already well into celebration mode.

Seeing everyone's excitement as the midnight hour approached only dampened our spirits. Tiffanie had been alive for the first five months of the year. How could we possibly welcome a new year when she would never be alive to share the joy with us again? It was a painful thought, and it made us dread a future without our daughter.

Walking toward the elevators, we quietly made our way through a large area filled with people. As a group of particularly festive partygoers passed us, we came face to face with a young woman, armed with a glass of something bubbly in her hand. She looked at us with obvious consternation. With an unforgiving glare and slightly slurred speech, she managed to say, "Smile for Christ's sake. It's New Years!"

Normally, I would have been quick to tell her why we weren't interested in celebrating. I shudder to think what I might have said, had I not been so blindsided by her unexpected reaction. Kathy and I were caught completely off guard. We were definitely not in a festive mood and this young lady was still sober enough to call us on it.

We understood how horrible and empty we felt inside. We just hadn't realized our facial expressions and body language conveyed those painful emotions to others. Without saying a word, we continued walking back to our room. There we could disappear from public view in relative safety, shielded from the festivities. This perceptive, though obviously inebriated, young lady was only guilty of stating the obvious. Our spirits had definitely been broken and it showed.

I relate this story only to warn you to be careful about how you spend the first New Years without your child. If you have the energy to go to a public celebration, watch out for the perceptive young woman with the drink in her hand. Try to blend into the crowd to avoid attracting attention to the grief that may seem to hover just above your head.

If you go to a local party, try to anticipate who will be there. A room filled with people who already know your child has died is preferable to strangers who may ask, "So, do you have any children?" We especially try to avoid that question as we struggle to get through our first New Year's celebration without our child.

You may decide to remain at home and spare yourself the party atmosphere. Kathy and I have slept through more than one of these celebrations. There is no right or wrong way to handle this particular holiday. I encourage you to do what fits best within your comfort zone. You may find that it changes from one year to the next.

For several years, our good friends Barbara and Scott Taylor generously invited our family to spend New Year's Eve at their home with a small group of close friends. In doing so, they created a warm, friendly environment, allowing us to feel protected and safe. We sought refuge in their home for several years as we faced subsequent New Years without Tiffanie.

Chapter 14 - After-Death Communication

THIS CHAPTER DESCRIBES OUR LIMITED EXPERIENCE exploring the possibility of achieving after-death communication with Tiffanie. I understand this topic is controversial and some readers may find it offensive. This discussion is not intended to frighten you or challenge your own religious tenets. If you find this subject objectionable in any way, I recommend that you simply skip this section, as well as any related references in the appendix or website.[66]

Much has been written about people, commonly referred to as mediums, who claim the ability to receive, interpret, and communicate messages from the dead. Grieving parents are in a very vulnerable emotional condition and are understandably desperate for the chance to talk to their son or daughter again. Many would grasp onto any opportunity offering the slightest hope of verifying their child is safe. Thus, it is not surprising that bereaved parents may be particularly drawn to the services of mediums in the hope of making contact with their children.

Some people believe the whole concept of after-death communication is totally bogus. Others point to various studies that seem to validate the existence of these abilities in some people.[67] It is safe to say that none of us can be certain whether or not actual communication with the dead is possible. We can only gather as much information as possible and draw our own conclusions. I have included a list of books related to this topic in the appendix, as well as on my website.[68]

At some point, anguished parents may attempt to communicate with their child in the afterlife. George Anderson, a widely respected medium, observes a pattern among the people who regularly request his assistance:

> I have noticed that bereaved parents make up the largest segment of those who come to me for a discernment. While the circumstances that bring them to me vary, their intent is always the same—to make sure their children are safe and happy in the

hereafter. Like any good parent sending their children across the street or off to camp or college, those parents with children in the hereafter are only doing their job, making sure their children are in good care wherever they are.[69]

If you decide to consult with a medium, you must exercise extreme caution. If you are not careful, you can unwittingly create an opportunity for scam artists to victimize your already emotionally-vulnerable family. Your first step should involve reading as much information about this process as possible.

Mediums may use a variety of other designations to describe themselves. In his book *Talking To Heaven,* another noted expert, James Van Praagh, defines and distinguishes several of these terms, including clairvoyance, clairaudience, and clairsentience.[70] Media personality Joel Martin and author Patricia Romanowski co-wrote a book describing George Anderson. Therein they describe him as a "psychic medium," defining the term as follows:

> …As an adjective, *psychic* means simply 'lying outside the realm of physical processes and physical science.' *Medium* is the most neutral word we know to describe the nature of George's role in the psychic process. He is truly a medium: a passive conduit through which the messages flow from the other side.[71]

Some of the most widely recognized people who claim this ability include John Edward, George Anderson, Sylvia Browne, and James Van Praagh, among others. There are a multitude of books written by or about each of them and most include amazing personal accounts of their sessions. In the beginning, I had some difficulty understanding how these "readings" actually worked. John Edward explains his approach in laymen's terms:

> …Like other psychics and mediums, I hear sounds, see images, and—the most difficult to explain—feel thoughts and sensations that are put into my mind and body by spirits on the Other Side. They do this in order to convey messages to people they have left behind on the physical plane.
>
> In some cases, I can give a good reading simply by passing on what I'm hearing, seeing, and feeling. But in most instances, I must interpret the information so that the meaning is understood…[72]

Since Tiffanie's death, Kathy and I have visited two mediums, Reverend Anne Gehman and George Anderson. Both appeared in a 1999 television documentary devoted to after-death communication.[73] Two years after Tiffanie died, a friend gave us her appointment, scheduled months in advance, for a reading with Reverend Anne Gehman. [74] We were told to bring one of Tiffanie's personal possessions. To the best of our knowledge, Ms. Gehman had no advance knowledge that we would be attending this session instead of our friend.

Our session was held at Ms. Gehman's lovely Virginia home and lasted slightly over an hour. During this, our first ever visit with a medium, Kathy and I had no clue what to expect. I had read virtually nothing on the topic and had serious reservations about whether this had any chance for success. However, we had heard bits and pieces about mediums. Enough time had passed since Tiffanie's death that we were willing to explore the possibility. When the appointment was offered to us, it seemed foolish not to at least try it once.

Kathy brought along Tiffanie's watch to the session and presented it to Ms. Gehman, who held it in her hand. As the reading began, Ms. Gehman indicated the first person who communicated with her was a priest with the initial "G." I actually remember two priests with that initial from my days as a young altar boy in Washington, D.C. Both priests passed away many years ago. It was not surprising to me that either of them might try to communicate if it were possible. Yet Kathy and I were confused and understandably disappointed that our daughter was not the first person to appear during this session.

Ms. Gehman then began interpreting messages that she attributed to Tiffanie. She described with amazing accuracy the nature of Tiffanie's illness and her hospital room. While most hospital rooms are quite similar, Ms. Gehman correctly referenced specific types of medical equipment used to treat Tiffanie's condition.

Being inexperienced and guarded toward this whole experience, we found it difficult to believe Tiffanie would communicate with us and not mention her younger brothers. Yet there was no direct reference to either boy during our session. Ms. Gehman also mentioned the names of several other people who were trying to communicate from "the other side," but most of these names were unfamiliar.

Ms. Gehman urged us to check these names with other family members, explaining that they could be older relatives we did not directly know. However, we were forced to ignore her advice. We did not want our family to know that we had resorted to something as drastic as visiting a medium in the first place.

Ms. Gehman then shifted her focus and began making predictions for the future. Kathy left the session with serious doubts about the entire process, while I had mixed feelings about the results. Ms. Gehman had described some people whose names we did recognize. She had been reasonably accurate in identifying that we lost a daughter who was hospitalized with an illness. She seemed to understand the nature of Tiffanie's infection and the equipment used at the hospital to treat her. Yet much of the information that did not involve our daughter made no sense to us.

John Edward describes some of the factors that can affect the accuracy of a reading:

> ...Any number of factors—the skill of the medium is a big one, but not the only one—will determine whether the information will be considered a hit or miss. We may not always understand how spirits choose their messages, or why they convey them with this symbol and not that one, but spirits don't play games or misstate. If I pass on twenty-five pieces of information and nineteen are validated, it doesn't mean I've gotten six 'wrong,' any more than it means that they've told six lies...[75]

A few years later, after we had read several books on the topic and educated ourselves about the process, Kathy arranged for our participation in a group session with George Anderson, a nationally-renowned medium.

This session was exclusively offered to parents who had lost a child. Thus, Mr. Anderson already knew that each participant had lost a child. I remember being excited at the prospect of receiving a reading by Mr. Anderson. I had read several books about his work and was impressed with the descriptions of his gift. In my research, I discovered that a medium has no control over who appears during a session. This immediately reminded me of the priest, (I'll call him "Father G") whom we were told was the first to communicate with us during our earlier session with Ms. Gehman.

My mother, Marguerite Collins, died on Christmas Day, over two years after Tiffanie's death. She had raised me as a single parent and we had a close, loving relationship. My mother had a fondness for talking, especially on the telephone. She suffered from serious leg ailments that greatly restricted her mobility and she never drove an automobile. Since she was often marooned inside her residence, the telephone became her primary source of communication.

My mother's telephone conversations were customarily long and legendary. I even remember a wrong number that Marguerite managed to stretch into a ten-minute conversation. I have great love and appreciation for the sacrifices she made to raise me as a single mother. Yet as the date of our visit with George Anderson approached, I began to worry that she would appear during our reading and take over the session. I remember visiting her grave several times in the days before our scheduled reading and praying to her, "Mom, I love you. But please let Tiffanie come through and talk to us. We need to hear from her!"

Our first session with George Anderson was held in 2001 at a New York hotel.[76] It required considerable planning to ensure that Kathy and I were there on time. We arrived early with two books written about Mr. Anderson, which he graciously autographed.

Kathy and I privately agreed not to disclose any information about ourselves or our family to Mr. Anderson's assistant or any other people in the room. We treated everyone who arrived early with great skepticism. We assumed they may have been planted in the session specifically to elicit our personal information in advance. Almost everyone brought along tape recorders, since Mr. Anderson openly invited each participant to tape the session. Kathy and I were no exception.

There were a total of twenty chairs in the room positioned in a semi-circle. In the middle was a chair set against the wall. Eight couples appeared for this session and one individual was present representing the ninth couple. The tenth pair of chairs remained empty.

At the scheduled time, Mr. Anderson entered the room and promptly seated himself in the lone chair as the door to the room was closed. He formally greeted everyone and gave a brief explanation of how the session would be conducted. Mr. Anderson is a nice-looking man who presents a neat appearance, yet there is a hint of genuine shyness about him. Although he speaks to hundreds of people at a time and has made national television appearances, he seemed surprisingly introverted.

As the session commenced, George Anderson explained that he would approach people in the room based on which of the spirits captured his attention. For each of the nine families represented, he correctly determined whether the parents had lost a son or daughter. For some people, Mr. Anderson seemed to provide detailed information only the family would likely have known. He made his way around the room in no particular order and his interaction with each family ranged anywhere from ten to fifteen minutes.

After completing the first five readings, Mr. Anderson suddenly turned in our direction and indicated that a "male presence" caught his attention. My mind immediately raced, fearing that "Father G," the same priest who appeared first during the Anne Gehman session, had done it again.

I was relieved when Mr. Anderson identified the man as my father–in-law, William Barry, who died five years before Tiffanie. Mr. Barry was a warm, wonderful man who enjoyed a close relationship with Tiffanie. In fact, a few days before her death, Tiffanie confided to her mother that she had a very unusual experience.

In a dream Tiffanie described as "very real," her grandfather appeared and kept trying to reassure her, "Don't worry. Everything is going to be all right!" When Kathy and Tiffanie discussed what had happened, both eventually dismissed it as "just a dream." Yet only few days later, Tiffanie died. So it was particularly comforting when Mr. Anderson indicated her grandfather was bringing Tiffanie to us.

We were told that Tiffanie and her grandfather were accompanied by another woman. Mr. Anderson later identified her as a "grandmother," but she made no effort to communicate. It was as though she merely wanted to be present to bring our daughter to us. I later went back to my mother's grave and thanked her for allowing Tiffanie to be the focus of the session. I had to smile knowing how much of a sacrifice that was for a special woman who loved to chat.

Early in the session, Mr. Anderson used the word "accidental" to describe Tiffanie's death. He indicated that he was being shown a "vehicle type accident," and indicated this reference could be simply "symbolic." Yet he seemed to backtrack quickly when he observed our negative reaction to this reference. I suspect this made Kathy a bit suspicious that he was only fishing for information. A close reading of the transcript verifies Mr. Anderson's reference to the vehicle included a cautious disclaimer that it might only be *symbolic* of an accidental death.

While Mr. Anderson did not seem to understand the actual cause of Tiffanie's death, he described her symptoms very accurately. What impressed me the most about this session was his obvious confusion about how Tiffanie died. If he was not a legitimate medium, he likely would have gleaned this information from advance Internet research. Yet during the session he struggled because he was receiving mixed signals and was understandably confused. He was interpreting a message about an "accidental" death, yet this seemed to conflict with other signs he received that Tiffanie had been "poisoned."

The word "poisoned" struck a meaningful chord with me. I remembered an earlier hospital conversation with an infectious disease expert treating Tiffanie in which he said, "Mr. Collins, you have to think of it [meningitis] as being like a poison. It goes from one organ to another shutting them down one by one." Kathy had remained by Tiffanie's side in the hospital room and was not with me at the time. Mr. Anderson's specific use of the word "poison" was a strong validation for me that he was definitely communicating with Tiffanie.

Throughout the first five years after Tiffanie's death, I had tortured myself emotionally, believing I was directly responsible. So many times I had lamented, "If only I had gotten her to a hospital as soon as I went to South Carolina. If only I had realized the sore throat could have been a sign of a more serious illness pervading her body." I remember going to the cemetery alone and crying uncontrollably, trying to apologize to Tiffanie through my tears.

After this first session with Mr. Anderson, guilt finally released its smothering grip on me. The message conveyed was that Tiffanie had "flu-like symptoms," so I could not possibly have recognized the severity of the illness. Sadly, because so much time was devoted to discussing my feelings of guilt, Kathy's need to communicate with Tiffanie was left unfulfilled. I believe that through Mr. Anderson's special ability, Tiffanie reached out to me because she had witnessed how severely I was being emotionally tortured.

Later in the session Mr. Anderson described Tiffanie as "not the doctor type. She is not going to go running to the doctor because she has the flu." Yet this was in stark contrast to the daughter we know and love. In fact, we always teased Tiffanie about being a hypochondriac because she would go to the doctor at the drop of a hat. Yet it was usually with good reason.

I remember when Tiffanie complained about some discomfort in her lower back and immediately diagnosed herself as having a back problem. Kathy and I made certain that she went to the doctor, but rolled our eyes at each other in disbelief. Tiffanie's diagnosis was confirmed after x-rays revealed the presence of minor scoliosis of the lower spine. So when it came to going to the doctor, Tiffanie was never reluctant and more often than not, her decision to go proved justified.

Kathy and I both felt Mr. Anderson's characterization of Tiffanie as one who avoids doctors was a significant discrepancy. He attributed this information directly to Tiffanie's words. Could it be a misinterpretation? That is certainly possible. However, it definitely added to Kathy's skepticism about whether Mr. Anderson was really communicating with our daughter.

Although Mr. Anderson made a general reference indicating that Tiffanie reached out to her family, we still felt unfulfilled. Again she made no specific reference to her brothers. Overall, Kathy harbored serious reservations about the value of this session. However, I concluded that Mr. Anderson was so accurate in his reference to "poison," as well as in his description of my guilt-induced anguish, the session had been personally productive for me.

Three years later, we decided to try another session with Mr. Anderson. We both felt the limited time available in a group setting may have restricted the chance for more extended and meaningful communication with Tiffanie. This time we scheduled a private session at the same location.

Again we flew to New York and arrived several hours before our scheduled session. When we met his assistant, she encouraged us to say "yes" during the session, even if we were not quite certain what Mr. Anderson was saying. She indicated that sometimes people don't immediately recognize certain information and warned that answering "no" can have a negative effect on the quality of a session.

George Anderson greeted us, shook our hands, and then positioned himself on the other side of the room about fifteen feet away.[77] When the session commenced, he again indicated a "male presence" had come forward, this time accompanied by two females. We concluded that it could be neither "Father G" nor my father-in-law when the male presence was described as "younger."

When Mr. Anderson related that the male presence stated, "... he's family to both of you," we actually had no idea who this was. We remembered the instructions provided by his assistant, so we responded, "yes." Mr. Anderson then stunned both of us when he said, "Which I take it he is.... He embraces both of you so...um... Let...He states to me he's the son that passed on..... Understood?"

Apparently, the shocked expression on our faces made Mr. Anderson immediately realize this was definitely not our son. So he suddenly seemed to be grasping for an explanation, saying, "Well, the problem is he's talking about it over there so he has to be somebody's.....He's not saying he's yours."

To his credit, Mr. Anderson then tried to clarify whether or not we recognized who this male presence was. When we told him that we didn't, he instructed us not to say "yes" if we did not know something. He suggested that we simply answer we "don't know," which seemed to be a more reasonable approach. We did not tell him about the prior instructions we had received.

As more information was disclosed during the reading, we considered the possibility that the younger male presence was Steve Carre, a mutual, very close childhood friend who died tragically in his early twenties. We finally concluded that it was apparently Steve who had brought our daughter into the session.

Although Mr. Anderson correctly identified one of Kathy's two miscarriages during this session, he provided little meaningful information about Tiffanie other than her name. Despite some initial confusion, he did indicate that Tiffanie reached out to her brothers.

In my opinion, Mr. Anderson spent far too much time trying to demonstrate that he was capable of coming up with our daughter's name, as well as its unusual spelling. We would gladly have conceded him that information had we realized how much valuable session time would be wasted trying to prove this minor point. If we had any significant doubts that he possessed these unique abilities, we would never have returned for a second session. We were there hoping for some type of meaningful communication with our daughter.

In retrospect, I suspect we caught Mr. Anderson on a bad day or he was simply exhausted from his earlier appointments. Mr. Anderson honestly acknowledges this process is vulnerable to human error.[78] Our second session aside, I still believe Mr. Anderson is blessed with an amazing gift. I have encouraged others to visit him and remain open-minded during the process. One of our friends subsequently consulted him and had a rewarding experience.

George Anderson's website can be accessed at http://www.georgeanderson. com.

In direct contrast to Mr. Anderson, John Edward is an extroverted, flamboyant medium who has used his television appearances to showcase his amazing abilities. He seems to thrive on interaction with other people and displays tremendous self-confidence in his ability to accurately interpret messages from the other side. Mr. Edward's website can be accessed at http:// www.johnedward.net.

Although Kathy and I hoped to schedule a session with Mr. Edward, the waiting list was so long when we last checked that he was no longer accepting names. Our best hope is to be fortunate enough to secure tickets to one of his mass concert-style appearances in the future. Thus far, we have not had the opportunity to see Mr. Edward in person.

James Van Praagh was the first medium who caught my attention after Tiffanie died. When I read his first two books, he gave me genuine hope that some day I might be able to establish communication with Tiffanie on the other side. James Van Praagh's website can be accessed at http://www. vanpraagh.com.

If you decide to experiment with a medium, don't make the same mistake we did with Ms. Gehman. Do your homework by reading any books or articles written about them. Research the work of other mediums so you can differentiate between their approaches.

No matter how impressive the research you find, you should still approach any session with a medium skeptically. If she requires you to provide a large amount of information before conducting a reading, be very suspicious. Place the onus on the medium to convince you that she has the ability. Don't automatically presume she possesses this gift.

It is also important to remember that a medium is similar to a language interpreter who converts messages from one form to another. I have had court cases where the interpreter's translation of a defendant or witness's testimony was questioned by someone else present who spoke the same language. Errors in interpretation are made by the best of interpreters, so obviously mediums are not infallible.

One negative aspect of using mediums may be that too much time can be wasted as they try to prove their abilities. Some may spend an inordinate amount of time trying to ascertain an obscure piece of information, believing this will convince us they are actually communicating with our children. Yet too often, no significant message follows due to time constraints.

As grieving parents, we may be drawn to these sessions because we want to confirm our children are safe. We desperately want to believe they are still connected to our lives. We hope they will reach out to us, as well as to their siblings. We definitely want them to know how much we will always love them. Our greatest fear during such a session is that these messages will not be conveyed if a medium runs out of time.

If you are willing to do the research, the cost is not too exorbitant, and you have a genuine interest, my advice is to try it. If you make every medium prove his or her worth, you can satisfy an intense curiosity and possibly derive a rewarding experience in the process. Please feel free to email me at tiffaniesdad@holdingontolove.com and let me know if you have a positive encounter with a medium. As far as Kathy is concerned, the jury is still out, but the verdict is not looking very promising. However, I remain open to the process.

Chapter 15 - A Special Chapter for Family and Friends

THIS CHAPTER WAS WRITTEN IN THE hope that grieving parents will share it with their family and friends.[79] If you fall into one of these categories, you should understand that it takes courage for a parent to openly share this information with you. If he has done so, it is a clear indication of just how much he cares about you. You are someone whom he wants to keep involved in his life.

Twelve years ago, I lost my nineteen-year-old daughter, Tiffanie Amber Collins, to an outbreak of meningitis. My wife, Kathy, and I were devastated, as were her young brothers, David and Christopher, ages eleven and nine, respectively. Over the years, some people have reached out to help us in very meaningful ways. However, too often, the words or actions of others have caused needless distress.

The fact that you are taking the time to read this material demonstrates your desire to offer genuine emotional support. Please understand this section was not written to insult you or hurt your feelings in any way. This chapter is intended to help you reach out to offer real comfort to a family who needs you so much more after they lose a child.

If you have made the effort to *be there* for a bereaved parent or family, you deserve praise for having the courage to try. Being a close friend or relative to a grief-stricken parent is a very difficult, often frustrating challenge. Kathy and I had a conversation with Jan Bowman Ingles, a lifelong friend who grew up in Washington, D.C. Jan was always inseparable from her close friend Rhea Nader McVicker, another product of our childhood neighborhood.

In 1997, Rhea tragically lost her twenty-two-year-old son, Nicholas Cristarella. About a year after his death, Jan remarked how difficult it was to be a close friend to a bereaved mom. She lamented that too often, she said the "wrong thing," and Rhea immediately corrected her. But, Jan continued,

"She is my best friend. So I pick myself up and try to learn from my mistakes. I just keep trying to be there for her!"

Jan's words gave us a deeper appreciation for the complexity of being a supportive friend or relative of a grieving parent. It really is a far more difficult challenge than we initially understood. Jan's selfless compassion and loyalty to her friend is a model for anyone who accepts the challenge of reaching out to a grief-stricken mom or dad. Supportive friends or relatives will respect the fact that each individual has her own timetable for healing. They won't impose their own expectations of when a friend or relative should have healed *enough*.

I hope to clear up one common myth. When grieving parents continue to read grief-related books, attend professional counseling sessions, or actively participate in support groups several years after their loss, this does not mean they are *trapped* or *stuck* in their grief. The loss of a child is life altering for parents, thus accessing grief support resources is a natural step for them.

Parents who participate in grief support groups many years after their loss are usually giving back to other newly bereaved families. They attend these meetings to instill hope in others that they too can survive. They become teachers as they share their coping strategies with those in need of emotional reassurance. Giving comfort to these devastated people is a wonderful gesture. In doing so, they honor the memory of their beloved children.

Although your friend or relative is grieving, this doesn't mean he will never be able to smile, laugh, or have fun again. But you must accept the fact that it won't happen over night. With the passage of time, genuine compassion, and emotional support from people like you, this special person in your life can gradually learn to enjoy living again. Don't give up on a parent or sibling because you feel the healing process isn't happening fast enough for you.

Remember you are in no position to impose a deadline. Everyone grieves differently because we are all individuals. Instead of trying to judge a person's recovery progress, focus instead on being supportive. A true, Jan Bowman Ingles-type of friend is invested in this relationship for the long haul. The relationship with your friend or relative is important, so commit yourself to being there for her.

Let's start at the beginning. When a family suffers the death of a child, they begin a long painful grief process that will affect them in a variety of ways for the rest of their lives. It will never end for them, but it will definitely get better with the passage of time.

When a child dies, you want to reach out and help the devastated parents. It is wonderful if you can muster the courage to be there for your friend or relative. He will definitely need your emotional support in the weeks, months, and years ahead. You will have to exercise great patience because in the beginning his mood may seem to fluctuate by the hour.

If you attend the child's wake or funeral, make an effort to sign the guestbook. Funeral homes provide this guestbook to the family when the services have ended. As grieving parents often experience some degree of memory loss months later, they may be unlikely to remember everyone who attended. If you signed your name and address, this information will be readily available to the family.

A sympathy card also offers a wonderful opportunity for friends, family, and co-workers to reach out to the distraught family. If you don't know the family very well, you can still express your condolences. Send a sympathy card, sign it, and include a brief explanation to identify yourself. Your thoughtful expression of compassion will be greatly appreciated.

On the other hand, if you *do* know the family, take the time to write a personal note expressing your sincere condolences over their loss. Don't rely on the preprinted message that appears on the card to convey your sentiment. Mailing a preprinted card bearing only signatures and expressing no personal outreach is equivalent to sending a form letter to a family at the most emotionally desperate time of their lives. When our daughter died, we actually received one expression of sympathy where even the signature was ink printed onto the card.

When a family has lost their precious child, a standard preprinted greeting card fails to communicate genuine concern. Take a moment and convey your individual condolences over their tragedy. If you are too busy to take a few minutes to express your regrets with a personal message, why bother to send the card at all? Either way, the message of indifference is the same.

Some people use a sympathy card to seize the moment. They write their own poems of remembrance or include other meaningful messages that have helped them through difficult periods in their lives. Others detail special memories they have of the child that has died. Those who didn't know the child personally may recall how excited the parents were whenever they spoke of him. Additionally, those who have suffered the same type of loss may include a brochure from a local support group, grief counselor, or special prayer that was helpful to them.

I have seen people transform sympathy cards into wonderful sources of comfort. Some will use the card to offer to do things for the family. If the death occurs in the fall, an offer to rake leaves can be a wonderful gesture. During the summer, few grieving parents can find the energy to mow the lawn. One woman offered to create a memorial garden in our yard dedicated to our daughter. Another volunteered to assist us in preparing thank-you notes, when we were "ready to deal with it."

If you send a card and express the intention of getting together, follow up with a phone call. By doing so, you convey a willingness to spend time with the family. If your card includes "If there is anything I can do…" language, include your telephone number. This reinforces your sincerity that you want to be there for them.

Depending on their age, surviving siblings often appreciate receiving their own individual cards from friends or relatives. Although most sympathy cards are sent to the entire family, siblings rarely see them. When they receive their own cards, siblings feel their individual grief is acknowledged. Whatever you do, don't urge the siblings to *be strong* for their parents. This only places undue pressure on these brothers and/or sisters to hide their pain, stifles their own ability to grieve, and inhibits honest communication with their parents.

At wakes and funerals, people often say, "If there is anything I can do…" Bereaved parents appreciate this gesture, but it is usually meaningless. Why? First, at this initial stage of shock, the parents are holding their breath merely trying to survive this formal part of the death process. In reality, they are so distraught they may not even remember your offer of assistance. Even if they do, they are unlikely to ask for your help. They simply don't know what type of assistance they will need in the weeks and months to come. In such intense pain and emotionally numb, they have no idea what their future necessities will be.

To offer the family comfort, you usually have to take the initiative. Hug them at the wake, funeral, or whenever you see them. A hug is almost never the wrong answer for a brokenhearted parent. Just about everyone who visits family members during these early days will say something akin to, "I am so very sorry," and either shake their hand or give them a hug. That is usually a perfectly acceptable way to approach these shattered people.

If grieving parents seem to want to talk, by all means provide them an outlet. If they ask about your children, try not to be defensive and just answer the questions. They don't want you to feel guilty because your children are still alive. However, if their child died in a car accident, this is definitely not an appropriate time to share the news that your child just obtained his or her driver's license.

The bereaved family becomes most vulnerable when the funeral is over and everyone else has returned to their own routine. This period marks the beginning of the dark days of isolation, when the family confronts the true magnitude of their loss. It is therefore the most important time for you to be there for them. I encourage you to periodically get in contact and schedule a visit. Give family members the opportunity to tell you exactly how they are feeling. It will be sad for you to hear, and it may be painful and awkward for you to witness them crying. At times you may find yourself sobbing right along with them.

However, try to remember that tears are an essential part of healing and you are providing an invaluable gift by offering this emotional outreach. The family understands you don't have any answers or magic cures for its pain. They know you are simply there to listen, hug, and comfort as best you can. They will appreciate that you made the effort to be there to offer your support and they will also never forget your kindness.

Please don't be one of those annoying people who call the family's residence when you are certain no one is home. I can still remember the obvious relief conveyed in the tone of some messages left on our answering machine in the early days. Those "Sorry I missed you, but I just wanted to let you know I am thinking of you" messages are nice, when they are sincere. Yet occasionally, the real message conveyed is, "I called at this time because I knew you wouldn't be home. Since I can't bring myself to talk to you in person, give me credit for leaving you a safe, but emotionally distant, message instead!"

You can also place a note on your calendar to send a "Thinking of You" card thirty days after the funeral in which you can express your willingness to get together whenever the family is ready. If siblings are involved, consider sending them a follow-up card as well. Inviting siblings to go to a movie, bowling, or out for a snack can be a wonderful gesture the family will likely appreciate.

If you determine the parents initially desire to remain close to home, respect their wishes in the beginning. Remember their world has been turned upside down and they may suddenly feel much less secure in their lives. Try to visit with them at home, or at least call them to express your genuine concern.

After a while, you should encourage them to leave their home and go somewhere, anywhere, with you. In the very beginning, movies are not recommended because parents may have short attention spans. A craft fair, a brief shopping trip, or an informal chat at your local coffee shop represent valuable opportunities to spend time with them in a non-threatening environment.

If bereaved parents express interest in accompanying you for a drink or a glass of wine, that is fine. However, let that be their idea, rather than your suggestion. Try to ensure that future get-togethers do not always revolve around alcohol consumption. The therapeutic benefit of your visit may be lost if parents merely use it to drink excessively to dull their pain.

You should also anticipate that the parents may initially be reluctant to accept your invitation. Don't allow this to dissuade you. Just keep inviting them until they eventually accept. Try to ensure the invitation will include just the two (or three) of you most of the time. If you always bring along other people, the parents may begin to suspect you are uncomfortable being alone with them. This can become a source of considerable resentment and totally nullify the positive impact of your good intentions.

There is no doubt spending time one-on-one with a sorrowful parent is an emotionally draining experience. Not long after Tiffanie's funeral, the mother of one of her friends dropped by the house for a visit. She and Kathy retreated to the outside deck where they sat together for over an hour, giving my wife an invaluable opportunity to talk openly about her feelings.

Occurring so soon after Tiffanie's death, this meeting was really therapeutic for Kathy, who was emotionally struggling. As she was leaving, the woman turned to Kathy and promised, "I will call you soon and we'll go out for a glass of wine and talk some more." Kathy was so touched by her visit that she called the next day to express her appreciation.

Although a few cards were received in the mail over the next several months, the follow-up call never came. About six months later, I received an unrelated call from the woman. When Kathy answered the phone, she asked why the woman hadn't called back so they could go out together. Without hesitation the woman replied, "Oh, I just didn't want to be sad anymore."

Kathy was crushed by her answer. This mother obviously felt she had paid her dues with her earlier visit and had since moved on with her life. The initial visit with Kathy was a wonderful gesture. However, raising Kathy's hopes that it might happen again definitely wasn't.

In the years since Tiffanie's death, several people have promised to invite one or both of us out to spend time together. While many friends followed up on these invitations, some never did. When we occasionally have contact with those who never followed through, they often repeat their pledge to get together, but it never happens. I strongly encourage you not to make promises you don't intend to keep. Although these parents forget a great many things due to the trauma of their loss, empty promises or convenient lies are not among them.

Some parents cling desperately to their strong religious beliefs as a source of comfort and strength to help them deal with their anguish. You might consider offering to pray along with them, accompany them to a church service, or drive them to a cemetery visit. You might also help them plan a special memorial service dedicated to their child on her next birthday.

However, if you are the strong religious type, be careful not to "force" your God on them if they are not ready. Not everyone is ready to turn to their Deity for strength when their child has died. Nor does everyone share your religious beliefs. They have suffered a significant blow to their universe and they may not be ready to deal with the damage this has caused in their lives.

I recommend that you tread lightly on the topic of religion and simply give them an outlet to express their feelings. This way, you will quickly discover whether they are clinging to their religious beliefs for strength, or angry at their God for what they perceive as allowing their child to die.

Many parents are very angry and confused about why their God has allowed this horrible tragedy to happen. Don't judge them or threaten them if they stop going to church. Just two weeks after Tiffanie's death, Kathy was warned by one well-intentioned friend, "If you don't go to church and praise God, you will never see Tiffanie again!"

Are we really supposed to judge the potential of other people to get into heaven? Years later, I confronted this same woman about her remark. To her credit, she did apologize. I suspect that to this day, she doesn't really have a clue as to why the comment was inappropriate.

In the early days of grief, parents often forget to eat and some lose their appetite completely. You could try to organize a rotating schedule of meals to be delivered by their friends, family, or neighbors. This will remind them to nourish themselves and allow them to remain close to home, which is something they may initially wish to do.

Several times after Tiffanie's death, my sister-in-law Dorothy Barry ordered food for all of us from one of our local restaurants (however, no one expects you to go into bankruptcy trying to feed your relatives or friend's family). Dorothy didn't just deliver the food and leave. She sat down and ate dinner with our family, thus providing a valuable outlet for all of us during a very difficult time. Her gesture was fantastic because with one gift, she managed to nourish our bodies and lift our spirits.

Grief can also have the opposite effect on the eating habits of some parents as the stress of their emotions may prompt them to overeat. You can tactfully help them as well. Invite them over to share a fruit salad, or ask them to take a walk with you so they will get some exercise to counteract the food consumption. Encourage them to join a local health club where you belong and sign up for an exercise or aerobics class together. Above all, *tactfully* try to give them something to do to relieve their stress instead of eating.

There are many ways you can reach out to the family, depending on their specific needs and your unique ability to assist. My friend Kevin McCarthy is a retired police official who now works as a school administrator. When Tiffanie died, I was in the middle of preparing for a complicated hearing for one of my clients. Since Kevin had a background as a detective, he volunteered to help with the investigation and conducted several crucial interviews with key witnesses that definitely helped me prevail.

Kevin took the initiative to identify my needs and followed up to ensure they were met. I was fortunate that Kevin had special qualifications and refused to take "no" for an answer. Only you can assess exactly how you might be able to assist your friend or relative in the early days of his or her pain.

When the time seems right, you might suggest that the parents consider attending a grief support group. You can become an invaluable resource for the family by investigating the resources available in your area. I suggest consulting with local churches, the Internet, and community newspapers for recommendations. If you contact a support group personally, you can gain insight into whether that organization might be an appropriate recommendation.

When you have finished your research, place the information in a folder and give it to your friends or loved ones. Briefly summarize what you learned during the process. Stress that you assembled this information for the family's consideration and there is no pressure to attend. The folder will be available as a reference whenever they have the energy or interest to review the material.

Bereaved families often fear their children will eventually be forgotten. Sadly, too often they are. Since you obviously care enough to read this chapter, help your friend or relative keep the memory of his child alive. Place the child's birthday and date of loss (often referred to as the sunset or angel date) on your calendar. A "thinking-of-you" card, a telephone call, or a visit on these special days is a very touching and most appreciated gesture. You might also leave a rose or small flower arrangement at the cemetery. Your friend or relative will be soothed knowing someone else visits her child's grave and remembers.

After Tiffanie's funeral, a reception was held in the church hall. Each table was decorated with a beautiful arrangement of Begonia flowers. Every year our friend Diane Kramer quietly appears unannounced on the anniversary of Tiffanie's death and plants a section of Begonias in our garden in her memory. When she does this, there is often no conversation whatsoever.

The fact Diane remembers and takes the time to pay such a meaningful tribute each year provides an emotional boost. This is just one of many examples of positive things you can do. Always look for opportunities to reassure your friend or relative that you will never let the memory of his or her child fade.

As time passes, bereaved parents have less opportunity to talk openly about their child. Nothing stops a conversation faster than a mother or father who begins discussing a child after his or her death. My wife and I were invited to a party in our new neighborhood a few years ago. We considered it an opportunity to meet some of our neighbors, so we decided to attend. When we arrived, there was a large gathering of neighbors mingling throughout the room.

Of course the inevitable question was raised by one couple, "Do you have any children?" Kathy explained that we had lost our daughter. Without missing a beat the woman gently patted her husband's arm and said, "Dear, I think it is time for us to go!" There was no "Sorry for your loss" or "I am sorry to hear that." No, just, "time for us to go!"

There should be a special label for these type of people. They go through life wearing blinders to shield themselves from unpleasant things. They don't want to know about the loss bereaved parents have suffered because they would have to actually consider their own children's mortality. When confronted with people who have suffered a death, they flee. Since the tragedy happened to someone else's family, they have the luxury of not having to think about it. I can only hope they never have to do so.

Even when you didn't know the child during his or her life, you can still reach out to a grieving friend or co-worker. One afternoon, I received a telephone call from Cathie R.B. Jackson, a talented, tenacious attorney with whom I had worked over the years on bar committees and special projects. Cathie requested that I schedule two hours on my calendar for the following Thursday and arranged to meet at my office. She was evasive about the purpose of the meeting, promising, "I will fill you in then."

I had no idea what this was about. However, Cathie had a reputation for being a very thorough litigator. I suspected she was going to discuss some fact pattern or legal issue in an upcoming case to elicit a second opinion. When the designated meeting time arrived, Cathie walked into my office and sat down. I was stunned when she announced, "I scheduled this appointment because I never had the privilege of meeting your daughter. I would like to use this time for you to introduce me to Tiffanie."

What followed was an extraordinary two-hour gift. Oh, the tears definitely rolled down my cheeks that afternoon. Yet I felt such an emotional lift to be able to openly talk to someone about Tiffanie. If I tried to do that with most people, they would leave skid marks trying to avoid the conversation. This is a gift that you as a friend or relative have the opportunity to give to a heartbroken parent. You must realize that some parents are in too much pain and may decline the opportunity, especially if they are newly bereaved. Others are very likely to jump at the chance.

Thirty-four years ago, my wife's childhood friend, Honey Ann Molo, was a bridesmaid in our wedding. Because she later relocated to California, she never actually met Tiffanie. During a rare visit to the area, she contacted Kathy and asked to see photo albums of Tiffanie. They spent an entire afternoon pouring over photographs as Kathy was given the chance to tell Honey Ann about our daughter. This is another example of a gesture you can make to show a family you care, even when you didn't know their child in life.

As a family member, even things you don't say can cause problems for a grieving parent. On the first Thanksgiving after Tiffanie's death, our family gathered for a traditional holiday celebration. For the previous nineteen years, Tiffanie had been with us on this special day. This year was the first time she was missing. Yet throughout the entire afternoon, not one person in our family mentioned Tiffanie's name. When we left that evening, Kathy was in tears. Sobbing uncontrollably as we drove home, she said, "They have already forgotten her."

I recommend that you find some special way during every family gathering to remember the child who is no longer there. Hanging a photograph of the child prominently in your home is usually a very meaningful gesture. If the loss was very recent, I suggest asking the parents' approval in advance to ensure they can emotionally handle it. Most will greatly appreciate your thoughtful gesture.

Carefully lighting a special candle in memory of the child can also be a touching family remembrance. Depending on your family's customs, a toast to the child is another way to honor his or her memory. If you are not related to the family and they have no other relatives in the area, or have declined to travel home during a holiday, consider inviting them to share Thanksgiving or Christmas dinner with your family.

Since Tiffanie's death, our family members have placed a beautiful wreath on her grave on her sunset date and Christmas. Yet during our first Christmas, they again avoided mentioning Tiffanie's name. At the time, we were in no emotional condition to understand how to change that.

Later, Kathy did insist that our daughter not be forgotten during these gatherings. Since then, some of our relatives have made a regular donation in Tiffanie's name to The Compassionate Friends, Inc., a support group dedicated to assisting grief-stricken families who have lost children. A number of our friends have also made periodic contributions to the group as a tribute to Tiffanie on special occasions.

If you normally exchange holiday gifts with bereaved family members, consider making a donation to a charity or non-profit in their child's name. It may be an organization with special meaning during the child's life or one dedicated to curing the disease that caused the child's death. Some families have created special scholarship funds in their child's name and a donation to that account is another wonderful way to remember their child. During holiday celebrations, hanging a special ornament dedicated to their loved one's memory can also touch the family's heart.

There is yet another area where your patience is required as a friend or relative of a family in mourning. If you sent flowers, orchestrated religious remembrances, donated a meal, or have done anything special for the family during or since the funeral, don't get upset if you don't receive a thank-you note. Although a written expression of gratitude may arrive in a couple of weeks or months, it could also take a year. In fact, it would not be surprising if you never received a thank you card at all.

This is not because the family doesn't appreciate your thoughtful gesture; it simply may be too painful a task for them to handle. Be patient and try to understand that each card forces the family to relive painful emotions all over again. While the rules of etiquette may require a timely response, the emotional pain involved in writing an expression of gratitude when a child has died ultimately may dictate otherwise.

If you are willing, you might offer to help them prepare these thank-you notes whenever they feel ready. If they don't immediately accept your offer, simply let it go. You have planted the seed and that is the best you can do.

Anticipating Personality Changes

When parents lose a child, I believe their personalities may undergo a significant transformation. Often their relatives and friends are anxiously waiting for them to return to *their old selves* again. It is important for you to realize that in all likelihood, these parents will never completely be the same people they were prior to this tragedy. Their core belief system may have been totally shaken and their attitudes about life drastically changed.

As I have tried to explain this over the years, some relatives and friends have seemed puzzled at the concept that losing a child may actually change who a parent is as a person. To help you better understand, allow me to use the following analogy:

Imagine a man who loses his leg as a result of a very traumatic car accident. In the beginning, he is consumed with tremendous pain and emotional anguish. After a very long time, his physical and emotional wounds begin to heal. As his pain gradually lessens, he can learn to walk on crutches as a temporary source of support.

Later in his recovery he may even be fitted with an artificial limb. After undergoing extensive physical therapy, he can actually learn to walk with his artificial leg, despite the immense trauma he has suffered. Yet no matter how hard he tries, he will never walk the same way he did before the accident. His life has drastically and unalterably changed. There will always be a part of him that is missing.

In our analogy, it is the loss of the man's leg. For devastated parents, it is the gaping hole in their hearts. Losing a child changes them emotionally. Hopefully, in time they do become functional and eventually learn to enjoy life again. Yet they will never be exactly the same without their child in their lives.

If they were introverted before, you may notice they seem a bit more outspoken. If they were extroverted, they may now be less willing to lead the conversation. Each parent has evolved as a person. As time goes on and people become more comfortable around them, they begin to find a *new* sense of normalcy in their lives.

With your loyalty, compassion, and emotional support, they can eventually stop going through life feeling as though they have three heads. Don't give up on them. In time, you can help them rediscover how to smile, laugh, and enjoy their lives again.

On behalf of these parents, I offer a heartfelt thank you for taking the time to read this chapter. Your determination to stand by and support them during the worst time in their lives is the most wonderful gift they can receive. Ask the relative or friend who shared this chapter to give you copy of "A Comfort Checklist for Family and Friends" in the appendix. In the end, your unselfish efforts may ultimately be the difference that helps them find renewed hope in their lives again.

What Not to Say to Grieving Parents

Over the years I have heard some incredibly insensitive remarks made to parents whose child has died. I have tried to include some of the most common ones below so you will not unwittingly fall into this trap.

"I have children of my own. I know what you are going through."

No. If another parent's children are alive, she doesn't have a clue what grieving parents are going through after their child has died.

"God has a plan."

While the speaker no doubt believes that, these grief-stricken parents may be struggling with their religious convictions and may be furious at their God. If so, this comment is not a comforting expression for them unless/until they can work through their religious issues.

"Everything happens for a reason."

This is a non-religious way of saying God has a plan. Dr. Beverly Anderson[80] attributes this type of comment to people who see your pain and feel compelled to "fix it" with some quick and easy explanation. They grow impatient with these parents' constant sadness and want them to move on with their lives. However, mourning families usually can't imagine anything that would justify their child's death. A comment like this is especially incomprehensible in the early days after a child's death. It does not comfort the parents and only serves to trivialize the magnitude of their loss.

"God needed another angel."

Cute clichés really don't make these mothers and fathers feel better. No one could possibly need their angel more than they do!

"The good ones die young."

I guess that means the rest of us are bad, since we are still alive.

"He is in a better place."

Someday parents may believe that too, particularly if their child suffered during his life. However, in the early days of loss, they just don't need to hear this. They believe there is no better place for their children than being with them.

"Well at least she wasn't your only child."

This response just infuriates me. There is no doubt that parents who have lost their only child suffer immensely. Yet having surviving children in no way lessens the agony their parents experience. These parents bear considerable pressure to reach out to their surviving children at a time when they are totally devastated by their own grief. Anyone who has children understands that each one is unique. Having other children in no way reduces the pain when one of them is ripped from their lives forever.

"You can have other children!"

Even if that is true, it in no way lessons the agony over a child who has died. Having another child, either naturally or through adoption, can never replace the one who was lost or the parents' special bond with him.

"Don't you think enough time has passed? You really need to get over it."

People who are waiting for families to get over their pain are totally clueless. Please spread the word: they will *never* get over the death of their child. In time, they will hopefully learn to better manage their grief, but they will always have a hole in their heart that will never fully heal.

"If anything ever happened to my child, they would have to bury me with her!"

The speaker seems desperate to make the conversation about her instead of the distraught family. Is it really this person's intention to encourage a brokenhearted parent to commit suicide? Or is she simply implying that the agonizing parents didn't love their child as much since they are still alive? Sadly, I have heard this unfortunate comment several times.

"That is so sad about your child. Recently we lost our dog and we are still getting over it!"

This is such an insensitive, ignorant remark it is difficult to take seriously. Yes, people love their animals. However, equating the loss of a pet to the death of a child is an insult. Please keep these types of comments to yourself. Someone just might consider comments like these as fighting words!

"Weren't you Tiffanie's Dad?"

I still am. I will always be her father.

"Oh, is that still bothering you?"

This remark was made a few weeks before the first anniversary of Tiffanie's death. When I declined to fill in for another attorney with a schedule conflict, he seemed amazed that I had not moved on from her death. It was an insensitive comment made by someone incapable of understanding my emotions.

"I need to leave. Wakes and funerals are really not my thing!"

This insensitive remark was made by a teenage friend visiting a sibling at her brother's wake. There is no explanation necessary here; his immature remark was extremely thoughtless and hurtful.

"Do me a favor, don't stand close to me."

This comment made to me by a high-ranking police official was intended to be a comical remark insinuating that since my child died, I must be a jinx.

"The President should never have gotten us into this war. Our soldiers died for nothing!"

This comment was overheard by a bereaved mother whose son died in military service. It is difficult to imagine a more insensitive remark. It was made by someone who was apparently trying to make a political point during a conversation. The fear that someone will make a similar statement may explain why some grieving military families are reluctant to participate in community-based grief support groups.

"When are you going to put a marker on that child's grave?"

Making the decision as to what message to place on a child's grave is an emotionally painful process. The person who made this comment to me had apparently concluded that enough time had passed for it to have been done. Of course, he hadn't lost a child, so how could he possibly know?

"When are you going to clean out her room?"

When to clean out their child's room is a highly personal, agonizing decision for parents. They will make choices about the disposition of their child's possessions only when they are emotionally ready. There is no deadline for this painstaking process, so don't try to impose one. This remark instills subtle feelings of guilt on the parents, even though they have done nothing wrong.

"Time heals all wounds."

This is another convenient cliché. If only that were really true, but it's just not so.

"I would have called, but I just didn't want to be sad any more."

This response is a total rejection of the grieving parent. It only reinforces the struggling parent's belief that he is a cloud over everyone else's sunny day.

"Did you ever get the autopsy or are those clowns over there just taking their time?"

Parents who deal with their child's unexplained death are under severe emotional stress as they wait for the coroner's report to be released. The findings may explain the cause of the worst tragedy of their lives. This casual comment was made to such a parent and it was amazingly disrespectful.

"Once you go back to work, everything will return to normal.

The decision as to when, or even if, parents go back to work can be an agonizing one. Whether they return to work or not, their life will never be *normal* again. They have a new *normal* to deal with for the rest of their lives.

"Thank God our son or daughter will be off to college in a couple of weeks. We can't wait to have the house back to ourselves."

I have heard this remark made several times by parents of high school students. They do not seem to grasp what an enormous blessing it is to have a child living at home. Bereaved parents would do anything to have their children back again. It is infuriating to witness these parents so casually taking their children for granted.

Miscarriages and Stillborn Children

Parents who suffer miscarriages or stillborn births are dealing with the loss of their child. If you have friends or relatives who suffer miscarriages or bear stillborn children, I encourage you to focus on offering comfort and support to them as grief-stricken parents. The actual cause of the miscarriage or stillbirth may never be determined. Do not try to *help* the parents by analyzing what might have gone wrong with the pregnancy.

Inferring the mother may have unknowingly engaged in some unhealthy activity that placed her pregnancy at increased risk only infers blame and imposes guilt on an already distraught mother. Do not ask questions about the number of hours the mother worked each week, her sleeping habits, how strenuously she exercised, or whether she smoked or consumed alcohol. None of that matters now.

If you want to reach out to your anguished relatives or friends, try listening instead of talking. Let them express their feelings to you because doing so is therapeutic for them. If you provide this outlet, they will always remember you were there for them during this very sad period in their lives.

Chapter 16 - Where Do We Go from Here?

GRIEVING PARENTS MAY FIND THIS NEXT sentence difficult to believe, especially if their tragedy was recent. They will eventually reach a point in healing when their thoughts are no longer totally dominated by the pain of their child's death. As their stream of consciousness returns, they resume having thoughts about work-related responsibilities, family obligations, financial concerns, and other normal, day-to-day considerations. While their children are never far from their minds, parents gradually become more functional.

The first time a bereaved mother or father goes through an entire day without consciously thinking about the child or visiting the cemetery, he or she can experience a feeling of immense guilt. The parent may have simply been overwhelmed by an unusually hectic day. She may have been confronted with some other crisis, such as another ailing relative, a vehicle breakdown, or a stressful incident at work.

There is no logical reason why parents should feel guilty. When this happens, it doesn't mean their child has been forgotten or is loved any less. It is certainly not indicative they have *moved on* with their lives. It is simply a sign that small steps of healing progress have begun. Although they carry a gaping hole in their hearts, they are now becoming as susceptible to the same every day life distractions as everyone else.

I hate the word *acceptance* that too many professional counselors seem to embrace. To me the term implies I have somehow cast aside the strong feelings and emotions that I still experience as a result of Tiffanie's death. Anger, depression, and frustration are still ever-present deep within me. If I have one of those particularly bad days, one or more of those emotions may rear its ugly head yet again.

So I do not *accept* Tiffanie's death. However, I do understand she is not coming back. It can take parents time to truly understand their child is gone from this life forever. Those other convenient terms, such as *closure, moving on*, or *letting go*, among others, should never be used in discussions with bereaved parents.

When a child dies, families usually begin dealing with the grief process right away. However, sometimes parents cannot fully grieve because they must deal with criminal prosecutions, civil litigation, or protracted investigations that require their attention.[81] Eventually, these intensely stressful distractions will end. When this happens, the grieving process can seem to begin anew. So what do we do next?

All of us must find our own way to deal with our child's death. Since we all grieve differently, there are no uniform procedures for us to follow. My first milestone was the reluctant realization that Tiffanie was really gone. You can only achieve this stage when you no longer find yourself pleading with your God for your child's return. So often we try to bargain with our God to send our child back in exchange for ourselves. When we are no longer anxiously anticipating a telephone call at a certain time or waiting for the front door to open, it is a sign we have reached this level of comprehension.

When we do recognize that our child is unable to return to us, the next step may be to decide how we can adjust to life without him. First, we must begin to discover our comfort zone.[82] Initially, we may have a very limited range of activities that we can emotionally tolerate. In time, our comfort zone will naturally expand and enable us to go more places and do more things.

We also have to identify and embrace our sources of comfort.[83] If we are deeply religious, we may turn to our faith for answers. Over the years, I have seen prayer and participation in organized religious services provide great strength to parents in mourning.

Some parents feel betrayed by their God because their child died despite their prayers. This reaction is also very understandable. If you fall into this category, I encourage you not to give up on your faith completely. Instead, consider participating in religious discussion groups with other parents who have lost children. While you may not always find answers in these sessions, the emotional outlet they provide may be very helpful in your healing.

If your beliefs were shaken, in time, you may be able to return to your religious institution and embrace your faith once again. Some parents choose to explore other religions in search of one providing them greater comfort or inspiration. There is no deadline for your decision. Take your time and proceed at your own pace. Ultimately, your decision should be based on you and your family's comfort level and beliefs.

Some of us are greatly helped by undergoing therapy or participating in grief support groups. Others have the loyal, unconditional support of relatives or friends who make the effort to be there for them. Remember that grieving alone is a long, torturous road and should be avoided. It may cause feelings of overwhelming guilt, unrelenting depression, and in some cases, fleeting thoughts of suicide. As we find the strength to embrace our sources of comfort, we can expand our comfort zones in the process.

Those of you similar to Kathy and me will want to ensure your child is never forgotten. We keep those photos on the wall, no matter how painful the memories they may bring back. Some of you may immerse yourselves in activities designed to pay tribute to your child. Additional forms of remembrance include memorials, scholarships, prayer services, special events, and support group ceremonies, among others.[84]

I understand that some parents take down their children's photographs because they find them too painful. For the same reason, they may be unable to watch videos of their child or browse through old family albums. In my opinion, anything that enables you to get through the day without causing harm in the long run is a good thing. So if this is your approach, do what you have to do. In time, you may be willing to reconsider.

Remember that forgiveness can be a very important component in healing. Give careful consideration to forgiving everyone who unknowingly offended you after your child died. They may have intended to offer comfort or show their concern, but they didn't know how to effectively do that. They never suspected that what they did or didn't say or do would cause you pain.

Yet I must exclude myself from this advice. I am simply incapable of forgiving those relatives who called me two days after Tiffanie died, refusing to attend her wake or funeral. They were afraid they might *catch* meningitis from being in the same funeral home, church, or even cemetery as my daughter's body. To me, that will always be a cruel, insensitive, and totally unforgivable act of emotional brutality.

It wasn't until five years after Tiffanie's death that I understood many of what I considered hurtful gestures or remarks by others were unintentional. I have also learned that it is ultimately my responsibility to educate my relatives, friends, and associates when they say or do something that offends my family. I had to learn to forgive these people because their hearts really were in the right place. We all have to learn how to reach out and educate people who really care. Most of them really do want to help us.

There is a separate category of people who intentionally say or do hurtful things. They really don't care enough to want to know the right approach to dealing with grieving parents. We are the people they simply prefer to avoid. Perhaps they believe we have bad Karma because we were unfortunate enough to lose a child. It may be that it requires too much effort to converse with us and always have to say the *right thing*.

Whatever the reason, they are imbeciles and not worth our time. If your religious or personal beliefs enable you to forgive them, you will probably be a happier person for doing so. Perhaps your act of forgiveness will get you one step closer to your version of heaven. I have simply written them off for the morons they are. For me, life is too short to devote one second trying to understand what makes them tick.

Ultimately, we have to learn to answer the "Do you have any children?" question without breaking down or fleeing in tears. This is part of the re-socialization process we all must face as we attempt to recapture some sense of normalcy in our lives. It may take considerable time to accomplish this without falling apart. We may experiment with several answers over time until we eventually choose one that feels right for us.

It is also critical that we learn to anticipate delicate situations likely to cause us pain. Receiving a wedding invitation can trigger raw emotions as you remember that your child will never enjoy this magical time. Baptisms, baby showers, high school and college graduations are all events that can cause you pain, especially if you don't realize their potential impact on you.

There are so many situations in which we can be blindsided by our grief. Thus, it is important that we learn to constantly anticipate whether some upcoming activity may be fraught with hidden emotional minefields. As we become more adept at identifying these situations, we can develop an effective strategy to navigate them with the least amount of discomfort.

I believe when we lose a child, our personalities undergo a significant transition. Many of our friends, relatives, and co-workers often wait patiently for us to recover. Yet we can never be the same person as before without our child in our lives. Our core belief system may have been totally shaken and our basic attitudes about life drastically changed.

Although losing a child whom we love so deeply changes us, we eventually do become functional and learn to enjoy life again. If we were introverted before, some may notice that we seem a bit more outspoken. If we were extroverted, we may now be less willing to lead the conversation. We have each evolved as a person. Before our family and friends can begin to understand the *new* us, we must grasp how we may have changed.

Our tolerance threshold may also have been drastically altered. We need to discover the emotional boundaries that define our new personality. Once we understand our new limits, we can communicate this information to those around us. This helps them better understand how to offer comfort and emotional support without causing us more pain.

As time goes on and people become more comfortable around us, we begin to find a *new* sense of normalcy in our lives. We eventually stop going through life feeling as though we have three heads and our fragile emotions are not as visible to those around us. We become more adept at managing our grief, and even handling the dark times whenever they revisit. We rediscover how to smile, laugh, and enjoy life again.

Our beliefs about what is important in our lives can also change after losing our child. In his book, the late Richard Edler recounted how greatly his life changed following the loss of his eighteen-year-old son, Mark. He described the new approach grieving parents often take in redirecting their lives after their child's death:

> Most people rearrange their priorities in life. Many strengthen their faith. Some change careers, do more charity work, or find a cause with special meaning. These are all positive steps we take in our children's name. It doesn't make the hurt go away, but it helps us heal.[85]

Carl Douglas, who lost his son Barry, offers this advice to bereaved parents as they begin to refocus their lives:

> The answer for bereaved parents, in memory of your loved one, is to do some little good each day. Make those whose path you cross feel special. Make your part of the world a little better place to live. Love your fellow man. When that occurs, I have to believe your loved one is up there looking down, watching you, smiling and saying, 'Mom and Dad, you've found the answer. Thank you for remembering me in this way.'[86]

Despite our tragedy, we never lose our love connection with our child. There may even be times when we sense their presence around us or experience the sensation they can hear our thoughts. At special times or places, we may sense a particular feeling of closeness with them. In those brief moments, feeling our child's presence is a priceless gift we will always treasure.

For the rest of our lives, we will nourish ourselves with special memories of our children. To the rest of the world, we may appear to have *moved on* from our grief. And yes, we will travel a long journey from those early days of paralyzing anguish. Yet no matter how *normal* or *recovered* we may seem to everyone else, a wound remains in our heart that will never fully heal.

Our children may be physically gone from this world, but their love sustains us always. We share an amazing bond with them that becomes the key to our ultimate survival. This love is so strong, it eventually empowers us to overcome our sadness and suffering. We can derive strength from this endless reservoir of love whenever we feel lonely or depressed.

Our children remain alive in our hearts. Regardless of how they died, we will always cherish the honor of being their parents. We can find new meaning by dedicating the rest of our lives to ensuring they are never forgotten. To accomplish this, we constantly search for different ways to remember them.

With each new form of remembrance, we feel their love and honor their lives.

Those friends and loved ones who understand this and support our efforts are awesome. They recall our child's birthday and sunset day. Because they understand how important it is to us, they always go the extra mile to remember our child.

Those friends or relatives who continue to insist we are *stuck* in our grief and need to *move on* may be partially right. If they are unable to comprehend our need to keep our child's memory alive, we may need to move on in our lives *without them*. They are in no position to constantly judge something so important to us that they seem incapable of understanding.

Despite the advice offered by some professionals, our survival has nothing to do with *closure, moving on, letting go* or *acceptance*. On the contrary, we will survive the horror of this terrible void in our lives by adamantly refusing to *ever* let go of our children. As we continue life's journey along our own grief path, we do so having discovered the most vital key to our survival. As long as we hold onto to our children's love, they will never be far away.

Notes

*See Works Cited in Appendix #1 for complete
information on each book referenced.*

Introduction

[1] tiffaniesdad@holdingontolove.com.

[2] http://www.holdingontolove.com.

[3] Schoeneck, *Hope For Bereaved,* available for purchase at http://www.hopeforbereaved.com., all rights reserved.

[4] See Appendix #1 and http://www.holdingontolove.com.

[5] See Appendix #2.

Chapter 1

[6] Rathkey, *What Children Need When They Grieve,* 145-6, all rights reserved.

Chapter 2

[7] *"Father of the Bride"* by Sandollar Productions, 1991, directed by Charles Shyer, starring Steve Martin, Diane Keaton, & Kimberly Williams in key roles, all rights reserved.

Chapter 3

[8] Grollman, Earl, *What Helped Me When My Loved One Died*, 65, all rights reserved.

[9] The Compassionate Friends, Inc. annually recognizes employers who address worker needs following the death of a child. See http://www.compassionatefriends.org. and access the "Employer Recognition" link.

[10] The Compassionate Friends, Inc. website is http://www.compassionatefriends.org. Access the link for "Brochure Program"

[11] A photo of the display case appears in Appendix #3(b).

[12] A copy of this painting appears in Appendix #3(c). See also http://www.davidcochran.com.

[13] A photograph of Tiffanie's marker appears in Appendix #3(d).

[14] Fitzgerald, Helen, *The Grieving Teen*, 69, all rights reserved.

[15] Garner, Bryan A., ed., *Black's Law Dictionary*, 8th Edition, 840, all rights reserved.

Chapter 4

[16] Hsu, Albert Y., *Grieving a Suicide*, 91, all rights reserved.

[17] Appendix #2 contains my personal account of the events leading up to Tiffanie's death.

Chapter 5

[18] Van Praagh, James, *Healing Grief*, 105, all rights reserved.

[19] Allen, Marie & Shelly Marks, *MISCARRIAGE: Women Sharing from the Heart*, 13 - (Reprinted with permission of John Wiley & sons, Inc., all rights reserved.)

[20] See http://www.holdingontolove.com.

Chapter 6

No citations.

Chapter 7

[21] O'Hara, Kathleen, *A Grief Like No Other*, 9. (Reprinted with permission of Perseus Books Group, all rights reserved.) See also http://www.kathleenohara.com.

[22] See Centers for Disease Control and Prevention, 1600 Clifton Road, NE, Atlanta, GA 30333 http://www.cdc.gov/men/lcod/index.htm.

Chapter 8

[23] The National Suicide Prevention Lifeline's website is http://www.suicidepreventionlifeline.org.

[24] See Chapter 13: "Remembering our Children."

[25] The author served as co-chapter leader of the TCF Burke/Springfield/Fairfax Chapter in Virginia from 2001-2006. Kathy Collins served from 2001-2007 and received the 2007 national chapter leadership award. Both later became regional coordinators for Virginia and the District of Columbia.

Chapter 9

[26] Heidi Horsley, Psy.D., L.M.S.W., M.S., is a grief expert, bereaved sibling, and adjunct professor at Columbia University. Her mother, Gloria C. Horsley, Ph.D., M.F.C., C.N.S., is a grief expert, therapist, and bereaved parent.

[27] Horsley, Heidi & Gloria Horsley, *Teen Grief Relief,* 32. (Reprinted with permission of Rainbow Books, Inc., all rights reserved.)

[28] O'Connor, Joey, *Heaven's Not a Crying Place, 79-80.* (Grand Rapids, Michigan, Fleming H. Revell, 1964, 1997), all rights reserved.

[29] Fitzgerald, Helen, *The Grieving Teen,* 150. (Reprinted with permission of Simon & Schuster, all rights reserved.)

[30] Dr. Beverly J. Anderson, B.C.E.T.S. is the Clinical Director/Administrator of the Metropolitan Police Department's Employee Assistance Program in Washington, D.C.

[31] Helen Fitzgerald, a certified death educator, has written extensively about grief and loss. See http://www.holdingontolove.com. and access recommended reading link.

Chapter 10

[32] See Appendix #4(e).

[33] Douglas, Carl with Pearl Douglas, *Barry Stories,* 94. (Reprinted with permission of Carl Douglas, all rights reserved.)

[34] McClafferty, Carla Killough, *Forgiving God,* 83 (Reprinted with permission of Discovery House Publishers, Grand Rapids, MI 4950l, all rights reserved.)

[35] Ibid, pg. 106.

[36] For information on the Stephen Ministries, see http://www.stephenministries. org.

[37] See http://www.holdingontolove.com.

[38] See Chapter 2: "Developing Your Comfort Zone."

[39] See http://www.compassionatefriends.org.

[40] See Chapter 14: "After Death Communication."

[41] See Appendix #2.

[42] See http://www.holdingontolove.com.

[43] Groban, Josh, *"To Where You Are,"* (Album Version), Josh Groban, Reprise, 2001, all rights reserved.

[44] Jackson, Michael, *"Gone Too Soon,"* Dangerous, Sony, 2001, all rights reserved.

Chapter 11

[45] Garner, Bryan A., ed., *Black's Law Dictionary*, 8th Edition , 1225. (Reprinted with permission of Thomson Reuters/West, all rights reserved.)

[46] Ibid, pg. 1293. (Reprinted with permission of Thomson Reuters/West, all rights reserved.)

[47] Ibid, pg. 1220. (Reprinted with permission of Thomson Reuters/West, all rights reserved.)

[48] Stephen H. Ratliff, Esq., 10511 Judicial Drive, Suite 102, Fairfax, Virginia 22030.

Chapter 12

No citations.

Chapter 13

[49] Ronald E. Smith, Esq., Lawrence, Smith & Gardner, 3900 University Drive, Suite 320, Fairfax, Virginia 22030.

[50] See Chapter 15: "A Special Chapter for Family and Friends."

[51] See Appendix #5.

[52] See http://www.thewall-usa.com.

[53] See http://www.oklahomacitynationalmemorial.org.

[54] See http://www.defenselink.mil. and http://www.pentagonmemorial.org.

[55] See http://www.columbinememorial.org.

[56] See http://www.vt.edu/remember.

[57] See http://www.madd.org.

[58] See http://www.compassionatefriends.org.

[59] Schoeneck, Therese S., *Hope For Bereaved*, all rights reserved.

[60] William "Bill" Baker has created an informative link dedicated to his beloved daughter, Kelly Elizabeth Baker to assist families interested in creating a scholarship in their child's memory. See http://www.holdingontolove.com.

[61] See http://www.nicksplace.org.

[62] See Appendix #6.

[63] See http://www.compassionatefriends.org.

[64] American Gold Star Mothers, 2128 Leroy Place, N.W., Washington, DC 20008, Main Number: 202-265-0991, Website: http://www.goldstarmoms.com.

[65] Tragedy Assistance Program for Survivors, Inc. (TAPS), 910 17th Street, N.W., Suite 800, Washington, D.C. 20006, Ph: 1-800-959-8277 or 202-588-8277, Website: http://www.taps.org. Email: info@taps.org.

Chapter 14

[66] See http://www.holdingontolove.com.

[67] Schwartz, Gary E., *The Afterlife Experiments*, all rights reserved.

[68] See Appendix #1 and http://www.holdingontolove.com.

[69] Anderson, George and Andrew Barone, *Lessons from the Light*, 51, all rights reserved.

[70] Van Praagh, James, *Talking to Heaven*, 29-39, all rights reserved.

[71] Martin, Joel & Patricia Romanowski, *Our Children Forever*, 5, all rights reserved.

[72] Edward, John, *One Last Time*, 43, all rights reserved.

[73] Schwartz, Gary E., *The Afterlife Experiments*, all rights reserved.

[74] See http://www.thecse.org/Ministers.htm.

[75] Edward, John, *Crossing Over*, 131, (Reprinted with permission of John Edward, all rights reserved.)

[76] See http://www.holdingontolove.com. for a transcript of the August 9, 2001 session.

[77] See http://www.holdingontolove.com. for a transcript of the December 9, 2004 session.

[78] Anderson, George & Andrew Barone, *Lessons from the Light*, 11-12, all rights reserved.

Chapter 15

[79] The reader is cautioned that some content duplication is necessary since friends or relatives who read this chapter presumably will not read the entire book.

[80] Dr. Beverly J. Anderson, B.C.E.T.S., is the Clinical Director/Administrator of the Metropolitan Police Department's Employee Assistance Program in Washington, D.C.

Chapter 16

[81] See Chapter 11: "Grieving through Litigation or Investigations."

[82] See Chapter 2: "Developing Your Comfort Zone."

[83] See Chapter 10: "Sources of Comfort."

[84] See Chapter 13: "Remembering Our Children."

[85] Edler, Richard, *Into The Valley and Out Again*, 108. (Reprinted with permission of Kitty Edler, all rights reserved.)

[86] Douglas, Carl with Pearl Douglas, *Barry Stories*, 118 (Phoenix, Arizona, ACW Press, 1999) (Reprinted with permission of Carl Douglas, all rights reserved.)

APPENDIX # 1

Works Cited

Reference cited relates to after-death communication.

Allen, Ph.D., Marie and Shelly Marks, M.S. *Miscarriage: Women Sharing from the Heart*, New York, John Wiley & Sons, Inc., 1993. (Reprinted with permission of John Wiley & Sons, Inc., all rights reserved.)

*Anderson, George and Andrew Barone. *Lessons from the Light: Extraordinary Messages of Comfort and Hope from the Other Side*, New York, G.P. Putnam's Sons, a member of Penguin Putnam Inc., 1999, all rights reserved.

Douglas, Carl with Pearl Douglas. *Barry Stories: The Spiritual Journey of Parents Who Lost a Son*, Phoenix, Arizona, ACW Press, 1999. (Reprinted with permission of Carl Douglas, all rights reserved.)

Edler, Richard. *Into the Valley and Out Again: The Story of a Father's Journey*, Torrance, California, Merryweather Publishing, 1996. (Reprinted with permission of Kitty Edler, all rights reserved.)

*Edward, John. *Crossing Over*, San Diego, California, Jodere Group, Inc., 2001. (Reprinted with permission of John Edward, all rights reserved.)

*Edward, John. *One Last Time*, New York, The Berkley Publishing Group, a division of Penguin Putnam Inc., 1998, all rights reserved.

Fitzgerald, Helen. *The Grieving Teen: A Guide for Teenagers and Their Friends* New York, NY, a Fireside Book published by Simon & Schuster, 2000. (Reprinted with permission of Simon & Schuster, all rights reserved.)

Garner, Bryan A., Editor. *Black's Law Dictionary*, 8th Edition, West St. Paul, Minnesota, Thompson Reuters/West, 2004. (Reprinted with permission of Thomson Reuters/West, all rights reserved.)

Grollman, Earl. *What Helped Me When My Loved One Died*, Copyright © 1981 by Earl Grollman (Reprinted by permission of Beacon Press, Boston, Massachusetts), all rights reserved.

Horsley, Dr. Heidi and Dr. Gloria Horsley. *Teen Grief Relief: Parenting with Understanding, Support and Guidance*, Highland City, Florida, Rainbow Books, Inc., 2007. (Reprinted with permission of Rainbow Books, Inc., all rights reserved.)

Hsu, Albert Y. *Grieving a Suicide: A Loved One's Search for Comfort, Answers & Hope*, Downers Grove, Illinois, InterVarsity Press, 2002, all rights reserved.

*Martin, Joel and Patricia Romanowski. *Our Children Forever*, New York, A Berkley Book, 1994, all rights reserved.

McClafferty, Carla Killough. *Forgiving God*, Discovery House Publishers, 1992, © 1992 by Carla Killough McClafferty. (Reprinted with permission of Discovery House Publishers, Grand Rapids, MI 4950l, all rights reserved.)

O'Connor, Joey. *Heaven's Not a Crying Place: Teaching Your Child about Funerals, Death, and the Life Beyond*, Grand Rapids, Michigan, Fleming H. Revell, a division of Baker Book House Company, 1997, all rights reserved.

O'Hara, M.A., Kathleen. *A Grief Like No Other: Surviving the Violent Death of Someone You Love*, New York, Marlowe & Company, 2006. (Reprinted with permission of Perseus Books Group, all rights reserved.)

Rathkey, Julia Wilcox. *What Children Need When They Grieve: The Four Essentials: Routine, Love, Honesty, and Security*, New York, Three Rivers Press, 2004, all rights reserved.

Schoeneck, Therese S. *Hope For Bereaved: Understanding, Coping And Growing Through Grief*, Syracuse, New York, Hope for Bereaved, Inc., 2007, all rights reserved.

*Schwartz, Ph.D., Gary E. *The Afterlife Experiments: Breakthrough Scientific Evidence of Life after Death*, New York, N.Y., Atria Books, 2002, all rights reserved.

*Van Praagh, James. *Healing Grief: Reclaiming Life After Any Loss*, New York, a Dutton book published by the Penguin Group, 2000, all rights reserved.

*Van Praagh, James. *Talking to Heaven: A Medium's Message of Life After Death*, New York, a Dutton book published by the Penguin Group, 1997, all rights reserved.

APPENDIX # 2

My Personal Account of Tiffanie's Tragedy

SOME OF THE FACTS, NAMES, AND locations presented in this account have been changed to protect personal privacy considerations.

In August 1994, my wife Kathy and I kissed our only daughter, Tiffanie Amber Collins, goodbye just outside her new dormitory at Clemson University in South Carolina. For the first time in her life, Tiffanie was on her own, facing the uncertainty of her freshman year. Wide-eyed and full of dreams, our daughter was ecstatic about the exciting new challenges ahead. She had been admitted into a health program and her dream was to pursue a career in occupational therapy working with senior citizens.

As Kathy and I departed from campus to begin our journey home to Virginia, we felt emotionally drained. We were happy that Tiffanie was entering this new phase of her life. Yet the idea that our precious daughter would no longer be running in and out of our home, actively involved in her daily activities, was difficult to accept. Tiffanie was outgoing with a very warm, engaging personality. We were confident she would have no problem making friends at her new school.

Yet Kathy and I found ourselves drowning in self-pity as we considered how much we were going to miss our daughter. We still had David and Christopher, ages nine and seven respectively, anxiously awaiting our return from this trip. We loved them deeply, but their range of activities was entirely different. We had learned that raising a girl poses an entirely different set of challenges.

Tiffanie's first two years at Clemson went well and she became active in her Kappa Kappa Gamma sorority. During her sophomore year, she lived on the top floor of Smith Hall, the housing space reserved specifically for her sorority. Despite Tiffanie's academic commitments, she satisfied the requirements to become a licensed aerobics instructor in South Carolina. She worked out religiously and kept herself in top physical condition.

In early April 1996, a glance at my law office calendar was a reminder that the end of Clemson's spring semester was rapidly approaching. Kathy had offered to make the trip to bring Tiffanie home when classes ended, but I was immediately opposed to the idea. I realized that after her exams, Tiffanie would need assistance moving out of the dormitory. Some of her possessions, especially her computer equipment, were cumbersome and heavy. With Kathy's history of periodic back problems, I knew this was cause for justifiable concern.

I also worried about Kathy's safety if her vehicle became disabled on a desolate country road. If I made the trip instead, she would not have to interrupt her work schedule and could preserve her government leave. I had retired from the police department during the previous year and opened a law office near our home. Thus, I was in a better position to arrange my court appearances and client appointments to avoid a scheduling conflict during this anticipated three-day commitment. Eventually, I convinced Kathy that it made more sense for me to handle the trip. We couldn't travel together because someone had to remain at home to care for our boys.

During the weeks leading up to the semester's end, we were growing very anxious to have Tiffanie home. I found myself impatiently checking the office calendar each day, as the month seemed to drag on forever. We had not seen our daughter since Christmas vacation as Tiffanie had traveled to Cancun, Mexico during spring break. Not having that opportunity to spend time together only made us miss her more.

When my departure date finally arrived, I spent a busy morning representing a client in court. After returning to the office, I moved hurriedly about, returning phone calls, paying outstanding bills, and photocopying materials to take on the trip.

I finished everything on my *to-do* list and prepared to leave. Walking towards the office door, I heard the voice of Jim Pinkowski, another attorney and my office landlord. Jim remarked to his attractive, young secretary, Renee, "Look at him. He is so excited about bringing her home. He just can't wait to hit the road to bring back the apple of his eye."

Jim and Renee were crouched over a document in the conference room, both smiling at me. "Yes, it will be good to get Tiffanie home," I agreed. I offered a friendly wave and then turned away, headed for the door. I knew there was no time for small talk with a nine-hour trip ahead.

During a quick stop at home to escape from my business suit, I opted for more comfortable attire. After changing into a warm-up suit and grabbing a cold soft drink, I returned to my minivan and headed southbound on

Route 29 towards Clemson, South Carolina. During my long journey, I passed through such cities as Greensboro, Kannapolis, and Charlotte, North Carolina.

Whenever I crossed the South Carolina border en route to Clemson, I stopped at the first rest stop and admired the paw prints painted across the parking lot to honor the beloved Carolina Panthers football team. About 1:00 a.m., I arrived at my destination and checked into the Clemson Country Motel. My no-frills accommodations offering no amenities whatsoever were offset by the modest price and convenient access to Clemson University's campus.

Rising at about 10:30 a.m. the next morning, I shaved, showered, and left my hotel room in search of a quick breakfast. I stopped at the "Tiger's Restaurant," a small, red-brick building I noticed after my arrival. The large sign in the front window, "Breakfast Available Until Noon," caught my eye.

I purchased a local newspaper from a vending box outside the restaurant. I then devoured a ham, egg, and cheese sandwich, a plate of home fries, and drank three black coffees. I realized long ago that my fondness for coffee and sodas was not healthy. Skimming through the newspaper, I noticed that almost every article featured some reference to Clemson University. It was obvious Tiffanie's school was the main industry and focal point of this small community.

I returned to my motel room about noon and checked for messages. I then emptied the contents of my briefcase onto a small rectangular table and began reviewing a court case scheduled for the following week. A short time later, I was startled by a sudden knock. When I opened the door, I was met by a rotund Latina woman dressed in a light blue uniform. The cleaning woman with "Maria" engraved on her white name tag had a great smile. I abandoned my futile attempt to converse with her when I realized she spoke no English.

I decided it made sense for Maria to clean the room then, rather than risk the possibility that she might not return later. I initially tried to communicate this by waving her into the room. Not surprisingly, she seemed a bit apprehensive about my intentions, since I was still standing inside the door.

I immediately returned the documents to my briefcase and locked it. I then walked out of the room and waved to Maria while pointing toward the small shopping center across the street. I then browsed around various stores, killing time while the room was cleaned.

About twenty-five minutes later, I glanced back across the street. Since the supply cart was now positioned in an adjacent doorway, I surmised it was safe to return. Re-entering my room at about 1:00 p.m., I resumed my case review.

I had been assigned to assist in an upcoming case, but my efforts to contact the client had been unsuccessful. From the file materials, I determined the Virginia Department of Motor Vehicles (DMV) had suspended my client's privilege to drive when it received no verification that liability insurance had been purchased for the current year. An official DMV notice had been mailed to the last address on record, directing that proof of insurance be provided by a specific deadline. The letter normally contained a standard warning that failure to comply would result in license suspension.

I could surmise from the address listed on the records that my client had moved to a new address and probably never received the notification. Apparently, when DMV did not receive the requested information, the license was automatically suspended. Three months later, my client was stopped by police for speeding. When the suspended-license status was discovered, the driving-on-suspension charge resulted.

If I received no contact from my client by the scheduled court date, I would consider requesting a continuance to another date. Of course, if the client failed to appear, a capias (judicial warrant) would be issued. As I sat there weighing my options, my thoughts were interrupted by another knock.

I opened the door, expecting Maria to be standing there. This time I was overjoyed to see my beautiful Tiffanie, standing in the doorway wearing an awesome smile. She stood 5'7, and weighed 122 lbs. She had beautiful strawberry-blonde hair with such a natural, unique blend of colors, it always commanded immediate attention. We quickly embraced, and she confirmed that her last exam ended an hour earlier - she was finished with her sophomore year. Tiffanie was upbeat about her exam, and felt confident she had done well.

I quickly returned the file to my briefcase. I would have all weekend to work on it, and the case was likely to be postponed anyway. It was more important to enjoy this brief time with my daughter, although there was little time available to talk. The plan was to move Tiffanie from her dormitory room into an apartment a couple blocks off campus.

When we arrived at Smith Hall, her roommate Jane was inside the room laughing with Katie, their close friend and next-door neighbor. We exchanged pleasantries and began moving Tiffanie's possessions out of the cramped dormitory room. I found it amazing just how much could be stored in such a confined area.

The move took two and a half hours, mostly because the packing was being done simultaneously. The computer table had to be disassembled, which also slowed our progress. When the minivan was loaded, we drove to her new apartment.

Tiffanie ushered me into the new living quarters and introduced me to Tammi, who was to be one of her new roommates, along with Jane and Katie. When Tiffanie's room was selected, the moving process resumed. It took about one hour until all boxes were stacked in one corner and the computer and workstation placed by the window. Tiffanie carefully hung her clothes in the small closet to avoid wrinkles. By now, it was early evening and we were famished.

During the ride back to campus, I promised to take Tiffanie to a nice restaurant. She left just enough clothes in her dorm room for a quick change, as well as sleeping essentials for one last night on campus. I dropped her off and returned to the motel, showered, and changed clothes. When I returned, we rode around trying to select a place to eat. We finally settled on a local restaurant not far from campus.

As Tiffanie and I entered the dimly lit establishment, we were ushered to a corner table. Here, we were discretely shielded from the main patron traffic back and forth. It was a remote spot, affording a welcome opportunity for conversation without kitchen noise or other distractions. Recessed lighting, apparently calculated to produce a romantic effect, cast only a faint light upon the table.

A small flickering golden lantern with bright-red illuminated glass would serve as the main source of our dinner light. The hypnotic rhythm of the flame caused an aura to appear over Tiffanie's face. "Too bad they wasted all of this romance on us," I remarked. "They probably think you are some dirty old man. That has to be why they hid us back here," she joked, and we both laughed.

Tiffanie recounted her spring break exploits in Cancun, Mexico. It was clear from her excited tone that she had the time of her life. The conversation then turned to home. Tiffanie possessed an insatiable appetite to learn every minor detail about the activities of her mom and two younger brothers.

I had sent Tiffanie a greeting card every week for the entire two years she was away. In the smallest handprint possible, I crammed in a multitude of details about the activities of each member of the family. Still, there was much she longed to catch up on since her last visit.

As I answered each question, I found myself mesmerized by Tiffanie's face. Not only had she become more beautiful, but I noticed a new air of maturity in how she carried herself. "She really is a grown woman," I thought to myself in reluctant amazement.

Tiffanie openly talked about her semester and expressed relief that her exams had ended. She seemed fascinated by her brothers' latest exploits. She could not believe that eleven-year-old, exceedingly-shy David was showing signs of coming out of his shell. Six months earlier, he had personally orchestrated a double date to the movies. Kathy and I had agreed to it because David had arranged for the girl's mother to chaperone from her rear seat in the theater.

Two days earlier, David had announced plans to run for president of his grade school. Tiffanie smiled as she realized a new David was emerging from the introverted, little boy she kissed goodbye in January. With his extroverted nine-year-old brother, Christopher, lobbying his classmates in the lower grades, Tiffanie reasoned that David had a good chance to win. Still, she laughed at the sudden change in David's normally-bashful personality. She was impressed by his willingness to throw caution to the wind and run for such a high-profile position in her former grade school.

Tiffanie ordered a light meal and mentioned a sore throat had been bothering her for the last couple of days. The previous day she had visited the campus clinic "Redfern" to be checked over as a precaution. "It's nothing to worry about," she assured me. "They gave me some medicine so I will be fine in a couple days."

I found myself studying the effect of the flickering candle on the natural blonde streaks in Tiffanie's strawberry-blonde hair. I was struck by the fact that she was going to be twenty years old in a couple of weeks. I wished that she had gone to college closer to home, so we could have a better opportunity to witness her transition to adulthood. "We are just missing so much," I thought to myself.

Tiffanie was beaming as she described campus life and how much she loved South Carolina and Clemson. Listening intently, I came to a startling realization: she was never coming back to live in Virginia. She had fallen in love with South Carolina - both its beauty and its people. Tiffanie even revealed a sudden interest in applying for graduate school at the University of South Carolina. Her research had indicated the school maintained a well-respected master's program in her field of study.

After dinner, we stopped at the local Winn Dixie grocery store for a few last-minute necessities. I then dropped her off at the dormitory where she would spend one final night on campus with Jane and Katie. Starting tomorrow, they would be officially living in the apartment.

Driving back to my room, I found myself regretting that Tiffanie had chosen to drive her car home from college. She would be returning to Clemson in two weeks to take some summer courses and continue her part-time job teaching aerobics. By driving home separately, Tiffanie would be forced to follow me on the highway during the nine-hour return trip. I regretted missing the opportunity to spend time with her.

Yet I also recognized that Tiffanie's decision to drive home was a smart one. During her time at home, she planned to visit her friends and former high school classmates. I suspected she would probably make an appearance at her brothers' elementary school, as she loved volunteering as a teacher's aide in their classrooms. To do all of this, she would definitely require ready access to "wheels."

I smiled to myself, anticipating the likelihood that Tiffanie would use her undeniable sex appeal to again charm the manager at our local Gold's Gym. Each time Tiffanie had done this, she returned home smiling with another complimentary two-week membership. She was a firm believer in rigorous workouts. Her aerobics training had taught her the importance of maintaining the same intense exercise regimen that she expected of her students.

The following morning, after running some last-minute errands together, we had breakfast at the local Cracker Barrel restaurant. To my amazement, Tiffanie ordered pancakes, something I always thought she detested. "They go down easy on my sore throat," she explained. She also clarified her distaste, noting it was the syrup, not the pancakes, she did not enjoy.

By 10:00 a.m. we were traveling north towards Virginia. Tiffanie was well-stocked with several bottles of water in the front seat of her shiny, aquamarine Saturn. We agreed she would signal for a restroom break by flashing her headlights.

A few hours later, we stopped for a bathroom break. When she returned from the restroom, Tiffanie took the opportunity to tease me. "I thought you were supposed to be a former cop," she chided me. "If you are so observant, how come I have been flashing my lights at you for the last half hour? I almost peed myself!" She laughed out loud and rolled her eyes at me.

I quickly pledged to pay closer attention, blushing a bit because she had nailed me. I had been absorbed in listening to music and thinking about my upcoming traffic case. I knew that losing the case would put my client at risk of receiving a jail sentence. I had been mentally reviewing the statute and case law information extracted from my legal research and planned to reorganize my trial manual as soon as I returned home.

Because we had eaten a filling breakfast, we agreed to skip lunch. I inquired about Tiffanie's throat and she confirmed that it was still bothering her. I decided to stop in Lynchburg, Virginia for dinner. We could attempt to locate an eatery offering soup to soothe her throat.

When we arrived in Lynchburg several hours later, we located a massive shopping mall advertising numerous fast food outlets. Unfortunately, none of the venders appealed to her. The range of fare offered was either too greasy or difficult to chew with a sore throat. After walking the entire length of the shopping area, we settled on a small restaurant with a limited menu. As

Tiffanie struggled to digest her chicken and dumpling soup, it was obvious she found it distasteful. However, she forced herself to finish in the hope that it might ease her discomfort.

As we briefly browsed through the mall, Tiffanie expressed a desire to purchase a Mother's Day gift for her mom. I discouraged her, saying, "Hon, you will have plenty of time for that when you get home and feel better. We have several malls there, and Mother's Day is a week away." Tiffanie nodded in agreement and we headed for the closest exit. Soon we were back on the road en route to northern Virginia.

Arriving in Fairfax, Virginia at about 8:30 p.m., we pulled into the local Dairy Queen to pick up some soft ice cream. I telephoned Kathy and took orders for everyone. About twelve minutes later, we arrived home.

As Tiffanie walked through the door, she was swarmed by her brothers hugging and kissing her. They were both so excited that she was home. Kathy gave Tiffanie a long, tight hug. She was beaming with pride as she absorbed the subtle physical changes in her only daughter. Their relationship was definitely a close one - more characteristic of two sisters. Kathy had taken the following week off from work so they could spend time together and go shopping.

The boys had made Tiffanie a few gifts and she expressed her appreciation for their efforts. Then Chris led Tiffanie upstairs to her bedroom. There he had taped a poster on the wall of Jim Carey, one of her favorite comedians. Chris had also placed "Welcome Home" posters on each wall in her room.

We then sat around in the kitchen finishing our ice cream and chatting about Tiffanie's trip to Cancun and, of course, her exams. We then gathered in the family room to view a Christmas video we made for Tiffanie's cousin Kim, who was away in Japan during the holidays. The family had performed various comic skits on camera, culminating with a group melody of "We Wish You a Merry Christmas."

Despite our careful planning, the funniest part of the video was unintentional. It occurred when Kathy, wine glass in hand, tried to dedicate a special cat ornament in Kim's honor as a reminder of the year she was away. As she went to hang the cute little figurine on the tree, it slipped out of her hand and fell on the floor. This was all permanently captured on videotape.

As a now blushing Kathy quickly retrieved it, she noticed the tail had fallen off. In the process of getting down on the floor to search for the missing piece, Kathy spilled wine on her shoes as we all howled with laughter. We knew immediately that our mission had been accomplished: to make Kim laugh even though she couldn't be with us for the holidays.

Tiffanie and I were tired from the long road trip and we retired for the night at about 11:00 p.m. Kathy was also weary from working a full day.

She was looking forward to spending her time off with Tiffanie. Chris had a soccer game scheduled for early the next morning; David's game would be later in the afternoon.

At about 3:00 a.m., Kathy was awakened by a noise emanating from Tiffanie's room. When she opened the door, she found Tiffanie sitting on the side of her bed coughing and feeling nauseous. After vomiting, Tiffanie seemed relieved and tried to go back to sleep. "You might be getting a touch of the flu," Kathy warned. "We will let her sleep in the morning. She can go to their soccer games some other time," she thought to herself.

The next morning, Kathy and I rose early. She made sure that Chris wore the appropriate color uniform shirt as his team was designated to wear blue for this game. Then we were off to the first soccer game of the day. I enjoyed coaching the team with my great friend, Dale Schneider. Kathy was impatient to get home to check on Tiffanie, but the game was exciting. Chris scored two goals and the blue team managed a 3-1 victory. At Kathy's insistence, I grabbed Chris and we left immediately, missing Dale's usual post-game wrap-up session.

Arriving home, Kathy hurried into the house while I removed the soccer equipment from the car. When I made my way upstairs to Tiffanie's room, I found her sitting on the edge of her lower bunk bed. She looked extremely pale and was holding her head. "Dad will rub your neck for you," Kathy said.

Kathy went on to explain that Tiffanie had awoken feeling very weak. She had developed a massive headache and pain in her neck area. I moved to the side of her bed and tried to massage her neck to relieve the discomfort. We quickly concluded that she must have the flu and decided to take her to our neighborhood health clinic immediately.

After Kathy helped our daughter get dressed, I assisted Tiffanie down the staircase and outside to our car. I became particularly concerned that she seemed so unsteady on her feet. The ride to the clinic only took five minutes. When I walked inside the front door with Tiffanie on my right arm, I was instantly dismayed. The waiting room was packed with a standing-room-only crowd.

As I considered leaving and taking her somewhere else, a woman in a white uniform approached. She looked at Tiffanie and said, "Honey, you look very pale. Let me take you in the back." Tiffanie was immediately escorted to the patient area. I was very relieved, but tried not to glance at the waiting mob, as they could not have been pleased at this sudden development. Kathy remained in the room with Tiffanie as I completed the various medical forms and tried to keep the boys occupied.

About ten minutes later, Kathy emerged from the room with a dazed expression on her face. I could hear ambulance sirens blaring in the background.

"They are taking her to the hospital by ambulance. They don't know what is wrong, but her vital signs are too weak for them to risk treating her here." As the words passed through Kathy's lips, we looked at each other in disbelief. "How could her vital signs be weak?" I thought to myself incredulously. Fortunately, the fire and ambulance station was located directly across the street.

As the ambulance crew pulled the stretcher bearing Tiffanie from the back room, the boys and I stepped outside of the clinic, positioning ourselves next to the rear door of the ambulance. "You will be fine honey, don't worry," I called to her. Tiffanie looked very pale, but she managed a smile and faintly waved at her brothers. Kathy climbed into the ambulance and in an instant they were gone.

En route to the hospital, Tiffanie looked up at her mother and apologized for being sick when she was supposed to be home on vacation. Kathy reassured her that she would be fine, and encouraged her to stay calm.

I also tried to maintain my composure. "This has to be the flu," I kept reassuring myself. I knew from my years on the police department that getting into an accident en route to the hospital doesn't help anybody. So I drove about ten miles above the speed limit, but obeyed all lights and signs. The boys kept peppering me with questions and were very concerned as to why their sister was sick. "She will be okay," I volunteered, trying to assuage them.

Once at the hospital, they settled into the waiting room. The boys watched the usual offering of Saturday morning children's shows on a large-screen television. I waited about fifty-five minutes before Kathy finally emerged from the back and explained the situation. The doctors had to place Tiffanie on a respirator to better control her breathing. The awkward device was making her choke badly and she began hyperventilating. The doctors had given her medication to sedate her.

Kathy also indicated the doctors did not know what was causing Tiffanie's condition. They had inquired whether she had recently spent time in the woods and they mentioned Rocky Mountain spotted fever and toxic shock syndrome as possibilities. Kathy then told me, "they have taken several tests to find out what is causing this. You can come back now."

The boys remained in the waiting room with Kathy while I walked into the patient treatment area. As I approached the temporary 10 x 12 room where Tiffanie lay sleeping on a stretcher, I gasped in horror when I spotted a large, clear plastic tube emanating from her mouth. Her eyes were closed and she was clearly sedated. But that horrible tube had a gruesome appearance and I was totally stunned to see my daughter in this condition. The sight of this mechanical device forcing Tiffanie to breathe in rhythm was sheer torture.

For the first time since this nightmare began, I became genuinely scared. I found myself taking very short, determined breaths to maintain my composure. My thoughts now raced in panic: "This can't be the flu." I walked to her side and held her hand for a few moments. "You will be okay, Hon," I whispered to her, choking back tears.

About ten minutes later, Kathy returned and urged me to take the boys home. We now understood this was going to take a while and the boys definitely did not need to be here. As I drove towards home with David and Chris, I could not get the image of that ghastly tube connected to Tiffanie out of my mind. The boys were filled with questions about what was wrong and when their sister was coming home. It was becoming more difficult to remain positive for them, when inside I was paralyzed with fear.

About forty-five minutes later, the telephone rang. It was Kathy. "You'd better get over here." Her words felt like someone had just driven a spear into my chest. I hung up and called our friends Diane and Jeff Kramer, who live just down the block. Jeff answered on the third ring. I explained that Tiffanie was ill in the hospital and we did not know why. Without hesitation, Jeff volunteered to keep David and Chris for us.

I pulled my van into the Kramers' driveway a few minutes later. As both boys exited, Jeff walked over and asked, "How is she?" With my voice breaking, I hesitated for a moment and then managed to say, "I don't know. Thanks for taking the boys."

I hurriedly backed out of the driveway and headed towards the hospital. On the way back, my fears intensified. I had seen many horrible things as a teenager working as a hospital orderly, as well as during my long police career. Yet that haunting image of a tube controlling my daughter's breathing frightened me far worse than anything I had ever seen in my life.

I arrived back at the hospital and was given the news that Tiffanie had been moved to the intensive care unit (ICU). She was lying on a bed in a cubicle-style room equipped with large computer screens. The nurse's station was directly across from her. Kathy explained that one of the top infectious disease specialists had arrived and was reviewing Tiffanie's chart. The nurse promised Kathy that the doctor would speak to us shortly. As we tried to remain patient, I paced nervously outside in the small, dimly-lit area.

We both experienced a sense of overwhelming panic and disbelief. We felt as though a bomb had exploded right in front of us and we were suddenly too numb to react. We found ourselves in a very busy place where we did not belong. Our healthy, vibrant daughter, who seemed to have the world by the tail, lay unconscious just down the hall. We tried without success to think of some logical explanation. Yet in our growing state of fear, we could not think clearly.

I paced the floor constantly, which only intensified the stress Kathy was feeling as she stood quietly in the corner. I felt certain she was wishing I would just stand still. But we had been married for almost twenty-two years. She knew walking back and forth was how I always dealt with stressful situations.

After about forty-five minutes, Dr. Leonard Douglas appeared at the door to the waiting room and introduced himself. The doctor explained that Tiffanie had been given medication designed to treat a multitude of infections, since they were unable to identify the particular cause of her illness at the moment. He assured us that the laboratory staff was testing to isolate the source of Tiffanie's infection. However, it would be twenty-four hours before any results would be known.

Dr. Douglas recited a litany of suspected infections potentially causing Tiffanie's condition. These included Rocky Mountain spotted fever, toxic shock syndrome, and bacterial meningitis. I had no experience with the first two conditions. I thought back to my old hospital job as a teenager and vaguely remembered that one patient's room had been conspicuously marked with several bright-colored quarantine signs warning of the presence of "meningitis." Otherwise, I really knew absolutely nothing about it.

The doctor indicated that it was important to find out where Tiffanie had been during the last few days. He also wanted to identify anyone with whom she had close contact. During this discussion, Dr. Douglas disclosed that he contacted both the South Carolina Center for Disease Control and the Redfern Clinic at Clemson, where Tiffanie had been treated a few days earlier.

Since the spring semester had now ended, Tiffanie's roommate and the other girls residing in her dormitory had already left campus and were en route home. Summer school classes were scheduled to begin in two weeks. The school's administration was checking to determine what, if anything, they could find out about Tiffanie's last few days there.

I contacted her roommate Jane's father, Charles, and explained the seriousness of the situation. Charles instantly understood the critical importance of tracing the chronology of Tiffanie's recent activities. He promised to attempt to contact both Jane and Katie. I also placed a call to Rev. Salvatore "Sal" Criscuolo, a young police chaplain I had known for several years during my earlier police career. Tiffanie had always thought "Father Sal" was cute and had a great personality.

Over the weekend, Kathy and I attended a brief religious service in the hospital chapel. I sat there silently, trying to reason with God. "She is only nineteen, just a few days from twenty. She has always been a good girl. She attends church regularly, even at college." God had to understand that in high school, Tiffanie had regularly risen at 5:00 a.m. on school days to attend spiritual inspirational meetings sponsored by an organization known as "Young Life."

I continued pleading my case, "She does not deserve to die when she has so much to offer in this life, so much potential, so much love." I believed that any merciful God would listen and spare our daughter. I was definitely worried, but this made complete sense to me. No loving, caring God could end this young woman's life now, when she was on the cusp of adulthood.

As I kept trying to think positive, Father Sal arrived and offered comfort and optimism that Tiffanie would find a way to pull through her condition. He promised to be available over the weekend and remained by our side throughout the afternoon.

The next few hours of uncertainty were slow and torturous. The nurses were very nice and understanding, and eventually placed two chairs for us in the limited space available in Tiffanie's room. They checked on her with great frequency, maintained meticulous notes, and closely monitored any progress in her vital signs. Listening to the sound of the machine apparatus connected to Tiffanie was unnerving. Kathy and I took solace from the hope this device was helping until her infection could be identified and cured.

We sat next to Tiffanie's bed overnight. As the hours passed, her blood pressure gradually began to drop. The doctors tried an assortment of medications searching for the right response. By morning, we noticed Tiffanie's face appeared slightly swollen.

Around 1:30 p.m. on Sunday, a nurse walked into the room and told us that a few neighbors had brought over a full-course lunch. "I put it in the conference room. You can eat it in there," she said. Kathy and I were now far too petrified to leave Tiffanie. The concept of hunger or eating was the furthest thing from our minds. We had consumed only coffee in the last twenty-seven hours, but we did not dare to leave our daughter. She needed all of the encouragement we could muster. We were not about to abandon her now.

After conferring with Kathy, I turned and thanked the nurse for her kind intentions. "Please tell them we very much appreciate what they have done. But we cannot leave our daughter." A surprised expression flashed across her face. "You both could really use some nourishment," she countered. I quickly dismissed her concerns, noting, "We need to be here. We cannot afford to be anywhere else but in this room. Please express our sincere thanks." On hearing these words, the nurse nodded slightly and left the room.

About ten minutes later, she returned carrying two white paper bags in her arms. "They brought sandwiches, salads, drinks, and desserts for both of you," she announced. Looking up and smiling appreciatively, this time Kathy spoke, "Please, you and the other nurses enjoy them. We talked about it and we really are not hungry. Thanks anyway." Realizing the futility of trying to convince us to eat, she turned and left the room with a firm grip on each bag.

Leaning over, Kathy whispered, "It was so nice of them to bring over the food. I hope they are not offended, but they will just have to understand." I nodded in full agreement as we continued to sit there hoping for the best while still holding hands. Silently, we were both praying in our own ways, pleading for Tiffanie's life to be spared.

Finally, at about 4:30 p.m. on Sunday afternoon, Dr. Douglas appeared and motioned for both of us to step outside. "It has been confirmed to be meningitis," he announced. He explained that a small percentage of the population actually carries some form of meningitis in their system at any one time. It is very rare and most people have the immunities in their system to fight off an infection. As a precaution, anyone Tiffanie had been around would have to take a vaccine.

Dr. Douglas noted the virus had apparently entered Tiffanie's system at a point when her immune system was weak, possibly due to her sore throat. I explained that it had been exam week and she had been studying. We guessed she probably had not been eating well or getting proper sleep as she prepared for her exams.

The doctor assured us Tiffanie had been receiving the most effective medication available since she first arrived at the hospital. All that could be done now was to wait and hope she responded. He cautioned that due to the large quantity of medication Tiffanie was being given, her face might begin to appear somewhat swollen.

Kathy returned to the room and waited by Tiffanie's side, holding her hand. I remained at the nurses' station trying to elicit as much information as possible from Dr. Douglas. He described meningitis as an infection that works its way into the body's bloodstream. He cautioned that it could best be described as a "poison" traveling through the body, shutting it down organ by organ. It was difficult for me to come to grips with the idea that Tiffanie had a "poison" in her body. The doctor assured me they were doing their best to combat it. He indicated the next twenty-four to forty-eight hours would determine their success.

I returned to Tiffanie's room and took my place next to Kathy. A short time later, a nurse told us numerous friends had been calling to check on Tiffanie's condition. I realized that Diane and Jeff were entitled to an update. I left the room briefly and called them from the closest pay phone. I struggled to deliver the information without breaking into tears. The tone of Jeff's voice indicated that he sensed the prognosis was far worse than I could bring myself to relay.

I then returned to Tiffanie's room and took my seat alongside Kathy. As the doctor predicted, Tiffanie's appearance began to distort from the various chemicals in her system. Her face had become fuller and her neck was slightly bloated. She looked very different from the elegant, slender model that had arrived twenty-eight hours earlier.

I handed a wallet-sized photo of Tiffanie to the duty nurse to show her how beautiful Tiffanie normally appeared. She commented on how stunning she was and then taped it to the wall in her room. It was important to us that these medical professionals understand this was "our" Tiffanie. "They have to do everything possible to save her," I thought to myself.

Kathy and I openly talked to Tiffanie periodically, hoping she could hear our words. "Hang in, there baby," "you can beat this, honey," "we love you so much and we are so proud of you." It took every ounce of our strength not to breakdown as we desperately tried to give our daughter bedside encouragement.

Soon we were on a first name basis with each of three nurses who cared for our daughter over a twenty-four hour period. They made every effort to be positive, but were careful never to downplay the severity of Tiffanie's condition. They were well aware meningitis is extremely dangerous.

I had learned from Dr. Douglas that meningitis can be fatal, and that some who survive suffer serious medical consequences such as brain damage or limb-loss. The road to Tiffanie's recovery might be a long one. We only wanted to get her onto that road. We would do whatever it took to nurse her back to health. I kept thinking how amazed Tiffanie was going to be when she finally awoke and realized how ill she had been.

As each hour passed, we tried to find hopeful encouragement from the various body fluid level checks performed by the nurses. If there was anything positive, the nurses were very good about keeping us informed. For the most part, Tiffanie's levels remained stable. We hoped this was a favorable sign indicating her body might be finding a way to fight this infection. At one point, feeling reassured that Tiffanie's levels had improved, Kathy and I walked down to the cafeteria for a cup of coffee. We then briefly went outside for some fresh air.

As the day passed into late afternoon, a young, neatly-dressed woman wearing wire-rimmed glasses appeared at the doorway to Tiffanie's room. She identified herself as being from the hospital's family services unit and requested to meet with us. While we were both very reluctant to leave Tiffanie, we definitely did not want to converse in the hospital room. We felt certain

Tiffanie could hear anything that might be said. On the woman's assurance this would be a "brief" conversation, we reluctantly agreed.

We followed her at a brisk pace to a small conference room just down the hall adjacent to the ICU. Once inside, the young woman seated herself. She began speaking in a very direct, matter-of-fact tone. "Your daughter's system is toxic. It is usually fatal. We need to start considering some final arrangements that will need to be made."

The icy tone of her voice was devoid of any trace of compassion. This horrible medical prognosis that Tiffanie was about to die was being delivered to us by a non-medical professional. Her cold, disinterested delivery provided this message in a far harsher manner than either of us could have anticipated was humanly possible in such a stressful situation.

Listening to her words in total disbelief, I found myself frozen, paralyzed, and unable to speak. Kathy, the usually shy, demure one, sat there staring directly into this woman's eyes. Without changing expression, Kathy instantly stood, turned her back, and walked toward the door. She then turned and faced the woman again. "I am not willing to give up hope on my daughter's life. I am going back to be with her." In an instant, Kathy opened the door and disappeared.

I watched in amazement as Kathy exited the room. I continued to sit on the couch, stunned and completely at a loss for words. I searched for the elusive strength to stand and follow Kathy. I had nothing but contempt for this woman and fought the urge to curse at her. Yet I had been deeply wounded by her heart-stabbing words and her icy tone. She had informed us that our daughter was dying with the same emotion one might display when ordering a pizza. She had given us a diagnosis far worse than any doctor or nurse had communicated thus far. She was trying to rob us of the one thing we had left: our hope.

I kept replaying her comments over in my mind, "Your daughter's system is toxic." I was not certain what that meant, but it sounded horrible. "It is usually fatal." I could not comprehend that anyone could actually be talking about Tiffanie and death in the same sentence. I wondered why this woman was rushing us to make funeral arrangements, when none of Tiffanie's treating physicians had expressed such certainty of a dire prognosis.

When Kathy left the room, the woman stood, appearing surprised at the abruptness of her departure. She then seated herself, obviously frustrated but determined. When she turned toward me, my mind raced in a thousand directions. As she started to address me, "Mr. Collins," I found the energy to stand and begin walking quietly towards the door. As I did, she called to me again. "Mr. Collins, if there is anything you or your wife need..." Slam. I heard the conference room door close loudly behind me.

I ambled down the hall feeling numb, discouraged, and a bit wounded. I retraced Kathy's footsteps leading to Tiffanie's room. I realized Kathy had very adeptly handled that crisis situation. I, the experienced law enforcement professional so accustomed to making snap decisions, had found myself too stunned to initially react.

When I rejoined Kathy in Tiffanie's room, we sat there quietly and did not speak of it again. Tiffanie was here in the room. We could not bear to think of such things. We held hands and both silently cried waiting desperately for someone to offer the faintest hope of better news.

Early on Monday morning, the decision was made to connect Tiffanie to a dialysis machine. The doctor explained that her kidneys were no longer able to function independently and this procedure would enable her body to continue to perform waste elimination. It was not a good sign, but after all, Tiffanie's organs had been severely shocked by this traumatic ordeal.

At 6:00 a.m. on Monday, I left Kathy's side and gave Tiffanie a firm, worried kiss on the forehead. I was scheduled to handle my court case on the morning court docket. I was a sole practitioner and my research files remained locked in the office. There was no one who could step in and handle the hearing for me. Hopefully, I could quickly resolve the matter and return to the hospital. There had been no time to create a trial manual and no prior meeting with the client to discuss it.

I prayed that Tiffanie would hold on for me as I rushed home to shower and shave my two-day-old beard. Changing quickly into the first suit I could find, I spotted the Jerry Garcia necktie Tiffanie had given me on Father's day. I immediately tied it around my neck, hoping it would bring both Tiffanie and I good luck. I grabbed my briefcase, but I still needed my research.

After driving to my office, I quickly retrieved the file and rushed over to the courthouse. Skimming the contents, I remembered printing a relevant case that addressed the key point at issue. Unfortunately, my only copy had been printed on recycled sheets of scrap paper shortly after I received the case.

I remembered that my client had been stopped by a state trooper for speeding. I located the officer in the lobby, introduced myself, and explained the urgency of my situation. He was understanding and immediately agreed to check his notes. After doing so, he confirmed that at the time of the traffic stop, my client claimed to have no knowledge of the license suspension. I thanked him for the information.

I knew the case law required that a person had to be aware of the license suspension in order to be convicted of driving on suspension. I also understood that when cases had obvious "notice" issues, many prosecutors tended to offer a reduction to "no valid operator's license." This criminal charge was less serious, carrying a potential, but rarely imposed, jail sentence, and a fine, but no loss of license.

In my limited legal experience, I had noticed a few attorneys who seemed to routinely encourage their clients to accept such an offer to reduce the charge. Yet I had discovered an opinion by a widely-respected circuit court judge contradicting such a disposition. According to this opinion, to be convicted of no valid operator's license, the defendant still had to be aware that the license was not valid.

I identified my client in the lobby of the courthouse by holding up a hastily-made sign bearing the case name. The judge assigned to this courtroom was a substitute whom I did not know. The prosecutor assigned was a man whom I had already grown to dread during my brief time in practice. He had a reputation for never dropping charges, even when there was evidence the defendant was innocent. He seemed to treat defense attorneys with contempt, as though they had committed a crime themselves. I had concluded that he was rude, obnoxious, and someone to avoid whenever possible.

With Patrick Jeffries assigned as the prosecutor, I would normally search carefully to find the "just cause" required by law to support a request for continuing the case, unless I had a great judge to offset him. A continuance usually assures a different prosecutor handles the case on the new date. The alternative was to take the matter to trial. Normally, it was fruitless to negotiate with Mr. Jeffries, because in my opinion his offers were never "reasonable."

However, I realized this day would have to be different. Today, I would have to talk to Patrick Jeffries about this particular case. I understood that requesting a continuance would force my client to deal with a delay, costing additional time away from work. Reluctantly, I decided to speak to the prosecutor.

In his usual gruff manner, Patrick Jeffries asked for the basic information on the case. I explained that I had been at the hospital continuously over the last three days as my daughter was extremely ill. I made it clear that I was considering asking to be removed from the case.

Revealing the slightest trace of compassion, Patrick Jeffries offered a suggestion. He volunteered to have the case called first on the docket. He would then explain to the judge there was an emergency and we could resolve the matter then! I was shocked at the kindness of his offer, and quickly agreed. It was then that Patrick Jeffries threw in the punch line: "If your client pleads guilty to no valid operator's license, I will offer a thirty-day suspended jail sentence and a two-hundred-dollar fine."

I desperately wanted to accept. If my client agreed to this offer, I would be out of there, quickly headed back to Tiffanie's bedside. I glanced down at my tie and knew Tiffanie would never want me to throw this client's fate to an unfair disposition. I assured him that my client would plead not guilty to either offense. I pointed out that for a conviction, there has to be proof that the motorist knew the license was not valid. It is clear from the trooper's account that my client did not know the license was suspended.

After verifying my information was accurate, most prosecutors would agree to drop the charge, especially under such dire circumstances. But Patrick Jeffries was not most prosecutors. He immediately made me feel as though I had foolishly disclosed some pivotal piece of information that would undoubtedly lead to my client's inevitable demise. "Since you have revealed this information to me, I need five minutes to check something because I don't accept that position. I will be back before the docket begins and we will call the case first." Patrick Jeffries then hurried down the hall.

As the judge entered the courtroom, the deputy sheriff announced his arrival, "All rise, Court is now in session, the honorable Michael Gadson presiding. Please be seated and come to order." Patrick Jeffries stood and authoritatively spoke up, addressing his comments to the judge. "Your honor, Mr. Collins has a driving-on-suspension case on the docket. His daughter is hospitalized and very ill and he wishes to resolve the matter today so as not to inconvenience his client. We have agreed with the court's indulgence to try the case first on the docket."

The young substitute judge looked over and I nodded in support of Mr. Jeffries' accurate recitation of the agreement. Judge Gadson agreed to hear the case. Mr. Jeffries then made a motion to amend the driving-on-suspension charge to driving with no valid operator's license. I did not object to the motion because I knew if my client was convicted of the latter offense, the consequences would be less severe.

Then I spoke up. "Your honor, the defense moves to dismiss the amended charge." To save precious time, I stipulated that the defendant was unknowingly driving a motor vehicle in that county after being suspended by the DMV for failing to provide insurance information.

I proffered to the Court that the evidence would demonstrate the DMV sent a notice to the last known address, advising of the need for updated insurance information. I pointed out that because the evidence demonstrated the defendant had moved to another address, notice of the suspension had not been received. I explained that my client had not become aware of the problem until being stopped by the state trooper. I referenced my prior conversation with the trooper and asserted that his testimony would verify my client was unaware of the suspension.

I summarized my argument for the judge explaining that the sole issue was whether or not the defendant could be convicted of driving with no valid operator's license without notice the license was invalid. I referred to a prior circuit court decision that strongly supported my theory of the case. I apologized to the Court that I only had one copy of the case printed on the back of scrap paper since I had been at the hospital continuously since Saturday morning.

The bailiff attempted to hand the decision to Patrick Jeffries first, but he waved him off. He obviously knew this case quite well. The judge briefly reviewed the court decision and then glanced over at the prosecutor. "Mr. Jeffries, your position on this issue?"

Patrick Jeffries rose and began his legal argument, explaining that the DMV sent a notice to the defendant at her last known address. He asserted that was all they were required by law to do. He noted that by having a driver's license in the Commonwealth of Virginia, a motorist impliedly assents to a number of things. One of those is that the DMV has been supplied with his or her correct address. Any license holder who changes residences and fails to notify DMV of the new address is responsible if subsequent DMV notifications are not received. He concluded that once the DMV sent the notice, the law presumed the defendant had received it. He then distinguished the court case I referenced by arguing that it was issued from the circuit court, not the Virginia Court of Appeals nor the Virginia Supreme Court. He assured the judge that he was free to ignore it and was certainly not bound to follow it.

I started to speak to offer further argument, but was quickly waved off by the judge. "Having reviewed the facts in this case and based on the arguments of both parties, the defendant's motion to dismiss is granted. Mr. Collins, I hope your daughter has a full recovery. Case dismissed." I expressed my gratitude to the judge and turned to thank Patrick Jeffries for agreeing to try this case first. When our eyes met, he seemed to glare at me with obvious contempt. Although I still managed a grateful wave in his direction, he abruptly turned his head and moved onto his next case.

I then shook hands with my client and walked briskly to the rear of the court. Once in the hallway, I sprinted to the parking lot. Within just a few minutes I was en route back to the hospital. While I was stopped at a red light, I glanced down at my tie and thought to myself, "Tiffanie brought me good luck."

At 10:22 a.m. I entered Tiffanie's hospital cubicle and breathed a sigh of relief. Tiffanie was still hanging in there. Kathy stepped outside and updated me out of hearing range. All of Tiffanie's levels had remained about the same except her heart rate, which had dropped slightly. That was not a good sign, but according to the doctor, it was to be expected with the tremendous strain being placed on her body's organs. We still had hope, however faint, and we were determined to cling to it.

When we returned, I leaned over and told Tiffanie about my case in the desperate hope she could hear me. When I was finished, I kissed her gently on the forehead and said, "Thanks for getting me through that one, baby. I wore the tie you gave me. I am wearing it right now to bring you good luck too." My lips trembled and my voice cracked a bit, but I did my best. She must not know how worried we were. She must believe in our complete confidence that she had the strength to overcome this and recover.

Periodically, one of us would rise for a restroom break or to bring back a cup of coffee for both. Since midnight, there was always one parent present in the room with Tiffanie. At around 1:30 p.m. on Monday, Tiffanie's heart rate dropped again. The doctor came into the room and indicated that because of the reduced heartbeat, he needed to start her on a new medication. When he told us the name, we were oblivious to the details and frozen in fear. After he left, we stood up to give yet another pep talk to Tiffanie. She should not panic. We feared she had overheard the doctor's remarks.

We then returned to our chairs and drank cold coffee, too worried to leave even long enough to freshen our cups. As the afternoon passed, Tiffanie's various level checks continued to decline. Nothing was positive but all news was tempered with comments from the nurses like, "Well, it has dropped a bit from last hour, but it is still relatively stable."

As Kathy and I sat through each discouraging update, we felt trapped and totally helpless. We were living in a nightmare and continued to tell ourselves this could not be happening. Tiffanie was too young, too beautiful, and too precious to our family to die. There had to be a way to save her.

Finally, at about 5:45 p.m., a nurse entered and said we would have to briefly leave the room. The doctor was going to inject yet another medicine into Tiffanie to try to bolster her heart rate. It was necessary that we step outside. Kathy and I rose reluctantly- we didn't want to interfere with any procedure that might change the direction of Tiffanie's medical prognosis. We both paused and each took one of Tiffanie's hands. Speaking to her softly as we professed our love, we encouraged her to continue to fight. We each kissed her again on the forehead and then walked outside of the ICU's automatic double doors, hand-in-hand.

Outside, we both could not hold back our tears. We were so distraught at how badly things had gone so far that day. We kept searching for some positive sign to grasp onto, but it hadn't come. We were frightened beyond description. At about 6:00 p.m., we heard a female voice speaking rapidly over the intercom system, "Code Blue, I.C.U...Code Blue ICU..." We heard a sudden commotion on the other side of those double doors.

Immediately, Kathy and I tried to re-enter the controlled access ICU area, but the duty-nurse frantically waved for us to remain outside. While we wanted to resist, we did not want to interfere with medical personnel trying to save our daughter's life. For a second, I considered the possibility the "Code Blue" was for someone else. Yet, there seemed little doubt the voices were emanating from Tiffanie's room.

At about 6:10 p.m., the doors to ICU opened and a nurse walked out to speak with us. She tried to remain calm and led us to a nearby waiting room. This was the same area where we had met earlier with the woman from family services. She assured that the doctor would meet with us there and explain everything.

A short time later, the doctor entered the room. The pained expression on his face conveyed the news we could not bear to hear. "I'm so sorry. It was her youth, the great physical condition she was in, and her will to survive that got her this far. Most people would not have been able to fight this long as valiantly as she did. I am very sorry, but she is gone. Her heart has finally given out from the strain of it all." The doctor's voice cracked, revealing his own emotional struggle, as he conveyed this message. His words impacted Kathy and I like a gunshot to the chest.

We immediately began to weep uncontrollably. Kathy grabbed the wall for support and cried. I collapsed into the nearest chair, sobbing openly. Although the doctor was willing to continue speaking, neither of us had the composure for that conversation. When he apparently concluded we were just two parents dealing with a tremendous shock, he and the nurse left the room to give us some privacy.

We remained there together, sobbing in disbelief. We might as well have been alone, because neither of us could offer the slightest bit of comfort to the other. Life, as we thought we understood it, had suddenly been turned upside down. In those few minutes of mutual solitude we were totally consumed by the devastating magnitude of our loss. We were struck by the reality that we could never hope to recover from such an enormous tragedy in our family. A short time later, Father Sal returned and hugged us, expressing his disbelief that Tiffanie could be gone.

As our thoughts continued racing, sheer panic set into both of us. Our beloved Tiffanie had just been ripped from our lives forever. There was nothing we could ever do to "fix" this. We could not bring ourselves to consider the next step. We could barely find the strength to get out of the chairs. Suddenly, we didn't understand anything in life anymore.

About twenty minutes later, the doctor returned to the room to check on us. Kathy looked up from her tears and said, "We need to see her." "Of course," he said. "When you get yourselves together, we will take you to her."

Kathy buried her face in her hands, searching for the strength to stand and walk to Tiffanie's room. I continued sitting in the chair writhing back and forth, totally distraught. On hearing the doctor's words, I slowly tried to compose myself so I could see Tiffanie again.

Another ten minutes passed and Kathy and I were still sitting there, deeply upset, but more in control. As we waited, we held each other's hands tightly. "For better or for worse," I remember thinking, "It can't possibly get any worse than this!" A few moments later, the evening nurse walked into the room and held the door open. In a very soft, gentle tone she said, "If you are ready, I can take you to Tiffanie now."

We stood immediately as if to prove our composure. We followed her down the hall and the automatic doors to the ICU again opened. The curtain to Tiffanie's room had been pulled closed. The nurse opened it just wide enough to allow us to enter. There lay Tiffanie, her face and neck still bloated - the consequence of so many medications injected in an effort to save her. But the breathing apparatus, the kidney equipment, all of the noisy, mechanical devices that had been connected to her, had vanished. Tiffanie finally seemed at peace.

One thing remained constant. The devastating effects of meningitis had not changed her beautiful hair or its striking strawberry-blonde color. I positioned myself on one side of her bed, while Kathy moved to the other. As we spoke to her and kissed her cheek, we both ran our fingers through her hair to drink it in one last time. It was one of her most outstanding physical attributes. It had defined her special beauty and distinguished her from so many other little girls throughout her life.

We remained in the room talking to Tiffanie and holding her hands for about fifteen minutes. Through our tears, with voices breaking, we professed our love. We told her how proud we were of her courage to fight back so bravely. We told her everything we could possibly think of to convey how much we loved her. We had to make certain Tiffanie knew that above all else.

My mind raced again and I began to panic. There was just no way we could ever leave Tiffanie here. She was still *our* Tiffanie. She couldn't be left alone, not here…not just abandoned in a hospital. In desperation, I assured myself there was just no way that I could possibly allow that to happen.

Finally, the same soft-spoken nurse entered the room and tried to comfort us both. "Tiffanie is no longer in any pain. We need to take care of her body, but she is in God's hands now. You need to take care of yourselves and be strong because you have a great deal of things to handle. Let us do what we need to do to take care of your Tiffanie. That is what she would want you to do." Somehow I found comfort in the tone of her voice and it seemed to ease my panic.

For one final time, Kathy and I bent over and kissed our only daughter goodbye. Gripping her hand, we kissed it, telling her how much we loved her. Then we turned slowly, looking back at her one last time, waving goodbye, as if Tiffanie could see us. When we were far enough out of the room, the nurse returned the curtain to the closed position.

Kathy and I held each other as we walked through the ICU exit. There we were met by Father Sal, who accompanied us. We walked slowly through the halls of the hospital very upset and crying, but in better control then we were earlier. Passing through the garage, we both expressed how much we hated having to tell David and Chris, who worshipped their big sister so very much. Yes, the nurse's words were very true. There was so much we now had to face. Informing David and Chris of Tiffanie's death was something that we absolutely dreaded.

Father Sal promised to meet us at the house to comfort our sons. We drove home, expressing our outrage openly that such a beautiful person would be robbed of her future. There was no reason a caring God would have taken Tiffanie's life. It made no sense to us, so how could we possibly make sense of it for our sons?

As we got closer to home, our level of panic increased. How could we ever tell David and Chris their sister was never coming home again? We endured the remainder of the ride in silence, aching with dread and sorrow. We were in a state of emotional shock. Although we recognized the need to be strong for the boys, we felt weak and physically wounded. We understood now more than ever before how totally powerless we really were.

As soon as we arrived home, I walked to the telephone and nervously grasped the receiver. I dialed the Kramers' number and Jeff answered just after the first ring. "We are back, Jeff," I managed to say. "Could you send the boys home now?" "Sure. How is Tiffanie?" he asked. "She's gone," I said with my voice breaking right along with my heart. "Please don't tell them." "Okay, I will get them right there," he promised in a stunned but soft tone. I sensed the boys must have been standing close to him.

I hung up the phone and took a very deep breath. Father Sal arrived and was waiting with us. I estimated the boys would be home in about three minutes and I realized breaking this terrible news was only the beginning of what would become a lifelong nightmare for all of us. We could never be the same people - the same family - without Tiffanie in our lives.

I resisted even trying to imagine the emptiness Tiffanie's death had brought upon us. For a moment, my thoughts raced frantically trying to find some magical solution that might bring her back to us. Yet I reluctantly understood there really was no way to undo the horror of this tragedy. I felt powerless and struck by the realization that we have absolutely no control over our lives.

Hearing the sound of hurried footsteps on our front steps, I was overcome by a new onslaught of panicked thoughts. I asked myself how we could possibly survive without Tiffanie in our lives. I then wondered *why* we would want to keep living at all.

APPENDIX # 3

Appendix #3(a) – A Family Remembrance

TIFFANIE AMBER COLLINS

Appendix #3(a) – A Family Remembrance

May 19, 1976 - May 6, 1996

Tiffanie Amber Collins

A Family Remembrance

Tiffanie, our daughter and sister, was the sunshine of our lives. She always had a way of bringing a positive outlook to potentially difficult times. She recognized early on that she didn't know all of life's answers. She developed a special bond with her Mom and Dad because she often consulted them about decisions in her life as each new challenge was presented.

Her mother, Kathy was her best friend, and they were often mistaken for sisters. Since Tiffanie started college, they spent many hours on the telephone. They had a very open, honest relationship and shared many secrets or experiences that Tiffanie probably would never have told her dad in a million years. Kathy was her role model, advisor, planner and sometimes just her loving Mom. They gave each other constant reassurance, mutual respect and total devotion.

Tiffanie was the perfect role model for her younger brothers. She often shared her ideas and experiences with them. She was always helping them to prepare for life's adventures. She loved them deeply and it was a comfort to her parents that she took such a tremendous interest in their lives and activities.

David and Christopher adored her. When she would return home from school, they would spend weeks preparing cards and homemade presents to welcome her home. Just a week ago Friday when she stepped through the front door of our home, she again saw that excited gleam in their eyes and firm hugs and kisses to know they were ecstatic that she was home.

Her father, Chuck loved her and they had a very special bond. He tried to always protect her and keep her out of harms way. He treasured her love and the way she would always negotiate where he drew the line. He always ended up setting the limits she wanted in the first place.

She was active in many organizations, activities and took a genuine interest in people of all ages. She was sensitive, and supportive to anyone who needed a sympathetic ear. It was no surprise when she decided to become an Occupational Therapist devoting her practice to elderly patients. She had a terrific sense of humor, a special charm and an elegant grace that defined her existence. Tiffanie approached life enthusiastically and took each new challenge head on.

We are proud of the many things Tiffanie accomplished during her short lifetime. Our loss is devastating, our are hearts broken, and our pain will last forever. We take solace from your cards, flowers, donated foods, telephone calls, personal visits, and most of all your prayers in knowing that our Tiffanie could mean so much to so many in such a short time.

Appendix #3(b) – Photograph of Foyer Display

Appendix #3(c) – Photograph of Family Painting

Appendix #3(d) – Photograph of Tiffanie's Marker

Appendix #3(e) – Photograph of Grade School Tribute

APPENDIX # 4

A Comfort Checklist for Family and Friends

Things that could be done for the family:
IMMEDIATELY AFTER THE CHILD'S DEATH:

( ) Answer the family telephone and record messages.

( ) Answer the door if the family is accepting visitors.

( ) Monitor visits tactfully to ensure they are kept brief.

( ) With the family's permission, make death notifications to relatives and friends.

( ) Wrap up any food items delivered to the home for storage.

( ) Clean up after visitors, if they leave any mess.

Things that could be done for the family:
DURING THE FUNERAL PLANNING PROCESS:

( ) Make an appointment for the family with a funeral home.

( ) Offer to review funeral procedures via http://www.ftc.gov/bcp/rulemaking/funeral.

( ) Offer to brief the family about funeral consumer information, or if they prefer, accompany them to the funeral home as a resource.

( ) Offer to help prepare the obituary notice for the newspaper and assist in locating a photo, if one is to be included.

( ) Assist the parents in deciding whether a donation to a particular charity is preferable to having flowers sent to the funeral home.

( ) Offer to spare the family by delivering the child's garments to the funeral home.

( ) If pallbearers or speakers for the funeral are needed, determine the family's choices, and contact them to ensure they are willing and available.

( ) Ask the family if they would like photos displayed at the wake or funeral. If so, assist them with browsing through family albums to select those appropriate.

( ) Determine if the family wants an after-funeral gathering. Such an event will require planning that a close friend or relative might be willing to handle for the family.

( ) Determine if the family desires a formal program for the funeral service. If so, offer to assist in its preparation.

    ( ) Determine whether a piano, organ, singer or choir may be desired.

    ( ) Offer to assist in the selection of music.

    ( ) Offer to assist in the selection of appropriate readings.

    ( ) Make certain everyone in the immediate family has clothing appropriate for the wake and funeral services.

    ( ) Offer to dry clean clothing items.

    ( ) If necessary, offer to get siblings fitted for appropriate clothing. It is not unusual for siblings to have outgrown their formal dress attire.

( ) Arrange child care, if necessary, while the parents make the funeral arrangements.

( ) Make an appointment for the family with the desired cemetery, if necessary. This is contingent on funeral home arrangements.

Things that could be done for the family:
DURING THE WAKE OR FUNERAL SERVICES:

( ) Arrange for the family's home to be protected. (Obituaries, other publicity, or word of mouth surrounding the tragedy may alert potential burglars that the home is likely to be empty during the wake or funeral).

( ) Encourage visitors to sign the guestbook.

( ) Monitor any surviving siblings during the wake. Be available to comfort them when their parents are greeting visitors.

Things that could be done for the family:
DURING THE FIRST WEEK AFTER THE FUNERAL:

( ) Send a sympathy card to the parents with your personal message.

( ) Send a separate sympathy card with your personal message to any surviving siblings old enough to read.

( ) Organize volunteers to donate dinners to the family at least during their first week after the funeral.

( ) Offer to spend time with the parents to provide an outlet for one or both.

( ) Offer to take the parents to the cemetery.

( ) With parental permission, make contact with the school guidance counselor before any children return to school to ensure all teachers are aware the children are grieving.

( ) Transport any younger siblings to after-school activities: e.g. football, gymnastics, dance practices or games.

( ) If there is a recital, performance, or game, offer to drive the family over to cheer for the siblings.

( ) Tactfully remind the parents to monitor any pending bills.

( ) Volunteer to address envelopes for thank-you notes *when* the family is ready

( ) Volunteer to research local court procedures and competent legal counsel to assist in handling the child's estate in the jurisdiction.

Things that could be done for the family:
DURING THE FIRST MONTH:

( ) Depending on your degree of contact with the family, send a "Thinking of You" card to the parents, as well as separate cards or notes to the siblings.

( ) Offer to spend time with the parents to provide an outlet for one or both.

( ) Try to encourage them to go somewhere with you (coffee shop, craft fairs, malls, etc.).

( ) Offer to take the parents to the cemetery.

( ) If the parents are unable to visit their child's grave, offer to visit the site regularly to ensure it is well maintained.

( ) Be alert for signs of any significant weight loss.

   ( ) If a drastic weight reduction is obvious, invite them to go out for a meal and don't be afraid to raise the issue with them.

( ) If a noticeable weight gain has occurred, tactfully invite them to join a health club, exercise class, or to join you for a walk.

   ( ) Invite them out for soup and salad.

   ( ) Being careful not to nag, try to involve them in any activity that is healthy and can help them lose excess weight.

( ) Research grief-related support groups in your community, especially those devoted to families who have lost children. Helpful sources include school guidance counselors, hospital social workers, and church officials, among others.

   ( ) Contact each viable group to verify information about how and when the group meets and identify a contact person and telephone number.

   ( ) Collect this information in a folder for the parents.

   ( ) Tell them it is for their information whenever they have the energy to read it.

   ( ) Be careful that they feel no pressure to attend. Don't even ask if they followed up on the information, unless they volunteer it.

( ) Research grief counselors available in your community, especially those with experience treating families that have lost a child.

( ) If the grieving parent is overtly religious:

   ( ) Offer to pray with them.

   ( ) Offer to accompany them to a church service.

( ) If the child or sibling who died is old enough to receive mail or even monthly bills, ensure someone is screening the child's mail for important information.

( ) If civil liability may be involved in the child's death, volunteer to make the initial effort to locate an attorney to review the matter for the family as soon as a parent is willing to discuss it.

The Work Environment:

( ) Employers should avoid making sudden changes to grieving parents' work duties. Familiarity may offer emotional security.

( ) Employers may also consider offering more flexible work hours, at least initially.

( ) Employers should ensure that co-workers are given information about how to be supportive to a grieving parent. See http://www. compassionatefriends.org for brochures to assist employers and coworkers in dealing with grieving employees.

Things that could be done for the family:
DURING THE FIRST YEAR:

( ) Continue to spend time with the parents to provide an outlet for one or both.

( ) Continue to encourage them to accompany you somewhere (coffee shop, craft fairs, malls, etc.).

( ) Offer to accompany the parents to the cemetery.

( ) Offer to help them plan a special celebration of their child's life on his next birthday.

( ) Place the child's birthday and date of loss on your calendar. On either or preferably both of these days:

   ( ) Send a "Thinking of you" card and/or

   ( ) Call the grieving parents to reassure them you are thinking of them and remembering their child and/or

   ( ) Leave flowers with a note on their child's grave.

( ) Research the environmental pros and cons of butterfly or balloon releases. If the parents wish to schedule either of these ceremonies, advise them about the environmental concerns surrounding the issue.

( ) On Thanksgiving, do something to ensure the child is remembered:

   ( ) Visit the child's grave and leave a flower.

( ) If you are not spending the day with the family, call to say you are thinking of them.

( ) Place a photo of the child on display.

( ) Light a special candle.

( ) Propose a toast in the child's memory.

( ) If the family lives away from their relatives or declines to travel out of town for a family visit, consider inviting the family to spend Thanksgiving with your family.

( ) During December festivities:

  ( ) Offer to accompany family members to a religious service, if they wish.

  ( ) If you are not spending the day with the family, call to say you are thinking of them.

( ) Do something to ensure the child is remembered:

  ( ) Visit the child's grave and leave a flower.

  ( ) Have a photo of the child on display.

  ( ) Light a special candle.

  ( ) Propose a toast in the child's memory.

  ( ) If you have a holiday tree, dedicate a special ornament in the child's memory.

  ( ) Place a wreath or flower arrangement on the child's grave, if possible.

  ( ) Present a gift to the family solely to remember their child, such as a donation to a relevant charitable organization

  ( ) Consider inviting the family to spend the holiday with your family.

( ) On the anniversary of the child's birthday:

  ( ) Call to say you are thinking of the family.

  ( ) If the parent is single or divorced, offer to spend the day with them. Do something special to remember their child. This could include watching old family videos or browsing photo albums.

  ( ) Send a "Thinking of You" card and/or call or visit to offer comfort.

  ( ) Leave a flower on the child's grave.

( ) During the month before the anniversary of the child's death:

( ) Inquire as to whether the family wishes to submit an "In Memoriam" message to appear in the local newspaper on the child's date of death.

( ) On the anniversary of the child's death:

( ) Call to say you are thinking of the family.

( ) If the parent is single or divorced, offer to spend the day with them doing something special to remember their child:

( ) Accompany them to a church service.

( ) Go to the cemetery together.

(   ) Send a "Thinking of You" card and/or call or visit to offer comfort.

(   ) Leave a flower on the child's grave.

Things that could be done for the family:
AFTER THE FIRST YEAR:

(   ) Continue to spend time with the parents to provide an outlet.

(   ) Place the child's birthday and date of loss on your calendar. On either or preferably both of these days:

    (   ) Send a "Thinking of you" card and/or

    (   ) Call the parents to reassure them you are thinking of them and remembering their child.

    (   ) Leave some flowers with a note on their child's grave, if possible.

    (   ) If you did not know their child, invite them to schedule a time when they can tell you about her. Encourage them to show you photos or movies, if they are emotionally able to do this.

Don't

(   ) Send a sympathy card without writing a message to convey your sincere, personal concern for the family.

(   ) Avoid leaving "Thinking of You" telephone messages unless the family refuses to answer the telephone. Always try to communicate your concern personally.

(   ) Don't make promises to get together unless you are determined to follow up.

(   ) Never expect them to "get over" their loss.

REMEMBER: When in doubt, my wife Kathy has often said "One of the greatest things any friend or relative can do for a grieving parent is to *listen!*"

APPENDIX # 5

Love Tributes to our Children

THE FOLLOWING ARE A FEW WONDERFUL examples of special efforts by parents and families to remember their children while making a positive difference in the lives of others.

Toys for Seriously Ill Children

*Two loving Virginia parents, Gregory Holt and Lori DiGiosia, sponsor an annual toy drive in memory of their five-year-old son, Ryan, who died of cancer in 2005. In his honor, friends and relatives are requested to donate new toys to the oncologist's office where Ryan was treated. Doing so allows other children undergoing treatment for serious illnesses to have exciting new toys to lift their spirits whenever they visit the doctor's office. This is a unique way to honor Ryan's memory while bringing comfort to other children dealing with serious medical conditions.

*In 2005, Claire Alexis Sachse was born prematurely in Pittsburgh, Pennsylvania, weighing only one pound, two ounces at twenty-six weeks gestation. This special little baby underwent extensive surgeries on her heart, eyes, and stomach. Facing immense medical challenges, it was obvious Claire Alexis enjoyed listening to music, having her parents read to her, and being held, cuddled, and loved. Despite her diminutive size, Claire Alexis displayed an amazing spirit, battling for her life for 252 days in the hospital until she finally succumbed.

Her parents Kathleen and Brett Sachse, both medical doctors themselves, felt a special bond with the people at their daughter's hospital. On Claire Alexis' birthday, they purchased sixty-five stuffed ponies for each baby then hospitalized in the same neonatal intensive care unit. A note attached to each pony read, "As parents and care-givers, we'd do anything to ease suffering

187

and accelerate healing of our NICU babies. We even bargain with our little ones. On a particularly tough NICU day, we told our daughter that if she got better, her daddy would buy her a pony. This pony comes to your NICU baby in hopes that he or she will get well soon. In loving memory of Claire Alexis." This was a generous, heartfelt gesture to reach out and comfort other sick children and their families in memory of Claire Alexis Sachse.

Combating Drunk Driving

*In 1999, eighteen-year-old Matt Dawson of Virginia, died as an automobile passenger in an alcohol-related traffic accident involving a teenage driver. Desperate to cope with life without her beloved son, Laura Dawson contacted Mother's Against Drunk Driving (MADD) for support. Laura was inspired by the level of outreach and services MADD provides to victims and their families. In 2001, she began volunteering and later became a certified "victim advocate," committed to providing guidance and support to other families. Laura has tried to increase awareness of the terrible consequences that can result from drunk driving.

In 2006, Laura was named President of the Northern Virginia chapter of MADD. In that role, she routinely educated teens and adults on the impact of drunk driving, including some offenders convicted of driving while intoxicated. Laura honors Matt's memory through her efforts to reduce the number of families devastated by drunk drivers and ensuring no one is ever left to grieve such a tragedy alone.

Scholarships

*Following the death of their beloved son Will in 2004, Sue and Paul Lowden created a scholarship at the Las Vegas Academy of International Studies Performing and Visual Arts in Las Vegas, Nevada. Will participated in several fundraisers for the school and actually performed on-site with his father Paul, an accomplished musician, on several occasions. This unique institution provides a challenging curriculum for students studying various aspects of music, dance, theatre, international studies, or visual arts. The Will Lowden Scholarship is awarded annually to three deserving students enrolled in a jazz studies curriculum. An original painting that depicts Will playing the bass with Paul accompanying on the piano hangs in the Lowden home as a tribute to the special bond and musical talents Will shared with his dad. A copy will soon be on display in the Las Vegas Academy's "Lowden Theatre."

*William ("Bill") and Andi Baker established the Kelly Elizabeth Baker Memorial Scholarship following the death of their beautiful nineteen-year-old daughter in 2005. This monetary award is annually presented to a graduating student at the Notre Dame Academy in Middleburg, Virginia, where Kelly attended school. Scholarship applicants are required to submit an essay explaining how their senior year of high school has enabled them to improve artistically, scholastically, emotionally, and spiritually. Tax-deductible contributions in Kelly Elizabeth's memory can be sent by check or money order endorsed to NVCF/Kelly E. Baker Memorial Fund, Northern Virginia Community Foundation, c/o Kelly E. Baker Memorial Fund, 8283 Greensboro Drive, McLean, VA 22102.

*In 1997, Dr. Jonathan Douglas Davis died as a result of suicide, five months after earning his Ph.D. in clinical psychology. Two years later, his grief-stricken parents, Martin and Jane Davis, established a unique scholarship in Jonathan's honor at James Madison University in Harrisonburg, Virginia. Each year, financial assistance is provided to one student enrolled in the university's graduate psychology program with a special focus on suicide prevention and awareness. The application requirements can be found at http://www.psyc.jmu.edu/gradpsyc/davis_scholarship.html. This wonderful tribute honors Jonathan's life, while taking positive steps to increase awareness and enhance suicide prevention efforts.

Substance Abuse Treatment Programs

*Following the death of her son Nicholas Cristarella, Rhea Nader McVicker created Nick's Place, Inc. to counsel young males struggling with addiction. Nick's Place, Inc. touches the lives of young men suffering from the type of addictions that so tragically cost Nick his life. Nick's Place, Inc. (http://www.nicksplace.org) is a private 501(c)(3) non-profit organization in Maryland that receives no state or federal funding. It provides temporary housing for men aged eighteen to twenty-five who have completed a drug or alcohol rehabilitation program. Residents remain in the program between three and twelve months. Instructions for making tax-deductible donations to Nick's Place, Inc. appear on the website.

Water Safety Classes

*Each year, Carl and Susan Johnson of Maryland organize a special Boy Scout Beach Safety Weekend. This event is dedicated to the memory of their son Michael, an Eagle Scout with Troop 495 who lost his life in a 1998 drowning accident at Rehoboth Beach, Delaware. The program, cosponsored by the Dewey Beach Patrol in Delaware, is conducted over the course of an entire weekend. It provides Boy Scouts with an understanding of rip currents and other potential ocean hazards. They are also taught about ocean rescues and life guarding procedures. Through these efforts, the Johnson family remembers Michael in a very meaningful way that promotes water safety and hopefully saves other young lives.

Soccer Tournaments

*In 2005, sixteen-year-old Vanessa Ilana Péan lost her life in a tragic Great Falls, Virginia traffic accident. Vanessa was a talented athlete who played high school varsity basketball and lacrosse. She also loved and excelled at soccer, competing in several leagues as team captain. In her honor, the Vanessa Péan Foundation (http://www.vanessapeanfoundation.org) was created as a 501(c)(3) charity to embody her unique spirit and creativity. The foundation raises funds for a variety of programs devoted to academia, athletics, and social service activities. The Vanessa Ilana Péan (VIP) soccer tournament (http://www.viptournament.net) is held each Columbus Day to pay tribute to Vanessa's life. A portion of the proceeds is used to maintain a soccer field dedicated to Vanessa and bearing a beautiful stone memorial in her honor. The remainder of the proceeds is used to award a variety of scholarships to high school students in Haiti.

Golf Tournaments

*An annual golf tournament is held in Roanoke, Virginia to honor the memory of Scott Robertson, a fourteen-year-old talented student and award-winning golfer. Scott, a ninth grader, died in 1982 of infectious mononucleosis. He excelled in academics and sports, and won his age division in several junior golf competitions. The tournament recently celebrated its 25th anniversary and has raised more than two hundred thousand dollars to provide college scholarship opportunities and support for "First Tee" programs for youth.

*The Tyler B's "Life Is Grand" Memorial Golf Outing, established in 2008, pays tribute to eighteen-year-old Northern Virginia Community College freshman J. Tyler Bentley. On Thanksgiving 2005, Tyler died while a passenger in a vehicle struck by a drunk driver. Tyler was a popular young man who overcame a birth defect and a series of surgeries. He was extremely personable, an avid golfer, and always had a positive approach to life. While others might have complained about a disability, Tyler's attitude was reflected in a comment he once made: "Life is grand!" The proceeds raised from the tournament are used for two purposes. The first is the annual J. Tyler Bentley Memorial Award created at W.T. Woodson High School in Fairfax, Virginia to honor a graduating senior in Tyler's memory. The remaining funds are donated to John Hopkins University Hospital to fund research at the Brady Urological Institute, which was instrumental in Tyler's treatment throughout his life.

Organized Walks/Runs

*In April, 2006, Frostburg State University student Danny Frank participated in the Relay for Life program (http://www.relayforlife.org.), an overnight event created to celebrate survivors of cancer, remember those who lost their lives, and raise funds to continue the fight for a cure. During this experience, Danny learned a great deal about cancer and was personally affected by the mixture of joy and tears expressed by those who had lost loved ones to the disease. When Danny died three months later of an unrelated medical condition, his grieving mother, Nancy, was determined to continue his commitment to the Relay for Life by organizing her own team called "From a Mom's Heart." Each year, she keeps Danny's dream and his memory alive by honoring those who died, their families, and cancer survivors everywhere, while continuing to raise money for further research.

*At the annual conference of The Compassionate Friends a "Walk to Remember" is held to pay tribute to all children who have died. Hundreds of family members travel from all over the country each year to participate in this march and honor their children.

Combating Childhood Diseases

*Adorable ten-month-old Bryce Michael Anderson of Virginia spent nearly seventeen months in five different hospitals after being diagnosed with leukemia in 2004. Throughout his painful ordeal, little Bryce bravely fought the effects of his disease, as well as complications from his bone marrow stem cell transplant. Despite his amazing spirit, Bryce succumbed to complications from his transplant in 2006 at twenty-seven months of age.

To honor their son, James and Emily Anderson established The Bryce Foundation to raise funds for cancer research on behalf of all children, and provide assistance to their families. The Bryce Foundation's programs are also designed to meet the needs of families with hospitalized children, while recognizing outstanding oncology nurses who provide excellent, compassionate care for their patients. The website for The Bryce Foundation may be accessed at http://www.BryceFoundation.org.

*In 2005, Claire Alexis Sachse was born prematurely in Pittsburgh, Pennsylvania, weighing only one pound-two ounces at twenty-six weeks gestation. This special little baby underwent extensive surgeries on her heart, eyes, and stomach. Despite her diminutive size Claire Alexis displayed an amazing spirit, battling for her life for 252 days in the hospital until she finally succumbed.

In memory of Claire Alexis, her parents, Brett and Kathleen Sachse, requested donations to the March of Dimes. They also participate in walks and runs sponsored by the March of Dimes to raise funds for research to prevent birth defects and premature births, and reduce the infant mortality rate. They established a March of Dimes website in memory of Claire Alexis in hope that their efforts will spare other families the pain of losing their children. The main website for the March of Dimes is http://www.marchofdimes.com. Brett and Kathleen Sachse ensure that Claire Alexis is always remembered as research funding continues to save the lives of other babies.

Online Remembrances

*Conducting an online search using the words "in loving memory" or "memorials" presents a host of beautiful tributes to children by their loved ones. While these sites are not limited to children, many are represented among these heartfelt dedications. Each website is as unique as the loved ones they honor and was created with love to ensure they will not be forgotten. While these online remembrances are far too numerous for inclusion in this book, check http://www.holdingontolove.com for more websites devoted to the memory of children.